The Reminiscences of
Vice Admiral Thomas R. Weschler
U.S. Navy (Retired)

Volume I

INTERVIEWED BY
Paul Stillwell

U.S. NAVAL INSTITUTE • ANNAPOLIS, MARYLAND
COPYRIGHT © 1995

Preface

Two considerable benefits from Admiral Weschler's oral history are the range of topics covered and the degree of detail included in the various topics. In this, the first of two volumes discussing his life and naval career, Weschler carries the story from his boyhood in Erie, Pennsylvania, through a tour in the Polaris submarine ballistic missile program in the late 1950s and early 1960s.

A factor throughout Thomas Weschler's successful naval service was the desire to emulate his older brother, Charles, who graduated from the Naval Academy in 1932, served as an engineering duty officer, and was subsequently captured by the Japanese at the outset of World War II. Charles died in 1945 while a prisoner of war. His younger brother graduated from the Naval Academy in 1939, then worked for two years in the commercial maritime industry because he couldn't pass the rigid Navy eye exams of the day. Once war came, Thomas Weschler taught briefly at the Naval Academy, then served in the aircraft carrier Wasp up to the time of her sinking in September 1942. His interest in gunnery developed considerably during subsequent combat service in the destroyers Sigsbee and Young.

After the war, Thomas Weschler became an ordnance subspecialist, first through postgraduate education, later as gunnery officer in the heavy cruiser Macon and on the staff of Commander Cruisers Atlantic Fleet. As part of the latter duty, he tells of the refloating of the battleship Missouri after she ran aground in 1950. His development as a naval officer continued with his study and teaching at the Naval War College and then command of the destroyer Clarence K. Bronson. The tour of duty that forms the heart of this volume came from 1955 to 1957 when Weschler, then a commander, was personal aide for the Chief of Naval Operations, Admiral Arleigh Burke. Weschler provides a great many insights into the admiral's personality, working style, values, and accomplishments. As this first volume concludes, Weschler tells of his service as executive officer of the guided missile cruiser Canberra and as an ordnance specialist involved in the development of the guidance system for the Polaris missile.

In the course of moving from the initial raw transcript of the oral interviews to this final version, both Admiral Weschler and I have done considerable editing in the interests of accuracy, smoothness, and clarity. Some material has been moved from one place to another in order to provide continuity. Unnecessary material has been deleted in other places. I have added footnotes to provide additional information for those using the volume.

Paul Stillwell
Director, History Division
U.S. Naval Institute
August 1995

VICE ADMIRAL THOMAS R. WESCHLER
U.S. NAVY (RETIRED)

Thomas Robert Weschler was born in Erie, Pennsylvania, on December 21, 1917, son of Charles Lee and Florence Marie (Illig) Weschler. He attended Cathedral Preparatory School for Boys and Academy High School in Erie. He entered the U.S. Naval Academy, Annapolis, Maryland, on appointment from his native state on July 18, 1935. As a midshipman, he was activities editor of the Lucky Bag; member of the editorial board of The Log; captain of the third battalion ketch; member of the ring committee and the class crest committee; and participated in battalion football and wrestling (star man for four years). He was also a member of the foreign language club and the stamp club at the Naval Academy.

He was graduated with distinction on June 1, 1939 (seventh in a class of 581 members) and awarded the degree of bachelor of science in electrical engineering. He was not commissioned in the U.S. Navy at the time due to defective vision. He subsequently served for a year as third mate in the U.S. Merchant Marine (Tide Water Associated Oil Company) and as assistant hull inspector, Charleston Shipbuilding and Drydock Company. He was commissioned ensign in the U.S. Naval Reserve on December 13, 1940. Through subsequent promotions and his transfer from the Naval Reserve to the U.S. Navy on September 3, 1946, he attained the rank of vice admiral, to date from August 1, 1973.

After his commission in the Naval Reserve, he returned to the Naval Academy from January 9 to June 3, 1941 as an instructor in thermodynamics. He then reported for duty on board the USS Wasp (CV-7). In that aircraft carrier he participated in the reinforcement of Malta in the Mediterranean; the Guadalcanal-Tulagi landings, including the first Battle of Savo Island; and the capture and defense of Guadalcanal. The Wasp was severely damaged by a Japanese submarine torpedo on September 15, 1942, near Espiritu Santo and subsequently sunk by U.S. forces to prevent her from being captured. Rescued by the destroyer Duncan (DD-485), he next was attached to Stinger Unit, Destroyer Base, San Diego, California, doing personnel administration work with the survivor group of the Wasp.

In January 1943 he was assigned to the Federal Shipbuilding and Drydock Company, Kearny, New Jersey, where the USS Sigsbee (DD-502) was building, and served as gunnery officer of that destroyer from her commissioning, January 23, 1943, until March 1945. During that period he took part in Pacific raids (Marcus and Tarawa); Gilbert Islands operation; occupation of Kwajalein and Majuro atolls; Hollandia operation; capture and occupation of Guam; Morotai landings; Leyte landings; Lingayen Gulf landings; Iwo Jima operation; and Third and Fifth Fleet raids in support of the Okinawa Gunto operation.

From March 16 until June 27, 1945, he served as executive officer of the USS Young (DD-580), in which he participated in the Mindanao landings (including Zamboanga, Malabang, Parang-Cotabato-Davao Gulf-Digos-Santa Cruz, and others). On July 25, 1945 he returned to Annapolis for instruction in ordnance engineering at the Naval Postgraduate School and completed the course in September 1946 at Massachusetts Institute of Technology, from which he received the degree of master of science. During the next three months he was assigned to the Bureau of Ordnance, Navy Department, Washington, D.C.

In January 1947 he joined the heavy cruiser USS Macon (CA-132) as gunnery officer and served in that capacity until February 1949, when he was ordered to the staff of Commander Cruisers, U.S. Atlantic Fleet, as gunnery officer and assistant training officer. While serving as such, he assisted in refloating the battleship Missouri (BB-63). A student at the Naval War College, Newport, Rhode Island, during the next 11 months, he remained there for two years after graduation as a member of the staff, in the Command and Staff Department (ordnance postgraduate billet).

He assumed command of the destroyer USS Clarence K. Bronson (DD-668) on July 19, 1953, operating in Korean waters. After participating in action under the United Nations Command and a long voyage back to the United States, he was detached in May 1955. He served as aide to Admiral Arleigh Burke, USN, prospective Chief of Naval Operations, and then for more than two years of Burke's CNO tour. In January 1958 Commander Weschler reported as executive officer of the guided missile cruiser USS Canberra (CAG-2). In May 1959 he became Bureau of Ordnance Technical Liaison Officer, Naval Industrial Reserve Ordnance Plant, Pittsfield, Massachusetts, later redesignated Bureau of Naval Weapons Special Projects Office, Pittsfield. For his participation in the development of the Polaris system he was awarded the Navy Commendation Medal.

In July 1960 he transferred to the Special Projects Office, Bureau of Naval Weapons, Navy Department, Washington, D.C., remaining there until August 1962, when he joined the 1963 class at the National War College, Washington, D.C. In July 1963, after graduation from the war college, he took command of the attack transport USS Montrose (APA-212) at San Francisco. In May 1964 he reported as assistant chief of staff (plans) on the staff of Commander Amphibious Force Pacific Fleet and in September 1965 assumed command of Amphibious Squadron Three. "For exceptionally meritorious service from October 15, 1965 to January 5, 1966, as Commander Amphibious Ready Group, U.S. SEVENTH Fleet, while deployed as a unit of the United States SEVENTH Fleet Amphibious Force . . ." he was awarded the Legion of Merit. During that assignment, he was responsible for the planning, embarkation, movement and execution of a series of two amphibious raids against Viet Cong forces.

In February 1966, he became Commander Naval Support Activity, Danang, Republic of Vietnam and was awarded the Distinguished Service Medal. He was cited, in part, as follows: ". . . [His] superb leadership, far-sighted planning and skillful control provided the vital catalyst to weld the procurement and operation of craft and equipment, and the efforts of men, into a dynamic, versatile and responsive organization that met the ever-increasing and changing support requirements of the combat forces aiding the Republic of Vietnam in its struggle for freedom and self determination . . ." He is also entitled to the ribbon for, and a facsimile of the Navy Unit Commendation Medal awarded the United States Naval Support Activity, Danang, Republic of Vietnam.

In March 1967 he reported as program coordinator for the DX-DXG (destroyer and missile destroyer) Program, Office of the Chief of Naval Operations, Navy Department. This program subsequently was designated the New Construction Destroyer Program and expanded to include the new nuclear frigates (DLGN-38 class), as well as the DD-963 class destroyers and associated missile ships. In May 1968 he also assumed the duty of Director, Ship Characteristics Division and Chairman, Ship Characteristics Board, in addition to his program coordination duties. He was awarded a gold star in lieu of the second Legion of Merit "for exceptionally meritorious service from March 1967 to May 1970. During this period Rear Admiral Weschler directed the planning, development and contract definition of a large-scale program to provide new destroyers and nuclear-powered guided missile frigates for the 'Fleet of the Seventies' and beyond . . ."

In May 1970 he assumed command of Cruiser Destroyer Flotilla Two and "for exceptionally meritorious conduct . . . from May 1970 to June 1971 . . ." was awarded a gold star in lieu of the third Legion of Merit. In July 1971 he reported as Commander Cruiser-Destroyer Force, U.S. Atlantic Fleet with additional duty from November of that year as Commander Cruiser-Destroyer Flotilla Two and "for exceptionally meritorious conduct in the performance of outstanding service . . ." in that capacity was awarded a gold star in lieu of the fourth Legion of Merit. The citation continues in part: " . . . Rear Admiral Weschler exercised dynamic leadership and managerial ability in maintaining a major force at maximum readiness and in accomplishing the mission of his vital command. Under his capable direction, worldwide commitments were met and significant improvements in the fields of management, maintenance, training, and logistic support were realized. He developed effective advanced tactical doctrine and promoted the development of new weapons systems to enhance the readiness of ships in current and future missions."

From August 1973 to June 1975, as a vice admiral, he served as Director, J-4 (Logistics), the Joint Staff, Office of the Joint Chiefs of Staff, Washington, D.C. He retired from active duty as of 1 July of that year. In 1976-77 he served as director of the center for continuing education at the Naval War College. From 1977 to 1981 he was director of the war college's naval operations department. Following retirement from a full-time position in 1981, he continued to maintain his affiliation with the school in subsequent years by teaching elective courses to war college students.

Vice Admiral Weschler is married to the former Katrina Quinn of Erie, Pennsylvania. They have two children, Kathryn Marie and Thomas Richard Weschler. Vice Admiral Weschler's brother, Lieutenant Charles John Weschler, USN, also an honor graduate of the Naval Academy (class of 1932), died while a Japanese prisoner of war after the capture of the Philippines.

Authorization

The U.S. Naval Institute is hereby authorized to make available to individuals, libraries, and other repositories of its choosing the transcripts of nine oral history interviews concerning the life and career of the undersigned. The interviews were recorded on 25 October 1982, 23 February 1983, 17 September 1984, 18 September 1984, 20 September 1984, 20 May 1985, 22 May 1985, 23 May 1985, and 21 May 1991 in collaboration with Paul Stillwell for the U.S. Naval Institute.

The undersigned does hereby release and assign to the U.S. Naval Institute all right, title, restrictions, and interest in the interviews. The copyright in both the oral and transcribed versions shall be the sole property of the U.S. Naval Institute. The tape recordings of the interviews are and will remain the property of the U.S. Naval Institute.

Signed and sealed this 11th day of June 1995.

Thomas R. Weschler

Thomas R. Weschler #1 - 1

Interview Number 1 with Vice Admiral Thomas R. Weschler,
U.S. Navy (Retired)

Place: Naval War College, Newport, Rhode Island

Date: Monday, 25 October 1982

Interviewer: Paul Stillwell

Q: Admiral, would you begin, please, by giving the date and place of your birth and telling something of your forebears.

Admiral Weschler: I was born in Erie, Pennsylvania, on December 21, 1917. I was the second with any sort of military connection in the immediate family. My brother was class of '32 at the Naval Academy, and I was '39. Others of the family had come from the Chicago and Milwaukee area, but no one was connected with the military.

Q: What business was your father in?

Admiral Weschler: My father was a shoe salesman.* His father had been a very successful maltster in the beer business. That trade had taken him from Erie to Milwaukee and Chicago and back to Erie. My grandfather worked for

---
*The interviewee's father was Charles L. Weschler, and his paternal grandfather was Leo Weschler.

his father in the malt business.

Q: Did your father work just in the area, or did he have a territory?

Admiral Weschler: No, it was just a very small-time operation. He was a salesman of children's shoes in a store at home.

Q: And what of your mother and her forebears?

Admiral Weschler: Mother was one of a very large family. Her father had been a tailor.* He had come over from Germany in 1842 and settled in Erie. He was married just before the Civil War. As a matter of fact, the Civil War was probably the making of the then family "fortune," because he set himself up right next to the railroad station, and every soldier who got out of the war had to buy a suit of clothes. My grandfather, the tailor, sold him that suit of clothes, so it was very productive--a forerunner of the ready-to-wear business.

Q: Did you have any other brothers or sisters besides the one at the Naval Academy?

---

*The interviewee's mother was Florence Illig Weschler, and his maternal grandfather was Daniel Illig.

Thomas R. Weschler #1 - 3

Admiral Weschler: Yes, I have two sisters and another brother. The two sisters are still living. One was a schoolteacher and subsequently married. The other is a nun and very successful in the field of education. She is sort of an anomaly in that she's a Ph.D. nuclear chemist and has worked twice at Oak Ridge, which is not the usual place for a Sister of Mercy.*

Q: No. What are the names of your brothers and sisters?

Admiral Weschler: The brother in the service who has been lost is Charles. The other brother who died fairly recently is Frank. He was a staff sergeant in the Army during World War II. My sister Florence is the married one, and Sister Mary Charles, born Marion, is the nun.

Q: What was the age range of the children in the family?

Admiral Weschler: There's about a 20-year spread through the children. Florence is the oldest, and I am second to the youngest, with my sister Marion being the youngest.

Q: What are some of the things you recall from your boyhood?

---

*Oak Ridge National Laboratory, Oak Ridge, Tennessee, which has long been involved in research and development in the field of nuclear energy.

Admiral Weschler: I'm trying to think of anything that might have to do with now. I always enjoyed the outdoors. There wasn't any question on that. I really didn't get on the water a great deal. I think a canoe was the largest thing I had been in before I went to the Naval Academy.

When I was 10 or 12, my brother was thinking about going to the academy. That got me pumped up on it, so I read every book that there was about the Naval Academy. I loved to read, and I was a very good student. I graduated from high school too young to go right into the Naval Academy, so I had to wait a year, going to another high school to take some extra courses.

I think the thing I remember most about getting ready for the academy was hoping my dad had enough political pull to get somebody to give me an appointment. My brother Charles got in on a third alternate and so did I, so I think that those who get third alternates ought to consider themselves lucky. It can pay off.

Q: Where did his interest develop that spurred your own?

Admiral Weschler: I'd have to go back now and say that I have a first cousin, Denys Knoll, who was class of '30 at the academy and who retired as a rear admiral.* Denny

---
*The oral history of Rear Admiral Denys W. Knoll, USN (Ret.), is in the Naval Institute collection.

was two years ahead of Charles, so I think that sort of spurred it. You remember that this was all through the Depression years. We were all good students, had all gone to Cathedral Prep. Cathedral Prep had a good reputation for putting people into whatever college they really wanted to go to. So with not much money, the service academies looked pretty good.

Of that immediate family, I have this first cousin, Denys, class of '30, and my brother Charles of '32. I have a first cousin, Bud Illig, retired BG, Army, West Point, '36, and then myself, Naval Academy, '39.* So four of us went to the academies and made careers of it once we got in.

Q: Was your family not of substantial means, so that this was about the only alternative?

Admiral Weschler: That's right. Their income was very small. I started work when I was 12, and we all contributed to the family to keep going. I think that made us prize education particularly. We all respected it. I think that's particularly true with people who are not that remote from Europe. They had a tremendous feel that education was the only way to be successful. I know my parents were determined that we were going to have college

---
*Brigadier General James M. Illig, USA (Ret).

if there was any way that they could engineer it for us.

Q: Was Cathedral Prep a local high school?

Admiral Weschler: It is a local high school, which was then in the basement of the cathedral. The name Cathedral Prep made it sound great. It had very strict discipline, and it had some of the most outstanding teachers you can imagine. I bless Sister Cornelia, who was a tyrant if ever there was one. She taught English. I feel I learned things from her I would never have learned any other way. She gave me a respect for language and what you can do with it, its antecedents and so on, that I've just never forgotten.

Q: What did you do in the way of sports?

Admiral Weschler: I liked to wrestle, and I was a little bit of a football player--not very much. As I indicated, I was young for high school, and I'm sort of sad now that I really hadn't slipped a year or two and been more of the age of all my classmates. I really grew tremendously while I was at the Naval Academy. I was probably 5-10 and about 160 when I went in. I was about 6-2 and 183 when I came out. I think if I had had some of that growth and some of

Thomas R. Weschler #1 - 7

the maturity, I would have enjoyed my classmates more. I know I would have enjoyed high school more. So I'm not one who's pushing people to graduate when they're 15 or 16. I think that there's a balance to those things, and I think you have to get physical and mental growth lined up together.

Q: You mentioned the outdoors. Did you go hiking and hunting?

Admiral Weschler: Oh, yes, hiking all the time. We moved to the outskirts of town--to a very nice suburb, as a matter of fact. So the days were spent outdoors, just out climbing the trees, hiking, bike hiking, doing all that sort of thing. I thoroughly enjoyed that. To this day, if the sun's shining, I simply can't stay inside. I don't care what it is that there is to do.

Q: Were you in the Boy Scouts?

Admiral Weschler: I was in the Boy Scouts, but I never got past second class. By that time, we had moved, and it was simply too far from where I was living to the troop I had originally belonged to. The kids in the neighborhood I had moved to weren't organized for scouting. So it was much easier just to get up and take off with the local friends

Thomas R. Weschler #1 - 8

than it was to go join the old group.

Q: Was this another neighborhood in Erie?

Admiral Weschler: Right. Same town. I'd had short trips, but I never spent more than a few nights away from home until I went to the Naval Academy. It was a fairly sheltered and close family or neighborhood existence.

Q: Did you have any hobbies?

Admiral Weschler: Yes. Chemistry was a passion. I still like chemistry. I did all the usual things with all the smokes and smells, and I really got an appreciation and an understanding of it. This prep school insisted on having chemistry and physics in the high school course and also geometry and advanced algebra. So it was a pretty good course, which was one of the reasons why I felt it would prep me for the academy.

Then I got into stamp collecting and thoroughly enjoyed stamp collecting, because I found I liked to travel. I hadn't done that much of it, but the place names were fascinating. I used to draw maps of the world from memory and try to position all the capitals and what stamp went with each one and so on. That gave me a great feel for geography. When I was doing some of those South

Pacific trips in World War II and would come on Funafuti and Tongatabu and so on, I had heard of the names before.

Q: What were some of the examples of the reading you mentioned?

Admiral Weschler: I read Shakespeare, which was something unusual. I was a nut on poetry--still am. So I read all of Shakespeare's sonnets. I got introduced to Browning and enjoyed him. There wasn't anything Rudyard Kipling wrote that I didn't read--novel, story, poetry. I tried my hand at writing a little bit of poetry. This Sister Cornelia I mentioned stimulated us along those lines. She would say, "All right now, a sonnet is a very tight thing. See if you can do it." She introduced us to scansion so that I learned what an alexandrine was and would try my hand at some of the Spenserian stanzas. I found it all fascinating--the combination of discipline and the rhyme, and, at the same time, trying to say something.

Q: That's not a usual boyhood pastime.

Admiral Weschler: No, but part of it was from her, and part of it was the challenge. There is an awful lot more challenge to poetry, particularly if you don't go in for free verse, than you're liable to think there is.

Q: Are you a fast reader?

Admiral Weschler: I am not basically a fast reader. Whenever I read something, I usually get two or three thoughts from it, and so I'm likely to do a lot of woolgathering while I go along. I enjoy reading because of the thoughts that it inspires, not necessarily from what's on the printed page.

Q: What would you read, say, for recreation, as opposed to the classics?

Admiral Weschler: Oh, all of the adventure stories-- Leatherstocking Tales and Jack London and any of Zane Grey, all that kind.* I also got into the science fiction of the day--Doc Savage was big. Amazing Stories, Popular Mechanics, Popular Science--all those things that went with my chemistry and this sort of thing. I wanted to find out what could be done.

Q: What about radio--did you have that?

Admiral Weschler: We had radio. I watched my dad and brother build the first set in the early 1920s after KDKA

---
*The Leatherstocking Tales comprised a series written by James Fenimore Cooper in the 19th century.

first went on the air, a 50,000-watt station.* I can still remember the smell of their drilling the holes in that hard rubber front and learning what a condenser was and hooking up the storage battery. I remember that very well, and certainly I built crystal sets and used to have the experience with them. But I didn't spend a lot of time listening to radio. It was not my cup of tea at all.

Q: Did you spend a fair amount of time with your brothers and sisters and your parents, or were you somewhat of a loner?

Admiral Weschler: I was mostly with friends. All of us got jobs when we got to be around 12 or 13. All of us peddled papers or magazines at one time or another. I was an usher in a movie theater. That lasted quite a while. That wasn't a bad deal as long as they didn't have the movies longer than about a week at a stretch. After that, they got so boring that it really was pretty tough to stay on with the job. But I enjoyed that. Again, it was a great opportunity for walking. It was about three or four miles from the house to the theater, and so you could walk down, work, and walk home. It was sort of fun just to be outside and think about things. I enjoyed that.

---

*Radio station KDKA of Pittsburgh, Pennsylvania, was the first commercial radio station licensed to broadcast in the United States. It began operation in 1920.

Q: So your brother essentially got you inspired to go to the Naval Academy then.

Admiral Weschler: That's right. And I should tell you one other thing. I read all the books about the Naval Academy--Dave Darrin and Dan Dalzell.* I got introduced to Ned Beach's father's books--not a lot of them, but I saw one or two.** My brother had had some books, including the typical introduction to the Naval Academy that you could buy there in Annapolis. I had one of those. When he came home each September, he knew that I was getting interested in the place, and so he would run through a couple of things that were going on.

I was 12 when he told me that when you were setting condition William, you closed the Victor doors, or something like that. But, anyhow, I thought, "Gee, what a fascinating thing--different conditions of readiness and doors that all have labels on them." So it was an introduction to damage control.

---
*The Darrin series comprised four novels for boys, each one covering a year in the Naval Academy course. Dave Darrin's First Year at Annapolis was published in 1910 and the other three in 1911. H. Irving Hancock was the author of the series; all four books were published by the Saalfield Publishing Company of Akron, Ohio.
**Edward Latimer "Ned" Beach, a Naval Academy classmate of Admiral Weschler, has written a number of books, most notably the submarine novel Run Silent, Run Deep. His father, also named Edward Latimer Beach, was an 1888 Naval Academy graduate who wrote popular fiction for boys.

Charles went on to be an EDO.* He was crazy about naval architecture and went to MIT.** So his interest in damage control and ship construction spilled off on me somewhat. I was particularly glad when I was program coordinator for the Spruance class and the Virginia class much later in life.*** I remember telling my wife that of all the things I've done, if Charles could be around again, the thing I would have appreciated more than any other was to show him those ships and say, "There you are, brother. I designed them; now you build them," which would have been fun.

Q: Did you find that his having been a predecessor helped make it easier for you when you got there?

Admiral Weschler: It didn't really at the academy itself. No matter what anybody tells you, the plebe year is its own mystery, and you've got to unravel it all by yourself. But it helped inestimably all through my naval career because Charles was successful. As a midshipman he was regimental subcommander and often led the regiment, because Lou Bryan, who was the commander, was captain of the football team and

---

*EDO--engineering duty officer, a technical specialist.
**MIT--Massachusetts Institute of Technology.
***The Navy's Spruance (DD-963)-class destroyers and Virginia (CGN-38)-class cruisers were surface combatants developed in the late 1960s and put into service in the 1970s.

was otherwise engaged in going to the games.* So people would know who Charles Weschler was, and my name wasn't always foreign to them, which was pleasant.

And people such as Lloyd Mustin and Corky Ward, and so on--were either class of '32 or '33 or '31 or Denny Knoll's class of '30, so that I was dealing with people I'd looked at in the yearbook.** I felt they were all friends, and, fortunately, they all sort of treated me as a friend, so it made the Navy seem like a lot smaller and more intimate place.

Q: It certainly was much smaller in that day.

Admiral Weschler: When I reported aboard my first ship, the USS Wasp, we had 2,200 people, counting our air group. I was told that the Atlantic Fleet at that time, I think, numbered something like 20,000 or 30,000, so I thought, "My golly, I know almost 10% of the fleet, and I've just been on one ship." So I thought I was really making progress.

Q: How did you wind up getting the appointment to the Naval Academy?

---

*Midshipman Louis A. Bryan, USN. Bryan died in 1966 while on active duty as a rear admiral.
**Midshipmen Lloyd M. Mustin and Alfred G. Ward, who were in the class of 1932, later became flag officers. Their oral histories are in the Naval Institute collection.

Admiral Weschler: As I commented, Dad didn't have that much political clout, but he was good to get a third alternate appointment for me--as a matter of fact, two third alternates. The first third alternate didn't pay off at all, but suddenly some other appointment became available, and I was the third alternate on that. I thought I'd lost out, because everyone had been recruited in June of 1935. But along about the 28th or 29th of June, I got word to stand by to report in mid-July, and then to report. Two men in front of me had physical disabilities. Then the second alternate was lucky enough to get an appointment to West Point, and he took that in preference to the Naval Academy. So suddenly I moved up to be the guy.

Then I went down there, and, lo and behold, I had some sort of a medical problem. I forget what it was now, but it was something that had me go back for a re-exam. Fortunately my roommate-to-be, Joe West, had exactly the same kind of difficulty.* My parents had gone back by this time, so Joe and his father and I sat outside on this bench in Smoke Park.** We looked at each other and wondered if we would we ever get into this doggone place. Then the next day we passed, and everything went swimmingly.

---
*Midshipman Joseph M. West, USN, class of 1939, eventually became a captain.
**Smoke Park is an area near Bancroft Hall, the large dormitory that houses all the Naval Academy midshipmen.

Thomas R. Weschler #1 - 16

I must say that it was a very happy day when I got in there. I had been looking forward to it for so long, and it really seemed the culmination of everything I had ever wanted.

Q: And then the trouble started.

Admiral Weschler: And then the trouble started. But I never minded. Plebe year, for me, is something about which I have absolutely no regrets. The only time I had any difficulty at the Naval Academy was youngster year.

I got to know Henry Singleton pretty well; he and I were both in the number-one math section.* He was from Texas, very smart. He is now the chairman of the board of Teledyne. About the middle of youngster year, he said, "This isn't challenging enough. There's too much else going on in the world. Let's resign, go to Rice, and then we'll get started in business."**

I talked about that once in a letter to my folks, and they were smart enough to say, "When you come home in September, we'll thrash it out. If you really feel that way then, okay." But by the time September came, I never brought the subject up, and neither did they. I never talked about it to my parents again until long after I was

---
*Midshipman Henry E. Singleton, USN, left the Naval Academy prior to the graduation of his class.
**Rice University is in Houston, Texas.

a commissioned officer and had it far behind me. Who knows what would have happened if I had gone with Henry Singleton? It probably would have worked out very successfully.

Q: What do you think kept you from going along with him?

Admiral Weschler: Because I knew I really liked the Navy. I think everybody tries an analysis. I made an analysis plebe year, and that youngster year, of what sort of a career I really wanted to follow. I set it all out: to try to be outdoors and working with people and intellectual challenge and sort of roughing it aspects and so on. I put it all down, and it ended up that I ought to be either a mining engineer, possibly a forester, or a naval officer. What Henry was proposing--becoming a mathematician and then perhaps going into business--didn't sound like the right sort of thing for me. So I think I was very happy and wise, the way it worked out, to stay with what I was doing.

Q: How well did you adapt to the discipline and regimentation and hazing and so forth?

Admiral Weschler: I think very well. I had a roommate who helped me a lot on that. Joe West had just come from a year and a half at VPI.* These were the days of <u>Brother Rat</u> and those southern prep schools and colleges which were some of the greatest in the world for hazing.** He gave me some good, practical words early on in our plebe year. He told me what had happened to him and what was likely to happen. We never hit the apex of what he prepped me for, so I felt quite comfortable that I was in the limits of what was tolerable, and I never really had a great difficulty.

Q: That's contrary to most people, who find it worse than they expected.

Admiral Weschler: If it hadn't been for this roommate, whom I trusted and who was so fresh from it, I might not have been so well prepared. Everything I imagined paled in front of what he had to tell me. So I thought he was a good foil to help me keep my balance.

Q: What do you remember about the quality of the academic instruction?

Admiral Weschler: Well, I never really thought there was a

---
*VPI--Virginia Polytechnic Institute.
**<u>Brother Rat</u> was a Broadway musical and 1940 movie about life at a military academy such as Virginia Military Institute. "Rats" were plebes, so a "brother rat" was one's friend in misery. Ronald Reagan was in the film.

tremendous amount of instruction. I didn't think that they intended it to be. I decided that they wanted you to read the book and understand it, and then if you had to ask a question to get it explained, they would be willing to do it. Otherwise, you simply walked in and wrote on the board what you knew. Since I didn't expect any instruction and really didn't seek any, I got along very well. I don't mean that there weren't people there who could be challenging. I was fortunate, too, in that as a star man I was usually in sections that had the best professors.* They, a lot of times, would recognize that what we were going through was quite simple and that all of us were doing very well. So they might take five minutes to check the lesson off and then would go off into other dimensions and things that were more exciting. I remember that particularly in math. I think that helped me enjoy the courses and keep stimulated by them.

Q: One quality that helps in that kind of atmosphere is a good talent for memory work. Was that a strong suit of yours?

Admiral Weschler: I have a good memory, or at least I used to. It's beginning to fade now, but in connection with

---

*A star man was a midshipman who wore a star on his uniform to indicate that he was at or near the top of his class in academic standing.

math I used to make it a point never to remember anything. I felt that people in the world had derived all these mathematical formulae before, and so I ought to be able to derive them if I really needed them. So I didn't use memory as a crutch in math.

Now, in connection with ordnance and some of these other things, I used every mnemonic device and acronym and aid that anybody else did. But in general I tried to have the reasoning. I much prefer logic to memory.

Q: What were your favorite subjects?

Admiral Weschler: Math and English.

Q: Why those two?

Admiral Weschler: English, because I've already indicated I find a lot of beauty in it and I'm fascinated with language. I want to know where words come from and why you use them the way you do and whether there isn't something that's more apt. I'm a great punster; if I hear words, I'm always trying to fit them together in strange ways. As for math, I think that everything has a thread and a core and an understanding. I'm enough of an engineer at heart that I want to get the pieces fitted together. I like the fact that math responds to logic.

Q: What about training in the strictly naval subjects? Which ones did you prefer there?

Admiral Weschler: I liked navigation very much. I thought astronomy and the stars were fascinating. To be able to use them to determine a ship's position I thought was quite remarkable. There again, there was room for reasoning, to remember whether it was left or right, plus or minus, and how you applied corrections and right ascension and all the terms. It just had a certain mystery about it that was fun to get into.

I enjoyed seamanship to the extent that it was necessary. I didn't turn up my nose at it, but seamanship was much better and more exciting when you were on a cruise. Then I could get all up into seamanship, but it wasn't that good in a classroom.

Q: Could you describe your cruises, please?

Admiral Weschler: I can describe them, because I think that's one of the reasons, also, why I knew I wanted to stay in the Navy. I've often told that to my wife, and I told it to my folks at the time.

My first cruise was aboard the old battleship Arkansas, and it was one of those wonderful midshipman cruises.* They were still having them full bore, in which you sailed from Annapolis and covered Europe. We went to Göteborg, Sweden, and came down the coast to Le Havre, France. On that particular cruise we swung down as far as Gibraltar, although we didn't go in. We visited Portsmouth, England, and then came back home to the States.

I especially enjoyed the nights at sea that were memorable. We were on that beautiful battleship crowded with lots of people. Then I found it magic, when night came, to be able to go out there on the fantail, and just sit there under the stars and listen to the sea. Everything was quiet, and there was a nice sense of order and security about it all. I've always thought that, "Gee, if I can do that, it's got to be a worthwhile career."

I must say, I didn't find a lot of time to sit on the forecastle or fantail as time went by, but the underpinnings of it all were still there. I often told people that, "If it's really getting too hectic, pick a good starry night and go sit aft, and I bet by the time you're done, you'll come back and say you can hack it."

Q: This probably also helped fulfill some of your desire to travel that you mentioned earlier.

---

*USS Arkansas (BB-33) was commissioned 17 September 1912. Following modernization in the mid-1930s she had a standard displacement of 26,100 tons, was 562 feet long and 106 feet in the beam. Her top speed was 21 knots. She was armed with 12 12-inch guns and 16 5-inch guns.

Admiral Weschler: That's right. As soon as that cruise started, I really found how much I enjoyed travel. To this day, if you tell me that there's a plane leaving for wherever, I'm ready to go. It doesn't make any difference if I've just gotten back from a trip. My wife now begins to say, "You go by yourself; I've had enough travel." But I really haven't reached that point.

The only other cruise which was quite a bit akin was another battleship cruise, in Texas, the first class summer.* Second class summer I rode a gunboat. It was very rare; there weren't very many, and it happened to be the gunboat named for my hometown, Erie. It had been christened by the mother of Denny Knoll. Erie was originally built for Panama Canal duty, but she was assigned to the cruise for that second class summer.** She took us up around New England, introducing us a little bit to aviation and the submarine world and to see a little bit more of the surface Navy.

---

*USS Texas (BB-35) was commissioned 12 March 1914. She had a standard displacement of 27,000 tons, was 573 feet long, and 95 feet in the beam. Her top speed was 21 knots. Her main battery comprised ten 14-inch guns, and her secondary battery included 21 5-inch guns. She served in both World Wars and was eventually decommissioned in 1948.

**USS Erie (PG-50) was commissioned 1 July 1936. She had a standard displacement of 2,000 tons, was 328 feet long, and 41 feet in the beam. She had a top speed of 20 knots and a main battery of four 6-inch guns. She was torpedoed and sunk while operating in the Caribbean in late 1942.

Thomas R. Weschler #1 - 24

Q: Where did your first class cruise go, to Europe again?

Admiral Weschler: Yes, to Europe again and another chance to visit France and England and to get down as far as Italy.

Q: Who were some of your classmates that you were close to during that period?

Admiral Weschler: Well, I've mentioned Joe, the roommate. I stayed with him four years. One that I met that youngster cruise whom I really enjoyed and have stayed close to over the years was Vice Admiral Foo Vannoy, Frank Wilson Vannoy, who retired after serving as ComPhibLant as his last duty.*

Jack Eversole--I wish that he had been able to keep going. He ended up an eye unsat, same as I did.** As a matter of fact, of the four of us in the room first class year, three of us ended up as eye unsats, and one was okay. A group of us then went with Tidewater Associated Oil, when we graduated, to try out the merchant marine. Of the four of us who went with the merchant marine, all four of us

---
*At the time of his retirement in 1974, Vice Admiral Vannoy was serving as Commander Amphibious Force U.S. Atlantic Fleet.
**John S. Eversole was honorably discharged on 1 June 1939, the date of the class's graduation because, like Weschler, he was unable to pass the vision portion of the physical exam. He was later recalled to active duty and retired in 1960 as a commander.

came back in the Navy the second that there was an opportunity. When the war was over, three of us stayed on in the Navy, and one of this group went to GE.* No one went back to Tidewater Oil.

Q: There were a couple of real brains in that class in Lou Roddis and Ned Beach.**

Admiral Weschler: I know Ned Beach; he's stayed a good friend over the years. Lou Roddis and I never knew each other that well. We were in different battalions, and the way things worked out, I just never really had a chance to see him. Tommy Walker was a reasonably good friend.*** Bill Ruhe, whom I think is one of the shining lights, has been a bosom friend all the way through.**** Paul Schratz is a good friend, and he was up here just recently and has done an awful lot of writing.***** Victor Taliferro

---
*GE--General Electric.
**The first two in class standing were Midshipmen Louis H. Roddis, Jr., who was later involved in the origins of the Navy's nuclear power program, and Edward L. Beach, the celebrated submariner and novelist.
***Midshipman Thomas J. Walker III, USN, became an aviator and eventually retired as a vice admiral.
****Midshipman William J. Ruhe, USN, became a submariner and retired as a captain. He later served as editor of Submarine Review, published by the Naval Submarine League.
*****Midshipman Paul R. Schratz, USN, became a submariner and a prolific author. He retired as a captain. His oral history is in the Naval Institute collection.

Boatwright, who lives over in Stonington now, was a fine friend in those days.* He was editor of the Lucky Bag, and I was activities editor, so we were thrown together quite a bit our first class year.**

Q: How hectic was the competition to finish at or near the top of your class?

Admiral Weschler: I must say I didn't really feel it particularly. As a matter of fact, until first class year I never really understood the company competition that was going on and all of the points that were involved. I was appointed battalion subcommander, and that was the first time I was aware that there was a color competition, which shows that I wasn't in gear for a long time. I don't think that the competition got through to you a great deal unless you were so motivated. I had done very well in not getting demerits all through the first three years, but first class year I was within an ace of having too many. Because of the stripes that I got, I was frequently in charge of formations, and formations have a tendency to be a little undisciplined when they're first class. The officer in charge is very likely to "get fried," and I did any number

---

*Midshipman Victor T. Boatwright, USN, stood fourth of the 581 graduates in the class of 1939; Weschler stood seventh. Boatwright, who retired as a commander in the Naval Reserve, lives in Stonington, Connecticut.
**Lucky Bag is the name of the Naval Academy yearbook.

of times.* So, having done very well for the first three years, I was just about at the bottom of the class in conduct by the time I graduated.

But in actual competition for academic stars, I wanted to hold on to my record. Everybody in my family had always had good grades, and I didn't intend to do differently. But I don't think the motivating force was intense; I think I was very fortunate.

Q: Did you get involved in sports while you were at the academy?

Admiral Weschler: I was in battalion football, and I was in wrestling. I started out for crew, and I think I really would have enjoyed that, but I was unsat in swimming, and so I had joined the "sub squad" and stayed with that.** That kind of threw me out of phase with what was going on. I've already commented that I felt about a year younger physically than I would have enjoyed with that group. So there were an awful lot of the fellows, the good athletes, I didn't really feel that close to. I had, I'm sure, a shyness in this regard. It took a while to get to the point where I had the self-assurance and was ready to mix with them.

---
*"Get fried"--to be put on the report, usually resulting in demerits.
**At the Naval Academy the "sub squad" was composed of the midshipmen who had trouble swimming and thus were given extra instruction.

Q: Was this evident also in your social life?

Admiral Weschler: No, not particularly. I enjoyed dating and had, from youngster year on, somebody coming down to almost all the dances. I was on the ring committee, the class crest committee, and the <u>Lucky Bag</u>. I enjoyed sailing. I'm into sailing now as my volunteer work almost full time. I'd joined the ketches; we had a ketch for each battalion, a 50-foot motor launch converted. We were allowed to go sailing every weekend from Saturday noon until Sunday evening. I did that religiously throughout second class and first class year, and I was captain of the ketch for our battalion that first class year. And we had a stamp club, and I was on that and a language club and a toastmasters' club, and I was on things like that.

Q: This sailing must have appealed to your sense of outdoorsmanship.

Admiral Weschler: I loved it, and also I thought it was the best-kept secret at the academy, because for 30 hours you were completely your own man. You climbed in that ketch, and you went where you wanted to go. There was no reveille, nobody said anything to anybody, and you could go all up and down that bay. You were just like anybody else who owned a boat. It was the most wonderful thing, and I'm absolutely thrilled that they introduced it.

I'm glad that sailing is now more of a recognized sport and actually an endeavor of the Naval Academy today as compared with then. I just don't think that there's any substitute, and I certainly think it gave us a sense of participation and responsibility. Although we got away from a lot of petty baloney, I think we learned an awful lot of other things, such as night navigation. You know, by the time you sailed up and down that Chesapeake and saw all the lights and avoided all the big freighters and everything that was moving around, you really had to be on the ball. You had to stand a good watch, or else you were in trouble. A nice combination!

Q: It sounds as if you got more than the usual ration of extracurricular activities. Were you more active than most people?

Admiral Weschler: I think so, and it suited me. I like to be busy, and everyone always says that if I'm not, I'll invent enough to make sure I am.

Q: These introductions you had to aviation and submarines--did either of those appeal to you at the time?

Thomas R. Weschler #1 - 30

Admiral Weschler: I thought that submarines did. I enjoyed aviation, but I knew I was having some difficulty with eyes. I wasn't an eye unsat, but all the time I was at the academy, I knew that when I went to a movie I had a hard time focusing on the screen in the dark. Although I could pass the physical when it would come around, each year it was a little bit more marginal. So I kind of put aviation aside long before that because of eye problems. But submarining I found of interest and talked of it.

During World War II, when there was a chance to have gotten into it, I said to myself, "I'm not going into that with my brother Charles a prisoner of war. I don't want to give Mother the extra concern of somebody in submarines." I know now that I never would have gone, because I just like being topside too much.

When I went into the merchant marine, I could have been an engineer or a third mate. I chose third mate automatically, and I obviously would today. So I know I liked being topside too much to be a submariner.

Q: I have heard about two classes in particular that didn't all get commissioned on time: 1933, because of the Depression, and 1939 because of eyes. I'm wondering why only '39 got picked on for the eyes.

Admiral Weschler: Forty did, as well. But the point was

that they had various limits. We were allowed to go down as low as 6/20 and still get a commission in the Supply Corps. But I was down to 4/20 or something like that--you know, the kind where they put a huge number up and you walk through it and you still haven't seen it. Fortunately, my cousin was an eye doctor, an excellent one, and I went to see him. He said, "Tom, I don't diagnose you as being long-term myopic. I think you're suffering from a lot of muscle strain. I can give you glasses right now that will let you see as well as anybody, but they'll be a crutch for the rest of your life. I'd rather give you a pair of glasses that you put on when you have to use them, but otherwise just see what happens and come back."

He recommended going into the merchant marine, because I'd look at the horizon and I'd be focusing on distance. He felt that would offset a lot of the strain, cumulatively, of four years of education and then working on things like the Lucky Bag. I just had done too much, he felt. I was probably latently myopic, and this had exaggerated the situation. He gave me a pair of glasses, and when the Wasp was sunk in 1942, the glasses went down with the Wasp. I got my next pair of glasses in 1962, 20 years later. I had gotten along perfectly well for that time.

The interesting thing is that now I have no problem at all with close range or medium range. It's the same situation that I had as a midshipman. If I go to a movie, I've got to put on a pair of glasses, and when I drive at night I put on a pair of glasses. But you tend to get farsighted with age, and I'm latently myopic, so the two events just come together and keep me in almost perfect focus. So it's not a bad way to go if you've got to have a difficulty.

Q: So if the war had not come along when it did, you may never have come back in the Navy.

Admiral Weschler: I was in the reserves, but it required the war to bring me back to active duty. Once I was on active duty, I was very fortunate and put in for augmentation and was accepted.* I was augmented in 1946 when I came back in as a regular naval officer.

Q: Could you cover some of your experiences when you were in the merchant marine?

Admiral Weschler: Yes, I tell you, I enjoyed it. I should say, too, that when I was at the Naval Academy, I read almost every book I came across on the big sailing ships and merchant ships of the world. In connection with that,

---

*Augmentation is the name of the procedure whereby an officer in the Naval Reserve receives a commission in the regular Navy.

I had had some contact with the merchant marine and what the Navy thought of the merchant marine, what the merchant marine thought of the Navy. I was shocked at the gap between the two. A lot of the hostility between the two depended on individuals, but there was some undercurrent in almost everyone on the merchant marine or Navy side.

When I went into the merchant marine, the Coast Guard people who administered the exams couldn't have been more tolerant and understanding and helpful. The men in our group were trying to be qualified as third mates or third assistant engineers. But things were different once we got aboard that first ship, which in my case was the Stanley Matthews, an old tanker. This was a 1918 or 1920 ship, and this was 1939. I thought that 19 years was pretty old for a ship. I now know that that's nothing, as witness our own Navy. Thirty or 40 years makes something an old ship.

The skipper was a wonderful gent from the Royal Naval Volunteer Reserve in World War I; I can't recall his name. Ted Banvard and I from the class of '39 were assigned to this ship.* The master called us up to his cabin one day, and he said, "I know that you're graduates of the Naval Academy, and you probably don't think anything more of the merchant marine than I think of your institution. But I'm willing to give you a fair chance to do your work. I know you have special assignments from the front office,

---

*Theodore J. Banvard later returned to active naval service and eventually retired as a captain.

and I want to make your life aboard comfortable. We'll just try to be objective about each other," or something like that.

It worked out very well, but you were always on trial with the group at first to see if you were going to be too uppity and turning your nose up at everything they were doing and not wanting to fraternize. But, actually, I have never met another such interesting group of people in my life as I met on there. This master, as I've said, was a British merchant captain who really believed in moon sickness. On a moonlit night if he caught you sleeping outside, he'd kick your tail. You had to get back in, because that moon would have maddened you for the night.

"Big Pig Bart" was the second mate, and he was that; he must have weighed between 300 and 350 pounds. His cabin was festooned with sausages and cheeses, and he kept a machete just inside the door. When we were in port he'd go ashore, and he could drink more beer than I've ever seen anybody drink. Then he'd come back about 2:00 or 3:00 in the morning and grab that machete and whack off some of that sausage and cheese and sit there and eat. What a guy! He was unmarried, and merchant marine pay was fairly adequate. He bought about a $6,000 pleasure boat that he was going to use in Bayonne, New Jersey. After he left it one day, it caught fire because he must have been smoking.

The thing burned down to the waterline, and he had no insurance. Well, that's the way it was. He shrugged and went right on again.

Wonderful René LeBlanc was a Frenchman who believed in navigation by every system known to man. He was right up to date. In those days H.O. 208 and H.O. 211 were the latest methods--Dreisenstock and Ageton. He knew them both, but he also had the Brazilian tables, Italian tables, and French tables. He could do the cosine-haversine formula, and he would work them all out. He loved to compare them and see the strengths and weaknesses. A fascinating guy to work with.

These kinds of people had been all over the world, sailed on all sorts of lines, and had gravitated to this ship. Each of them really had a brain and had something to offer, but every one of them had a phobia or some funny side to him that made him happy to be in that merchant marine environment and away from the rigors of service.

This ship operated in the U.S. oil trade, so that all we did was take black oil--which we picked up in Texas or Aruba or Lake Charles, Louisiana--and brought it up to Bayonne, New Jersey, where we pumped it into the refinery. Then the clean product went out from there.* I sailed most of the time up and down the eastern seaboard to the Caribbean but had about six months in clean smaller ships

---
*In this sense, "clean" refers to refined oil products, as opposed to "dirty" crude oil.

running up to Boston and up the Hudson River, thus seeing a lot of New England from seaside.

Q: What sorts of duties did you have?

Admiral Weschler: Well, we bounced around. We were like ensigns; we had to keep an ensign's notebook. We sketched and described every piece of equipment on every ship we served in. We had to keep track of a copy of every paper that the captain or mates had to fill out. We were being prepped to join the marine department of Tidewater Associated Oil. It was run by a man named Kelly; he was class of '21 and he had been a constructor.* He had once been connected with the salvage of a submarine.

Kelly wanted us to come along gradually, with an eye to one of us being his relief. He was willing to give us 10 or 15 years of experience before he stepped down. So we moved around. We were on one ship, then another, and then another. We kept moving, so that in a year and a half we had been on about six or seven different ships. The last ones were new diesel ships that the company, Tidewater and Tidewater Associated, had just recently acquired.

Q: This is what the captain referred to when he said, "You

------
*Richmond K. Kelly was a member of the Navy's Construction Corps; he resigned from the service in 1929 when he was a lieutenant.

have your assignments from the front office."

Admiral Weschler: Yes, that's right. He knew that. In addition, we stood watches as makee-learns with the mates to whom we were assigned.* He would rotate us with the mates with a series of 4:00 to 8:00s and a series of 12:00 to 4:00s, and that sort of thing.

Q: Being familiar with both, how would you compare the merchant marine deck officer training with Navy?

Admiral Weschler: As far as what merchant marine deck officers were required to do, the training was fine. But it was very simple, because all that amounted to was watchstanding and keeping the ship's security. They didn't have to worry about many of the things naval officers do. They weren't prepped for search and rescue; that wasn't likely to come along. The crew just went about its own business and didn't worry about anybody else. There weren't any weapons or sensors to operate. They didn't have radar in 1939 and 1940 when I was working with them. All we had was a direction finder, which was used on rare occasions. So it was a less complicated kind of watchstanding than for the naval officer, and the mate had

---

*Makee-learn essentially amounts to on-the-job training--watching and then doing.

Thomas R. Weschler #1 - 38

no responsibility for the people on board. That was the function of the chief mate and the captain and certain of the day operators and the union representative and people like that. So it was a much simpler task, but I thought they did it well.

I must say I learned some things about frugality in manpower that I think our Navy could still learn. By golly, you really thought twice before you asked a person to do something, because the second you did, it was overtime. The captain had only so many hours of overtime he was allowed to expend before he was on the carpet with the front office. So the only one who authorized overtime on the ship was the chief mate or the captain himself. I don't think that's bad.

Q: Were you reasonably content with this life or still disappointed you weren't in the Navy?

Admiral Weschler: Well, I'd have to say that I enjoyed it as a change, and it was the best job that was available when I came out of the Academy. The salary was not that munificent--$125.00 a month. But that was $25.00 better than most of those who were not commissioned had gotten from industry. And at least I had something to look forward to. This marine department was a big job; our marine manager was making $25,000 a year, which in 1939 was a pretty fantastic salary to aspire to. So I could see a career, and that gave me some satisfaction, because this at least gave me some new sense of direction.

But I did miss the Navy, and I found it to be one of those eye-opening things that once you're yanked away from the Navy, you get a chance to know how much you like it. When I came back, there wasn't any question as to whether or not I was going to stay. After we got married, a couple of times my wife would ask me, "Tom, are you really satisfied?"

I would tell her, "Darling, if there's one officer left in the U.S. Navy, I want to be that officer." So she never pressed me on that, because she found out how strongly I felt about staying in.

Q: How did you happen to hook up with this particular company?

Admiral Weschler: Because it was the only one recruiting. Mr. Kelly came down to Annapolis and looked around and really wanted to get some people. There was a different flavor about the interviewing. He came back a second time to see us, and so there was a feeling that this was more than run of the mill. All the others were so impersonal, and even though they had nice, pleasant people like yourself who would come around and talk with you, you

Thomas R. Weschler #1 - 40

figured, "Well, he's probably done this every day of his life for the last three months, and he can't remember anybody whom he's really seen." But this man Kelly would talk to us about what he wanted to do and why. Knowing his background and what he was after, there weren't that many schools he could recruit that kind of people from. So Tidewater was the only game in town that was merchant marine, and a very persuasive fellow who was sketching the future so you could fit into it.

Q: What was the specific act that brought you back into the Navy? Did the service redefine the eye standards?

Admiral Weschler: I had applied for the Naval Reserve, and I had heard nothing from Fourth Naval District. Being from Pennsylvania, that was where my papers went. I had written there a couple of times to see what was going on. The specific thing that got me in was that I was about to be drafted in December of 1940. I got my papers saying that I had to report the first week in January for Army draft. I said, "This is ridiculous to have a Naval Academy graduate being drafted into the Army when I have applied to the Naval Reserve. There has to be something useful I can do in the Navy." So I got hold of Greham Halpine, a friend who lived in Annapolis and was then serving in Washington. He became interested, so between Halpine and the Fourth

Thomas R. Weschler #1 - 41

Naval District and myself, we managed to find the papers and to get myself approved to be an ensign.* I think January 3, 1941 was the date that my reserve commission started.

Once that was approved, then the Naval Academy, since I had done well there, was looking for some young people to augment the teaching staff. I got my first set of orders to the Naval Academy as a professor. I had a new physical exam taken, and it showed that my eyes had come back remarkably. As a matter of fact, I read 20/15 when I came back in. The Bureau of Medicine and Surgery rejected this and said, "You must have tested the wrong man." But the doctor insisted that was perfectly right, and that's when the term "latent myopia" entered my life. They wrote that, "Although he can see 20/15, he has latent myopia." That's what kept me out of aviation.

But I was cleared enough then to go to the Naval Academy, and at the academy I got myself changed from E-V(G) to DE-V(G).** I was converted to the broadest category a reserve could get into. As soon as that was done, then I applied for sea duty, and I joined the Wasp in June of 1941.*** So I was at the Naval Academy only one

---
*Lieutenant Commander Charles G. Halpine, USN, retired in 1937 and then was recalled to active duty in 1940.
**From Engineering Volunteer General to Deck and Enginering Volunteer General.
***The USS Wasp (CV-7) was commissioned 25 April 1940. She had a standard displacement of 14,700 tons, was 741 feet long, 81 feet in the beam, and extreme width of 109 feet. She had a top speed of 29.5 knots and could accommodate approximately 80 aircraft.

term while my physical condition was checked out, my designation changed, and I was determined to be adequate to go to sea.

Q: How did you spend that time at the academy?

Admiral Weschler: I joined the "steam" department.* I taught thermodynamics and internal combustion engines to the class of '42. I had known a lot of the class of '42. They were plebes when I was a first classman, and so it was a pleasure to be back there that quickly. At least somebody I knew was still around. I taught them.

I thoroughly enjoyed it, and I thought I did a good job as a prof. I was familiar enough with what was going on that I thought I knew the highlights, and I could go through the lessons and say, "This is baloney. This is really what's salient. Don't worry about that; these are the things to really get." I think it helped a great deal; I wish someone had done more of it for me. It would have been useful to separate wheat from chaff. But I enjoyed it.

As I told you, both of my sisters were teachers. I taught at the Naval War College from 1951 to 1953 and then taught here again another six years after retiring, and now I'm teaching an elective. So I think teaching is something

---
*"Steam"--marine engineering.

Thomas R. Weschler #1 - 43

that I enjoy and that my family enjoys.

Q: Could you pick up the tale as you joined the Wasp? What kind of operations was she involved in?

Admiral Weschler: Well, to set the stage, this was the summer of 1941. As you know, the United States was doing everything short of actual warlike acts to assist Great Britain in its war against Germany. The Wasp was on what we called neutrality patrol. We had that line of demarcation with no offensive action allowed on our side--or the west side--of this line that the President had sketched out in 1939. We operated out of Bermuda, and our mission was that if we could find any German ship, we would put an airplane over him and tell the British where this German ship was as he went by. That was very helpful to the Brits; they could just stand on the line, and when that ship came steaming across, they would just happen to be where he was coming through. That happened with a couple of passenger liners and support ships that were operating out of the Caribbean.

    I should mention, too, that when I joined the ship in 1941, Mickey Weisner was aboard as the assistant navigator.* He was just about to get married, and I had

---

*Ensign Maurice F. Weisner, USN, Naval Academy class of 1941. In 1979 Weisner retired as a four-star admiral.

Thomas R. Weschler #1 - 44

decided that I wasn't interested in getting married with the war coming up, or I suspected coming up. So I bought a new convertible, and my major contribution to Mickey Weisner's love life was that he borrowed my convertible for his honeymoon. To this day I've never met Norma Weisner, but I know that she enjoyed my car.

Q: You had an odd situation in seniority then, didn't you? Some people that graduated after you were senior to you.

Admiral Weschler: Coming in as I did, I joined the class of '41. I run with '41--with but after. So that Mickey Weisner and Whitey Withrow and all these gents whom I'd known in '41 were my seniors, and I ran right at the tail end of the class.* But it didn't bother me at all. I was so glad to be back in, I could have been tail-end Charlie and I was. It just seemed like having been almost drafted and then only being allowed to go to the Naval Academy to teach, and then finally getting my eyes back up again, then being able to get a set of sea duty orders and wearing a uniform and going aboard a ship at sea in the Navy, that was just too much for anybody to accept in six months. That's why I say you could have told me I was any rank, and it wouldn't have bothered me. It was just so

---

*Ensign William H. Withrow, USN, was another shipmate in the Wasp.

much fun to be there.

Q: Did you express any preference on the duty, or was Wasp the luck of the draw?

Admiral Weschler: Luck of the draw. I simply said I wanted to go to sea duty and the sooner the better. That's where they sent me. And when I got aboard, I was very fortunate. I was made aide to the exec.* That doesn't sound like much; really, today we call it personnel officer. There was an officer out of '38, John Smith, who had had this job.** He wanted to move on to be a qualified officer of the deck and gunnery division officer. He had looked up my record and saw that I had a good set of credentials, and a couple of my classmates aboard told him I was a pretty good guy, and he said, "You're my relief." So I got aboard and joined him.

I was going to tell you about neutrality patrol and operating out of Bermuda. I don't think we'd been there more than about two weeks when we got the word that we were to load a couple of Army and Marine squadrons and a whole bunch of their gear, and we were going to join some larger group of ships. This was when we were going up to relieve the British and occupy Iceland. It was the first time I had seen Army and Marine aviators operating from a carrier,

---
*Exec-executive officer.
**Lieutenant (junior grade) John C. H. Smith, USN.

and, really, they didn't do it that often. I don't think we saw it ever again for the Army Air Forces and not until almost '43 or '44 for the Marines. So that was fascinating.

It was the first time we operated with a fairly major convoy. We had American Legion and Wichita and all sorts of ships with us in a fairly good-size formation. To me it was good size--probably 15 or 20 ships in total--and a lot of fog in the North Atlantic at that time. So it was a very interesting passage and particularly so for me, because I'd never gone that far and into those waters before.

After we completed the delivery of aircraft to Iceland, we picked up our air group in Norfolk and carried out some other operations at sea. Then we went into Newfoundland and just missed the President and Winston Churchill, who had been at Argentia for their conference.* We had a brief return to Iceland and anchored in Hvalfjordur. I remember it particularly for a wicked wind one night--almost a hurricane. We steamed at nearly five knots to the anchor to keep from dragging. I had a chance to go ashore for a conditioning hike with the Marines. That was an association I kept up for the next 40

---

*President Franklin D. Roosevelt and British Prime Minister Winston Churchill had their first face-to-face meetings at Placentia Bay, Argentia, Newfoundland, 9-12 August 1941. Out of their conferences and those of their staff officers came the principles set forth in the Atlantic Charter.

years, as often as I could.

Then to Bermuda. On December 7, 1941, I had been ashore and came back to the ship. I guess it was about 5:00 o'clock in the afternoon when we heard that war had started and couldn't believe it. We were under way before midnight, heading for Martinique because the carrier Bearn was in Martinique, and there was an emergency op order that if war was declared, we had to make sure that the French could not get their ships turned over to the Germans to operate against us. So we were the plug in the bottle for keeping the Bearn in Martinique. We steamed over there, and nothing happened. They were deciding to stay put, and they didn't make any move at all during the war.

Then the Wasp went over to St. Thomas, where we had a submarine scare. Somebody thought he saw a German sub, and that was the first time that I heard all about that and saw aircraft launched and people going out and dropping depth charges. Then we returned to Bermuda.

So it was a very busy six months of getting into the war and getting going.

Q: Who was the exec for whom you worked?

Admiral Weschler: Fred Dickey.* He was not Naval Academy; he was an aviation radioman in World War I and had

---
*Commander Fred Clinton Dickey, USN.

done very well. He got into the aviation training program, qualified as an aviator, and so he was a very special kind of person. I can't think of the name of the fellow who was his buddy. That I'd like to know, but he was Howard Hughes's right-hand man for starting Hughes Aircraft.* He and Fred Dickey had been aviation radiomen together. When I met him through the Polaris program later on, Fred Dickey's name was "open sesame" to getting me invited to everything that the Hughes Company was doing. He just couldn't do enough for a friend of Fred Dickey's, which I found to be very interesting.

My first skipper at that time was Black Jack Reeves, later Vice Admiral J. W. Reeves.** He was very successful in World War II and ended up as Commander Western Caroline Sub Area and later commander of NATS.*** When he left the ship, he was relieved by Forrest Sherman, so we had two very interesting captains.****

Q: What can you say about serving under those two?

Admiral Weschler: Black Jack Reeves wouldn't take any guff, and he was absolutely adamant in what he was going to

---

*Howard R. Hughes (1905-1976) was an eccentric American entrepreneur who was a test pilot and also had interests in the movie industry, oil-drilling, and Trans-World Airlines.
**Captain John W. Reeves, Jr., USN.
***NATS--Naval Air Transport Service.
****Captain Forrest P. Sherman, USN. As an admiral, Sherman served as Chief of Naval Operations, 1949-51.

do. But everybody felt that if they had to go to war, there wasn't anybody they'd rather go to war under. Black Jack Reeves insisted upon things being done precisely and properly; everything had to be ready for war all the time.

Learning to stand deck watches under him was probably the best experience any JO could ever have had.* When you were a JO for Black Jack Reeves, you were looking constantly for anything in that ship that wasn't absolutely perfect, and if he found it before you did, you really had it. But if you saw it and did something about it, then you were not only home free, but he really thought you were a pretty good guy.

Q: Of course, he had to see you do it before he said something favorable.

Admiral Weschler: No, no. Because he'd come on watch and see how things were around there and sense the improvement. He'd have been out perhaps before and then come back again. You didn't have to grandstand for him. As a matter of fact, that was probably sure death. But I knew that when I came on watch, I'd better look over the side. And if the scuttlebutt wasn't clean, I'd send for the flight deck boatswain. I was a fairly young ensign, but I didn't

---

*JO--Junior officer.

hesitate to call any head of department, all of them full commanders.

For instance, I'd say, "Commander Kernodle, the flight deck looks awful.* You'd better get somebody up there doing so and so." He took it, because he knew that if he didn't get it from me, he'd get it from the captain in about two minutes. So it really made me willing to speak up. As I say, I learned so much from Captain Reeves. I don't mean he was tolerant, but if he thought you were trying, he would give you a chance. He was fair to that extent, but you didn't try to snow him or give him any baloney. That wouldn't go over at all, and he was very, very short-tempered if he thought you were incompetent.

Q: The department heads were probably glad that you had given them this tip-off.

Admiral Weschler: As I say, it was easier to get it from an ensign and to blow your stack at him a little bit and then do something about it than it was to face the captain's wrath, because it was not unusual.

I'll never forget, we had a chief engineer named Rogers Elliott.** He was an absolutely wonderful guy and

---
*Commander Michael H. Kernodle, USN, air officer of the Wasp.
**Commander Rogers Elliott, USN, was the chief engineer of the Wasp.

had been in submarines. The captain came up one day and thought that the whistle was leaking steam. He had complained about it the day before, and they had fixed it. So he sent for the chief engineer and said, "Chief engineer, look up there at that whistle." He did, and he looked back again. The captain said, "I told you to look up at the steam leaking out of that whistle." And he looked up. Reeves said, "I told you to look at it."

He was there for over an hour looking at that damn steam leaking out of that whistle. It didn't leak anymore, I'll tell you that. But it didn't make any difference to him to have this commander standing up there making a fool of himself looking at that steam. That was the way it was going to be. And he sent for the communication officer when he didn't like the way the radios were being handled, and the communication officer stood watch for about six hours up there handling all the radio circuits and so on, personally. That was the way it was.

But I don't want to leave a picture that the captain made the Wasp an unhappy ship; it was not unhappy at all. We always knew whom everyone was going to gripe about, and so the rest of us get along perfectly well. We all knew he had good standards, so we felt ready for war if war were going to come, and we had one of the best leaders we could possibly have for it.

Q: How did the crew look on him?

Admiral Weschler: Same way, same way. And they knew that he was fair. You know, he liked going ashore as much as anybody, so difficulties on the beach were no real problem. If you got tanked up or were in a fight or something like that, that was tolerated. It was what you did aboard ship that mattered. If you could haul yourself together and come up the brow and go below without making a big scene, you were probably okay--no matter what somebody else was saying about you.

Q: As the personnel officer, you probably saw a lot of mast cases.*

Admiral Weschler: I saw a great deal of them, and in those days the exec was able to handle a lot of things. Only the very major things had to go forward to the captain. And, you know, there were certain allowances. Heads of departments were allowed some leeway. A man might be an hour or so AOL, and the head of department concerned, not wanting it go to any further, took care of it.** So it

---
*Captain's mast is a sort of court in which the commanding officer listens to requests; awards either non-judicial punishment, that is, for lesser offenses than those which merit courts-martial; or issues commendations. Most often captain's mast is used for punishment.
**AOL--Absent over liberty, that is, being late in returning to the ship.

was the usual kind of ship where people were looking out for their own, and I thought it was a very happy and pleasant group. I learned an enormous amount from it.

Wasp had a lot of top-notch officers on board. I should mention Dave McCampbell, who was later one of our top aces in World War II; he was the landing signal officer aboard Wasp when I first arrived there.* He was a lieutenant then, myself an ensign. The impression he made was one of total competence, really professional. In his manner he struck me as a real hell-for-leather kind of individual, great ashore and fun to know.

When he climbed into that cockpit, he seemed welded to the aircraft, the way that he could function. One of the big ways that landing signal officers are successful is in establishing a feeling of confidence with those who are landing aboard, that the LSO really knows what he's doing. Dave McCampbell was that in spades. He was able to bring them in well, and they felt very confident in having him there as the LSO. All I can say is that the initial impression of a JO seeing him was that this was a gent who was going to write history, because he had that capability, and he went on to prove it.

While I was there, his exploits had really just begun

---

*Lieutenant David McCampbell, USN. In 1944, as a commander, he was Commander Air Group 15 in the carrier Essex (CV-9). During that tour, he shot down 34 Japanese airplanes, the top figure for a U.S. Navy pilot during World War II. His oral history is in the Naval Institute collection.

Thomas R. Weschler #1 - 54

with our support of the Guadalcanal landing, and I didn't really have much more contact with him after that.* I just wanted to convey that thought of how he came across to us.

Q: You say you spotted him as a comer ahead of time. Were there any you spotted then who didn't fulfill the promise you expected?

Admiral Weschler: That's an interesting one. I don't really have any that come to mind as having been potentially great who didn't come off well later on. We had such terrific people aboard. One we lost who was marvelous was Commander Jack Shea.** He was killed when the Wasp was sunk, and they named the field at Naval Air Station South Weymouth for him--Shea Field.*** He was one who came across very well. Mike Kernodle was our air officer before Shea, and he later commanded San Jacinto and did very well for himself. We had a lot of good people in there. I can't remember anyone, though, who was really a

---
*As he related in his own oral history, McCampbell also worked with the British pilots during the trips to Malta.
**Lieutenant Commander John J. Shea, USN, became widely known for a touching letter he wrote to his young son before he died. The letter and an article about Shea appear in The Hook magazine (published by the Tailhook Association), Fall 1983, pages 25-27.
***On 15 March 1946 the field at Naval Air Station Squantum, Massachusetts, was named Shea Field. When that station closed in 1954, the name was transferred to the field at South Weymouth, Massachusetts.

flash in the pan, who gave you a great deal and then, later on, bombed out.

Q: Selection was so rigorous before the war, you probably had to have good people.

Admiral Weschler: That's right. And those who were, say, lieutenant commanders and commanders were the ones who were caught in the acceleration, so that suddenly they were captains and earned stars by the time the war was over. There was nothing at all unusual in that happening.

Q: Were most of the officers still regulars at that point?

Admiral Weschler: Yes. I'd say they were about 90%. There were already some reserves when I got there. There were more reserves in aviation than there were in the surface Navy, because the AvCad program had been going on for some time.* In 1935 the Navy started to recruit aviators from other sources than the academy. So the squadrons might have had some reserves in them. The flight deck crew or hangar deck crew might have had some reserves

---

*AvCad--aviation cadet, a program instituted in 1935 whereby individuals enlisted in the Naval Reserve, then were trained as aviators and sent to the fleet before being commissioned as officers. In 1939 the program was modified so that individuals were commissioned upon successful completion of flight training.

in them. But as far as the ship's company deck force was concerned, I was one of the first of the reserves to come into that group. They started coming at fairly regular intervals in 1941, and inside of a year I'd say we were approaching a third or more of reserves.

The same was true of enlisted. We still had that crackerjack group of petty officers who were all pre-World War II recruits, the men who were all going to go on and be chiefs and warrants and lieutenants and so on as the war progressed. They were all now the second class and the first class.

As a matter of fact, that first year I was aboard, two of our enlisted men were considered for the Naval Academy. One of them was a first class gunner's mate, and I never saw him again until I was working on the Spruance-class destroyers in 1968. I looked across the table at Franklin Steward Bergen, and I said, "Captain, I know I've seen you before."

He said, "I don't think so, Admiral."

I said, "Well, let's play 'Where have you been?'"

He told me the ships and no, no, no, no. Finally he said, "Well, I was an enlisted man aboard the Wasp."

I said, "I was on the Naval Academy selection board in 1941. I remember you now. You were a first class gunner's mate when you were 22."

He said, "That's right."

Though he didn't go to the Naval Academy, he was commissioned and eventually became a captain in the regular Navy.*

Q: That's remarkable.

Admiral Weschler: The other one was Sergeant Doehler. He had left a month before I got there. Sergeant Doehler was a Marine sergeant. He's now retired Brigadier General Doehler.** That was the caliber of guys that you had coming through there. I can name handfuls of petty officers who eventually retired as lieutenant commanders, commanders, and in a couple of cases even captain. There was a tremendous cross section of talent.

Q: How could Bergen make it that fast? I thought advancement was quite slow in the prewar Navy.

Admiral Weschler: Well, that was my impression, but I know that's true that he was recruited and was a first class petty officer at 22. I had a first class yeoman, Norman Byers, who was killed when the ship was sunk. He explained it to me, because I challenged him on that. I said, "What

---
*Bergen, who was born in 1919, enlisted in the Navy in 1936. He was commissioned as a reserve officer in 1943 and subsequently augmented into the regular Navy. Bergen retired as a captain in 1969.
**William Francis Doehler graduated in the Naval Academy class of 1945.

did he do? How did he do it?

As I remember, Bergen had had a bonus from his school where he was number one in the class, and they made him a third class petty officer on finishing the course. It was something like that. Then he just went on from there. So it was an amazing story.

Q: You were sort of an anomaly. You were officially a reserve officer, but essentially you were a regular.

Admiral Weschler: That's right.

Q: How were you viewed by your contemporaries?

Admiral Weschler: The Naval Academy grads treated me generally as one of their own. The reserves treated me as one of their own. I was happy to be friends with both groups, so I had the best of both worlds. Every Naval Academy guy was kind enough to say things like, "Gee, Tom, you ought to be ahead of me. You ought to be right up with your class. This is ridiculous," and words to that effect.

I was very close to the reserves and enjoyed being with them. They said, "Gee, it's a tough break for you, but we enjoy working with you and knowing you, so it's pleasant to have you around." So I really was in both camps. The camp lines tended to disappear as the war went along, but there was a little feeling still.

Q: What was the caliber of the reserve officers that early?

Admiral Weschler: I thought they were top-notch. They were mostly from places such as Harvard, Princeton, Yale--wonderful Ivy League colleges and a couple from the West Coast. We didn't have any reserve programs that weren't in some of the best colleges in the country. One of the things that that unfortunate period in the late '60s, early '70s cost us was most of our finest affiliations with Ivy League schools. I'm not picking them out because I think they're wealthy and I think everybody who goes there is great. But from the Navy's point of view, these graduates were an investment in long-term influential support. The NROTC graduates from these fine institutions were going to go on to make their mark in the country, and they would never forget the Navy. Admiral Holloway was so wise in getting this program going after the war.*

I'm here in Newport now, and there's hardly a person

---

*In 1946, the Holloway Plan was enacted to establish a Naval ROTC program that would pay for the college education of individuals and grant regular, rather than reserve, commissions upon graduation. It was named for Rear Admiral James L. Holloway, Jr., USN, who had much to do with its development. See "A Gentlemen's Agreement," U.S. Naval Institute Proceedings, September 1980, pages 71-77.

on Bellevue Avenue--and a lot of them are very influential--who was not in the Navy at one time or another during World War II.* They don't remember anything that was more exciting, and they have great respect for the Navy today and cheer for it and support it. This is the kind of cadre in civilian life that helps get the Navy what it needs. So it isn't just what they can do when they're on active duty. It's what they do with their contemporaries and the leverage that they can apply politically that is so effective. I think we're going to feel it in years to come.

Q: You probably know Kemp Tolley from the class of '29.**

Admiral Weschler: Oh, yes.

Q: He was an instructor at the Naval Academy right about that period, and he said he was more impressed being with the young reserve officers than the midshipmen. He thought they were more sophisticated, they talked about more important things. They talked about the world problems and political things, whereas the midshipmen were buried in a mass of details, petty things involved in academy life.

---
*A number of the upper-crust members of Newport society live on Bellevue Avenue.
**Rear Admiral Kemp Tolley, USN (Ret.), whose oral history is in the Naval Institute collection.

Admiral Weschler: Yes. I think that's quite right. I think that aboard ship, the reserve for the first year might be behind the Naval Academy graduate in terms of the routine of what was going on aboard ship. But in terms of understanding the discipline and seeing what was going on in the big picture, he was more mature than the average midshipman. The midshipman, having come from a disciplined life, wasn't prepared for his new role. These others, coming from a less rigid life, could see where the right balance was. I found the reserves' outlook to be quite eye-opening.

Q: Was there any difference between the two categories in the way they went along with the captain's program of a very taut, shipshape operation?

Admiral Weschler: No, they were quite willing to play ball with what he wanted. After all, we were learning to stand watch; none of them were qualified OODs before they came.* We were all brand-new ensigns who were going through this. Captain Reeves didn't believe in having a lot of officers of the deck. He would get about four qualified, and then those four stood all the watches. If one of you was sick, three of you stood them. It didn't make any difference that there were perhaps another 20

---

*OODs--Officers of the deck.

ensigns running around. He wasn't going to bother qualifying them. He had his stable that he liked, and they were the ones he was going to stay with. If he didn't like you as a watch stander, it wasn't hard for him to get you moved out. So the fact that four of you, say, got qualified and then stayed there was in itself a vote of confidence, and you were sort of proud.

Nobody knew more about what was going on in the ship than the officers of the deck did. Even the heads of the departments didn't hear the captain and the navigator and others shooting the breeze about what was going on. We were up there enough, and we'd pass the word to one another and to our friends of what we had heard was going to happen. We were a well-informed group, and I'm sure we were a little stuck on ourselves.

Q: How did you happen to break into the rotation? Did the merchant marine experience help there?

Admiral Weschler: No, I'd have to thank the exec for it. Commander Dickey knew that the personnel officer billet didn't turn me on 100%. I wanted to get myself into something active with the ship topside and to know the functioning of it. So he said, "Okay, I'll start breaking you in on deck watches." He made me a JO, and I stood JO watches for probably five or six months before I could qualify for top watch.

During that time, I know that I impressed the captain a couple of times because of his comments to me. I went around to each of the divisions and got everything explained to me, so that I knew what a 1.1 was and what its rate of fire was and how many watch standers there were up there and what division had it.* That way, if I wanted to do something, I knew the chain of command. A couple of times on the bridge the captain wanted to get something done, and a name was needed. I'd volunteer, "Well, we can call So-and-so, and he'll take care of it."

He'd say, "How did you know that?"

So, as I say, because of that attitude of trying to find out and knowing what was happening, I think he finally decided that I wouldn't be too bad if I got on the team.

Q: You did this on your own initiative?

Admiral Weschler: The exec had put me up there for JO watches, but the rest of it was my own doing, simply because I wanted to know. I always do like to know, so I just applied that same approach. Well, it paid off. The captain thought that if I wanted to know, that was a pretty good attitude, and maybe I'd know about the right things at

---

*A 1.1 was an antiaircraft gun with a barrel diameter of 1.1 inches, commonly found in quadruple mounts. Because it was prone to jam when in operation it was soon replaced.

the right time if I were on watch.

Q: I'm surprised the senior watch officer didn't have a more formalized program.

Admiral Weschler: Part of it was that we had a senior watch officer who was also the aerographer. The aerographer was busy as could be in a carrier, because he had to be up for the morning soundings and the evening soundings and making up the weather forecasts and so on. So Sherman Betts didn't get around to do an awful lot of senior watch officering.* The captain didn't trust the next person. So he was almost prohibited from talking to us about what he was going to do. By that time, we were down to the ensigns, and the ensigns looked out for themselves. The two seniors moved out of the watchstanding as soon as enough of us qualified.

During my early period as an officer of the deck was an incident that I ought to tell you about. That was Wasp's collision with the destroyer Stack.** We were coming south after having been up around Newfoundland and Maine a short while and were heading for Norfolk. We were accompanied by the Stack and the Sterett, and the fog was very thick. There was an operational requirement to be in Norfolk that necessitated good speed. So instead of

---
*Lieutenant Sherman W. Betts, USN.
**The collision was on the morning of 17 March 1942.

slowing in the fog, the captain was placing some reliance on radar. The only radar that we had that could do anything on the surface was a fire control radar, which was a Mark 4. One of our former officers of the deck, Lieutenant Lewis, was up in the director tower, and he was reporting where the destroyers were.*

We were making about 20 knots in this very thick fog, so thick that from the bridge you couldn't see the lookouts who were on either side of the flight deck forward. That was about 350 feet maximum, and there was less than that visibility. To be pressing on like that and feeling that the radar was going to let you know if anything got in the way was probably asking an awful lot of the radar in those days. But the only things we could imagine that would be out there were fishing vessels. Anything else, because of the submarine scare, was probably traveling in convoy or staying fairly close to the coast. So we really didn't think there was much chance of hitting anything.

Anyhow, as we were coming along, the radar was reporting that the Stack was getting closer. We asked him what his intentions were, and he said that he felt he was getting off station, and he was simply coming in to sight us and regain his station. We reported to the destroyers that we weren't sure of their positions. Time went by, and there were echoes, but we couldn't be sure where Stack was.

---
*Lieutenant William E. Lewis, USN.

This was on the morning watch.

Suddenly, somewhere along in here, there was a thump, as though we had run into a heavy sea.* Except for the fact that there had been a momentary dull, red glow forward just at that time, there wasn't anything to indicate that there had been a collision. Then I got a report that there was heavy smoke on the forecastle. I had the deck at this time, and I sounded fire quarters and reported to the navigator, who was the supervisory watch officer at the time, that I had a feeling I had collided with the Stack. I'd sounded fire quarters because of the report of this heavy smoke up forward. At that time, we got word from the engine room that we had lost all vacuum. I ordered "All stop." The navigator took over the watch from me at that time and said, "I relieve you." He ordered all ahead standard and said, "I know the captain wants to hold to the schedule."**

I said, "We've got a destroyer wrapped around the bow." By that time, the captain had come to the bridge and was getting reports of what was going on, that fire quarters was being set.

The navigator said, "I feel there is no destroyer up there. If there were, the lookout would have reported it, and according to your radar, the last report you had to

---
*The collision was at 0550 in the morning.
**The navigator was Commander Donald F. Smith, USN.

show where he was, was 500 yards out." By this time our crew were looking over the side and could hear people on this destroyer down there yelling.

So Wasp was plowing ahead again because of the navigator having gone back to standard speed, and we had a destroyer wrapped around the stem. We learned a little later that we hit it just about the break of the deck, which was about a third of the way aft. So Stack was being held partly heeled over, pressed against the bow and being pushed through the water almost with its outboard rail underwater. The destroyer's captain hollered up, "What are your intentions?" Of all the phrases when you're being pushed, I thought that was a classic: "What are your intentions?"*

In any event, Captain Reeves got the word that there was a destroyer on the bow. He said, "All stop, back two-thirds," and he backed out, and then he went back up to speed again. As soon as we started moving, he tried to raise Stack on the radio. We lost sight of her as soon as we backed out. We didn't know whether our bow had been plugging a hole which was now flooding or just what had gone on. We tried to raise her by every means known to man. We made a report that she had been holed and was in we didn't know what state there in the North Atlantic. And

---

*Admiral Harold E. Shear, USN (Ret.), was an ensign in the Stack at the time of the collision. In his Naval Institute oral history, he discussed the performance of the destroyer's commanding officer.

we never did establish contact with her. We used the bullhorn and radio, went around the area and tried to pick her up again with radar. We simply had no luck. So after putting in about three or four hours in the area trying to find <u>Stack</u>, we got word back through the beach that she had made a report that she was proceeding to Philadelphia and could make it on her own. So we went on to Norfolk.

When we got in there, obviously soon there was an informal investigation and then a court of inquiry. The captain and I were cleared of all responsibility because, in effect, the captain of the destroyer had been steering a collision course to find the <u>Wasp</u>, and he found it by making perfect contact at the bow. The reason why we didn't have any report from the port lookout was that the yardarm of the <u>Stack</u>, as it went by the bow, took the phones off the head of Wasp's lookout. Thank heavens, they weren't strapped that tightly on him that he went over the side with the phones!

It was a question, as I say, of the conning officer thinking he would be able to see the <u>Wasp</u> before he made contact, but the fog was so thick he couldn't. And he hadn't been thinking of his relative motion. He was steering to close, and in steering to close, without extra speed, forgot that he also had a component dropping him aft. So that instead of making contact and being able to cross ahead of our bow, he really made contact and dropped onto the bow--too bad.

Q: Did you have a PPI scope on the radar at that time?*

Admiral Weschler: We didn't have any surface search or air search radars at that time. The only radar yet installed was this fire control radar, which had no PPI. That's the one we were using. And the destroyer didn't have anything, so they were counting on the Mark I eyeball. Stack was repaired and worked with us again later on but obviously with a new skipper, because he was relieved, lost some numbers, and so on.**

Q: Did the fire control radar have a minimum range?

Admiral Weschler: Yes, but we didn't know that then. For example, we didn't know what multiple echoes were. When you got in to a certain point, the energy was bouncing back and forth to give a string of echoes anywhere from, say, 1,000 yards in to zero, and which was the target was hard to say. The last time Lieutenant Lewis was really certain

---

*PPI--planned position indicator, is a circular type scope that gives a picture as if looking down on the scene from above, with one's own ship in the center and other ships shown at appropriate ranges and bearings.

**Commander Isaiah Olch, USN, was commanding officer of the Stack at the time of the collision. He had been in command since the ship was commissioned in 1939 so may have been due for transfer in any case.

what the range was, it had been about 500 yards. He'd watched them close from, say, about 2,000 to 500. So we were fairly certain that he was continuing to come in, although we couldn't tell him where he was. All we could say is, "We have confused echoes." And none of us knew enough to interpret what that really meant.

Q: And you certainly didn't want to start maneuvering when you had no idea where he was.

Admiral Weschler: That's right, and we still had this other destroyer who was doing perfectly well staying over there, who didn't lose us. I just thought I'd mention that for the record.

Aboard <u>Stack</u> the captain had the conn, because he was maneuvering to do this. I found out later on who was the officer of the deck there with him. It was John J. McMullen out of '40.* I since have met and talked with John McMullen about that situation, about what was going on and what their fears were, and then this horrible experience of being wrapped around the bow and of us continuing to move so that they couldn't get away. And then, when we finally backed loose and they came free, they wondered for a moment what was going to happen.

---
*Ensign John J. McMullen, USN.

The thing that saved them was that the stem of Wasp came right in at the forward starboard lifeboat davit. That davit was stout enough that, even with that pushing, we didn't really make more than a few feet of dent into the ship. We never got into the keel. We could have sliced them in half. They were really pretty fortunate. No injuries, incidentally, in either Stack or Wasp from this event.

Q: When the navigator ordered the ship back up to speed again, was that countermanded before you could hit the destroyer again?

Admiral Weschler: The sequence of orders was this: we were making standard; then we went to stop, and we still had way on and were continuing to push. We didn't have the order off long enough for us ever to have pulled apart. We were continuing to drive in. He took the deck from me and ordered all ahead standard. So we continued to press in. It wasn't until the captain came on the bridge and took the conn and ordered all stop, back two-thirds, that we got out of there.

Q: That probably didn't help your navigator's career at all.

Admiral Weschler: He didn't get socked for it, as I recall. He later went on and had a ship command, but that's as far as I know he went I was not generally impressed with him as a seaman.

Q: John McMullen that you mentioned--this is the fellow that owns the Houston Astros, isn't it? He's a naval architect.

Admiral Weschler: That's right. I didn't know he owned the Houston Astros. He used to be president of U.S. Lines, and he has John J. McMullen Associates, which is a consultant and shipbuilder. He's had quite an illustrious career.

Q: Douglas Fairbanks was on board your ship for a while.* What was his role?

Admiral Weschler: Captain John Hall came aboard, and he had with him as an aide Doug Fairbanks, Jr. This was when <u>Wasp</u> was operating with the Home Fleet and when we twice made that resupply of aircraft to Malta, had the Spitfires aboard. Captain Hall was there as the observer for Admiral

---

*Lieutenant (junior grade) Douglas E. Fairbanks, Jr., USNR, was a well-known movie actor of the period. He has written a book on his World War II service: <u>A Hell of a War</u> (New York: St. Martin's, 1993).

Stark, to let him know how we were doing with the Brits.*
Doug Fairbanks was a jaygee and was assigned to a stateroom on about the second or third deck in "torpedo hollow." He was down there "with the boys," and a welcome addition. He looked a lot like his father in terms of manner and capability and really didn't take himself too seriously.** That was pleasant to find out, especially because he was very well connected, not only through his own capabilities but because of his wife's antecedents and so on. But he really just joined the group.

I had a roommate by the name of Dave Bill, a classmate who's since retired, class of '39.*** Dave Bill was notorious for never having the right clothes at the right time, so that you never knew when he was going to come in and grab something out of your drawer. If you came in and the last pair of skivvies was gone, you knew that Dave Bill had made a raid. Well, we were still having Saturday morning inspections whenever there was a lull; there was enough of the old prewar routine that carried over.

Shortly after Doug Fairbanks had come aboard and was living nearby, we were due to have an inspection. Dave had been ordered to radar school in November 1941. It was up

---
*Captain John L. Hall, Jr., USN; Admiral Harold R. Stark, USN, became Commander U.S. Naval Forces in Europe in April 1942 after being relieved as Chief of Naval Operations.
**His father, Douglas Fairbanks, Sr., was a swashbuckling actor during the silent-movie era and was for a time married to actress Mary Pickford.
***Lieutenant (junior grade) David S. Bill, Jr., USN.

to about March that I'm talking about now. He had packed his cruise box to go to radar school. His orders were canceled, and the cruise box sat there in the cabin until the ship was sunk; he never did get rid of it or unpack it. So all his clothes were in there. For this Saturday morning inspection, he had everything he needed except a pair of white pants. So up he went to find the nearest room that looked like it had white trou, and he remembered Doug Fairbanks. He said, "Well, he's an aide type; he's bound to have a lot of uniforms." So he dove in there and grabbed a pair of Doug Fairbanks's trou, the very ones that Doug intended to put on.

About five minutes after Dave was in, Doug was running around saying, "Does anybody have a pair of white pants to get up for inspection?" Anyway, that was Dave, and it also shows that Doug was very human and would get caught in situations. He stood qualifying deck watches while he was aboard. He had no basic responsibilities except assisting Captain Hall and observing and writing reports and things like that. He stayed with us only those two months that we were with the Home Fleet.

Q: I take it that he was not at all aloof from the rest of the officers.

Thomas R. Weschler #1 - 75

Admiral Weschler: No. He loved bridge, and he played bridge in the wardroom and mixed very convivially. The captain, of course, was delighted to have him aboard. He was a good tennis player, and Captain Reeves loved to play tennis. So while we were in the Orkneys, they'd go over and play tennis. So he was a welcome addition and something to write home about which was not classified. He made his contribution in simply being one of the fellows.

Q: I take it he didn't ask any special favors because of his fame.

Admiral Weschler: Not at all. Not at all. And I think that the average one of us, if anything, leaned over backwards not to give him any deference or special treatment. We wanted to make sure he felt at home, and we didn't want him to feel we were a bunch of star-struck young men who were blinded by this movie idol. We treated him normally, and I think it came across very well.

Q: Did you have any impressions of Captain Hall?

Admiral Weschler: I wish I had known him better. I just saw him as a sober and capable individual. I know he had a

Thomas R. Weschler #1 - 76

good sense of humor, because I could hear him standing on the wing of the bridge, talking to the captain, and he seemed to be having a wonderful time. I had no professional dealing with him.

Q: Hall was a noted Naval Academy athlete, so maybe he got in some of those tennis games also.

Admiral Weschler: He may very well have, yes. And I don't know where he went afterwards in the war. I don't recall. But I know I remember seeing his name mentioned in Morison's history once or twice.*

Q: He was an amphibious commander, particularly in the Atlantic, developing doctrine and tactics and so forth.

Admiral Weschler: Well, I missed that.

Q: What do you recall about the Wasp's transition from the Atlantic to the Pacific?

Admiral Weschler: It was all very rushed. We'd been in the Med. We hightailed it back to Norfolk, had orders to go through the Panama Canal and get out to San Diego as

---

*Rear Admiral Samuel Eliot Morison, USNR, produced a widely read 15-volume History of United States Naval Operations in World War II.

quickly as we possibly could. The Guadalcanal operation was set at that time for the first of August, and we didn't get back into Norfolk until late May. It was just a fantastic struggle to get radar installed, go through the canal, get into San Diego, pick up the air group, get to Pearl for briefings, on to Fiji for rehearsal, and then get to the operation by the first of August.*

Along the way, Black Jack Reeves got pulled, and Forrest Sherman stepped aboard.** There was no formal change of command with everybody getting together. They saluted in the cabin, and we were under way with a new captain on board.

Q: What can you say about Captain Sherman in comparison with Captain Reeves?

Admiral Weschler: Well, it was obvious that we had a completely different man when Captain Sherman came aboard. But except for seeing Captain Sherman sitting in the chair on the bridge soon thereafter, I really wasn't aware of what his personality was. He did seem a lot more reflective than Captain Reeves. Since we were going into a major operation now, he was reading through all the op

---

*In fact, the U.S. invasion of Guadalcanal was delayed briefly; it took place on 7 August 1942.
**Captain Forrest P. Sherman, USN, relieved Reeves on 31 May at Norfolk. The ship left for the Panama Canal on 6 June and went through on 10 June as part of Task Force 37.

orders, and he would listen to what was going on. He didn't like some of our procedures, and so he was organizing things for better watch-standing. He would tell the navigator, who would tell the senior watch officer, who would tell the officers of the deck. We'd all get the word simultaneously what the new setup was going to be.

I think it's important, too, to note that under Captain Reeves we had started a system of command duty officers on the bridge. In addition to the officer of the deck, you also had a senior officer who would sit up there on the bridge in a supervisory role. What his authority was was never very well established, and we officers of the deck were always alert for our prerogatives. If the command duty officer intervened, we would ask, "Do you have the deck, sir?"

Whoever had the duty would say, "No, damn it." He would then let us go on and do what we were doing, though we noted the advice, which was often very good. Captain Sherman had a hard time accepting that and adjusting to it. He liked it being a little more clear-cut. He didn't change it. He still had it up there, but he didn't really push it as much as Captain Reeves had done.

Sherman was much quieter. He didn't do all the looking around and chewing out of everybody if the scuttlebutt wasn't clean and that sort of thing. He was just a different personality. But he watched for a lot of other things. He was terrifically interested in the way the air group operated and in getting a full briefing on the range capability of the aircraft with all sort of weapons loads. He was thinking a lot more combat-oriented than we had any reason to do before or than Black Jack Reeves had shown any interest in doing. We hadn't been flying strike missions; we had been flying antisubmarine warfare patrols. In the Atlantic all you really were worried about was the submarine threat. Now we were going out where there would be anti-shipping strikes, and the ship had to be ready to go in and provide support in amphibious operations. So he was prepping himself for that.

Q: I'm surprised to hear you say that Captain Reeves was not more combat-conscious, because didn't you face a considerable air threat going into the Med?

Admiral Weschler: I gave the wrong impression then. He was equally combat-conscious, but we were in air offensive operations and task group attack operations in the Pacific. In the Atlantic they were generally ASW and ferry operations.* They called for different outlooks. We didn't have the same sense of initiative and responsibility toward what we were doing in the Atlantic as we did in the

---

*ASW--antisubmarine warfare.

Pacific. We were operating as part of the Home Fleet with a British op order. We were almost in cotton batting within this carrier group and surface task group that the Brits put together in order to deliver Wasp with the Spitfires inside Gibraltar to launch aircraft and then get out again.

We weren't allowed to go in harm's way any more than absolutely necessary. We were allowed to go into the Med only far enough that the Spitfires with wing tanks could take off and get to Malta, and then we were to get out of there. So under those circumstances, with the deck full of Spitfires, there was little that the Wasp could do to protect herself. We didn't have the bulk of our own air group aboard. We'd left it in the Orkneys, and it was operating out of there. When we came by Gibraltar, in order to give us some sort of protection, we had Fairey Fulmars, Swordfish, and Albacores--all British planes--put aboard to work with us until we could get our own air group back.

So there was a completely different feel to the two oceans. The Atlantic was exciting, and the ASW and mine threats were of concern, but we couldn't get into the task group picture the way we did in the Pacific.

Q: It was strictly an expedient thing at that point.

Admiral Weschler: That's right. We did a very fine job, and it was just what was needed. Twice we provided the deck that was big enough to accomplish something that they were after.

Q: What do you recall about the flag officer who joined the ship once you get to the Pacific?

Admiral Weschler: Admiral Leigh Noyes came aboard in San Diego.* He didn't bring a full staff, so Captain Sherman became the chief of staff to Admiral Noyes, who was commander of our particular little group. Well, the captain took that very seriously, and Admiral Noyes equally, so the two of them were together almost all the time. Sherman's role became about half commanding officer and half chief of staff. Once he was satisfied that the ship was operating satisfactorily, his effort went elsewhere.

There was no less respect for Sherman than Reeves. We knew that this was a man with brains, and he knew his signal book. We had not done much signal work before, but now we were using signal flags a lot more, and he was really up on them. And the radio was being used a lot more. We had not had that much TBS, and we were not in

---

*Rear Admiral Leigh Noyes, USN, was Commander Task Force 18, which comprised the Wasp and five transports headed for the Tonga Islands.

major formations.* Now we were beginning to get into larger formations, larger groups of ships.

I want to make sure that you get the impression of a person who was after the big picture. I thought Admiral Leigh Noyes did not have the big picture, and that Captain Sherman was really the one who was carrying him.

Q: There was another pretty famous name on that ship, Wallace Beakley.**

Admiral Weschler: He was the air group commander. He was not there when I first came aboard. I have Wallace Beakley strongly in mind from a time during our initial voyage in the Pacific. I had a classic run-in with Wallace Beakley which made sure that I remembered him, although I don't know whether he remembered me all that much or not.

Q: What was your run-in?

Admiral Weschler: The navy yard at Norfolk had put aboard this CXAM radar, which was a development version of an SC air-search radar. With that we got sort of a radar plot and some new, young officers aboard to man that. Wallace

---

*TBS--the short-range voice radio equipment used to communicate between ships.
**Lieutenant Commander Wallace M. Beakley, USN, who eventually retired as a vice admiral after serving as Commander Seventh Fleet and Deputy Commander in Chief Atlantic Fleet.

Beakley, as CAG, became officer in charge of radar plot and coordinated its functions with the ship and his air group. He was the interlocutor to the captain for what was going on.

I really didn't know an awful lot about all this. It was secret within the ship as to what was happening, and nobody talked a great deal about it. We were out in the Pacific and had just about reached Tongatabu. I had the OOD watch one day when there was the announcement that an aircraft contact had been made. This group back of the bridge sent word up to the bridge that an aircraft contact had been picked up at such and such a range and bearing. I asked, "Friend or foe?"

With that, Wallace Beakley came charging out to the bridge and said, "We will answer any questions from the captain. The rest of this is classified information, and you have no right to know."

I said, "Commander, that just can't be. I'm not going to have any report of an aircraft reaching me and not be able to know if it's friend or foe, if you have any identification, so that I can take the right action for the ship." Captain Sherman happened to come out just about that time; his cabin was aft on the island. He came walking up, and he heard the two of us. Sherman said, "The officer of the deck is perfectly right. If you have any indication, I want that provided to the OODs so they know whether or not to go to general quarters, or whether they should launch fighters, or whether they should do anything in connection with your contact. If you know it's friendly, that's something else again."

Wallace Beakley was not very cooperative and was not happy about the outcome. But he never groused at me again, and the next time I saw him was when he was chief of staff of the Naval War College as a rear admiral. I was a commander and had just been selected for duty on the faculty up here. I walked into his staff meeting one day and introduced myself. He was kind enough to say he remembered me. We took it from there. We stayed good friends. I mean, I really respected him. He was a great aviator from Dover-Foxcroft, Maine. I like anybody from Maine. He was very much along the lines of Black Jack Reeves. He liked things done in certain ways and precisely right and didn't want to be crossed. As long as you did it his way and on time and perfectly, then everything was okay.

Q: Why was there that attitude, even toward people in your own ship, that they didn't need to know about radar?

Admiral Weschler: I tried to find this out at our reunion this September, the 40th year of the loss of the Wasp.

Jack Birch, who had the duty that day in radar plot when I asked the question about friend or foe, said that he doesn't blame Wallace Beakley as much as he did one of the other officers who was in there.* One of the other officers had been to this radar school and had been given the impression that <u>nobody</u> should know about what this was, that in some way you could easily compromise its capability if you let too many people talk about it. He imbued that group and everyone associated with it so fully with this idea that no one was to know what was going on.

The radar had been there almost two months before I ever knew it could give a range and bearing on an aircraft. I didn't know what it did. So the first time I heard that it gave a range and bearing on an aircraft, it was only logical to ask for some other information. That's why I think Beakley was a little angered that anyone had even given us the range and bearing of the aircraft. Heretofore, the information had been on a slip of paper that would be passed to those who were to know. It was all that business of just learning how to be operational. We didn't have CIC in those days; this was the beginning of combat information centers and the beginning of fighter direction. It took time.

We have situations along the same lines today; there are still plenty of people in the Sixth Fleet who are

---
*Ensign John W. Birch, USNR.

unaware of all the tools that are available to provide information. The information comes in, but a lot of times it doesn't even go to the flag officer who's in command of the operating force. It goes to somebody else, and if he decides that it's okay, he may pass it along. Admiral Watkins, as a matter of fact, said this last month--that he is trying to make sure that our operational intelligence gets to those who need to know.* So it's not a simple problem, and it's still going on today.

I indicated we were sent to the Pacific to support the invasion of Guadalcanal. I think that Admiral Noyes contributed to some pretty poor decisions during that operation.

Q: Such as?

Admiral Weschler: For Guadalcanal Admiral Fletcher was the overall task force commander and the support for commander of the carriers.** He had Saratoga, Wasp, and Enterprise. He had given Admiral Kelly Turner and General Vandegrift the word that he was going to keep his carriers around

---
*Admiral James D. Watkins, USN, was Chief of Naval Operations at the time of this interview. He had previously served as Commander Sixth Fleet.
**Vice Admiral Frank Jack Fletcher, USN, Commander Task Force 61, the overall commander of the expeditionary force sent to invade Guadalcanal.

Guadalcanal for only about 48 hours.* Then he was going to withdraw them because he didn't want them around there if the Japanese fleet were to come. He didn't want to take a chance on losing them, and besides he had to refuel them and watch out for them.

Well, that was not a good attitude. Here was our first amphibious operation going into Tulagi and Guadalcanal. Admiral King had said we had to get a foothold in the Solomons in order to hold on to the line of communications with Australia.** So you would have thought that the supporting forces would be ready to stay around Guadalcanal and Tulagi until the commander ashore said, "I'm ready to look after myself," Henderson Field operating, and in some way giving some sign of readiness.*** However, these were the general guidelines Admiral Fletcher had imparted to one of his subordinates in the force where he was responsible for the whole operation.

Admiral Noyes had our carrier task force, and we'd had word throughout the day after the landings, August 8, that some Japanese ships were coming south. But we didn't get any further word on them later in the day. The possibility

---
*Rear Admiral Richmond Kelly Turner, USN, commander of the amphibious task force for Guadalcanal; Major General Alexander A. Vandegrift, USMC, Commanding General First Marine Division and commander of the landing force.
**Admiral Ernest J. King, USN, Commander in Chief U.S. Fleet and Chief of Naval Operations.
***Henderson Field was an airfield on Guadalcanal, much sought after by both the Americans and Japanese in their quest to control the island and its environs.

existed that there was a seaplane tender in the group, and so the general philosophy was, "Oh, they're going to stop at Rendova and put in a seaplane base, and maybe we'll see them around tomorrow." But that night, which was the night of the first Battle of Savo, the carriers began to withdraw by about noon, so that by sunset we were already 40 or 50 miles from Guadalcanal. About 2300 or so, we got the first indication that there were aircraft scout planes over Ironbottom Sound, and by 1:00 o'clock, shots were being fired, and there was definitely a lot of hoopla, and you could see flares.* We were by now about 60 or 80 miles away from there.

Three times during the night, Captain Sherman said to Admiral Noyes, "I recommend you tell Admiral Fletcher that we should turn around and go back in there. They need our support." But Admiral Noyes never sent a single one of those messages forward. I think Captain Sherman had been reluctant to leave in the first place and then had prodded him through the night, trying to get him to turn around, but it never did any good.

I just had the feeling from having seen Admiral Noyes--and this is strictly an ensign talking, looking at somebody--that Admiral Noyes didn't have the picture. He didn't really understand amphibious operations, and didn't

---

*Ironbottom Sound, so nicknamed because of all the ships sunk in it during the struggle for the area, was a body of water essentially surrounded by the islands of Guadalcanal, Florida, Tulagi, and Savo.

have a feel for what they should be doing. The only thing the commander seemed to be saying about carriers was, "We've got to get them refueled." And, Lord knows, they could have gone longer than that without having to withdraw.

Q: That's the general charge against Fletcher--that whenever a problem came up, he went and fueled.

Admiral Weschler: He went and fueled, yes. You know, it's that old business of capabilities versus intentions. The admirals could have plotted the tracks of the Japanese ships coming south and known they could have reached Guadalcanal. So it just seemed wrong to have withdrawn that night. We should have stayed at least until morning light to have given them the protection and then been there to strike if anything was around. The Japanese would still have been within range, and we could have done some good. Had we stayed, General Vandegrift wouldn't have called Admiral Turner and Admiral Crutchley, the British admiral, back in to talk with them.* And it might have been a whole different situation.

---

*Rear Admiral V. A. C. Crutchley, RN, was in command of a screen comprising U.S. and Australian ships. Because he had been called to a conference on board Turner's flagship, the transport McCawley (AP-10), he was not on hand to command his ships during the Japanese attack. They were poorly handled by the U.S. officer who took his place, and four cruisers were sunk.

Q: What was the feeling of the crew? Were they disappointed to be heading away?

Admiral Weschler: Oh, yes, I think we all were. We couldn't understand why we were withdrawing so quickly, because we had prepped for this mission. We had gotten there on the seventh, and by the evening of the eighth, here we were wandering off. We could hear from the beach that everything wasn't that rosy, that the transports hadn't been off-loaded. They were rushing to try to get things off, and they had to withdraw all of the transports the next morning. They didn't dare let them stay there with the carriers gone.

Q: Both Fletcher and Noyes disappeared soon thereafter to other assignments.

Admiral Weschler: Yes, and so did Admiral Ghormley, who was ComSoPac.* They felt he didn't really have the total picture either, and that's when Admiral Halsey came on the scene. I remember that Leonard Gross, an ensign, was the most vituperative about capabilities versus intentions and

---

*On 18 October, Vice Admiral William F. Halsey, Jr., USN, relieved Vice Admiral Robert L. Ghormley, USN, as Commander South Pacific Force and Area, the commander of the theater in which the Guadalcanal operation took place.

our withdrawing.* He left our ship and was assigned as a communications officer on ComSoPac's staff. So we said, "It serves you right, Len. You can get down there and can tell Admiral Halsey how to do it." I don't know what happened to Gross after that. He was a very smart guy, and he really knew what he was doing, but his claim to fame was in capabilities versus intentions.

Q: That battle is one of the worst examples that could possibly be cited.

Admiral Weschler: Yes, it really was too bad the way that thing worked out.

Q: Captain Sherman has been portrayed as an extremely ambitious person, always looking for his next stripe or star. Did you see any of that?

Admiral Weschler: No. As a matter of fact, as I say, it seemed to me that he was always trying to get Admiral Noyes's attention about the kinds of things Admiral Noyes ought to be thinking about. I always thought Admiral Noyes was sort of afraid of his own shadow. I don't know whether he was a real aviator or not. I think he was just one of those who had gone to some senior officers' course and had

---

*Ensign Leonard Gross, USNR.

gotten the requisite flight hours.*

He'd walk up and down on the quarterdeck, in greens, wearing his aviation pigskin gloves, and that's really the only time I ever saw him. I always had the impression of him as being sort of a mannequin, rather than really being a flesh-and-blood naval officer who was in the thick of decisions and ready to take over and set the course.

Q: Sherman, of course, was one of the ultimate strategists. You mentioned the big picture. How was he as a seaman?

Admiral Weschler: I have no reason to be critical of him as a seaman. Certainly the ship was well handled, and I have to say that one of the reasons why I think I'm still here is in some way a credit to his preparations for war, thinking ahead to the tasks that were going to come up.

Wasp continued to operate in and around the Solomons into September of '42, and we were rumored to be going to Noumea, New Caledonia, for a visit. One day, in preparation for our expected visit to Noumea, the first division boatswain's mate, Spiewak, began breaking out the paravanes.** I had never heard of paravanes, and so I

---

*Noyes, who was in the Naval Academy class of 1906, did not enter flight training until 1936, as a captain, after he had completed his tour as commanding officer of the light cruiser Richmond (CL-9). He commanded the carrier Lexington (CV-2) briefly after becoming a naval aviator.
**Boatswain's Mate First Class Chester N. Spiewak, USN, who eventually retired from the Navy as a lieutenant commander.

asked him what they were. He said, "Well, we're going into mineable waters, and ships have these paravanes to stream out and cut the moored mines."

I said, "Gee, and are you going to do the rigging?" And yes, he was. I said, "Well, I'm very interested in that. How about giving me a call whenever you're going to get it done?" So that was one day.

The next day was September 15, when we were still providing general support for resupply operations to Guadalcanal. We always went to general quarters at first light and usually stayed there until the aircraft came back from their longest patrol to make sure there wasn't anything in the area, and usually that would be, oh, noonish or could even go on to about 2:00 o'clock. So it was getting on to almost 2:00 o'clock, and we had had rations at stations and so on. At 2:00 o'clock they sounded secure from general quarters.

We recovered the aircraft and were just beginning to refuel and rearm them and get ready for the next patrol. I dove down to my bunk, which was in the forward part of the ship, right next to the chain pipe. There was a series of five decks that went down, and in the fifth deck was my room. The chain pipe came right through it, so there was never any doubt as to whether we were anchoring or not. It was far enough down that we called it "torpedo hollow," with the thought that if ever we got hit with a torpedo, we'd never get out of there.

I had just lain down and was stretching out, really going to enjoy a few hours of sleep, when the phone rang, and the voice said, "This is Spiewak, first class boatswain's mate. I'm about to rig paravanes. You said you were interested in learning a little bit about it, and if you want to know, come on up."

I thought for a second, "Oh, my, do I really want do to it?" And I said, "Yep, I do." So I said, "Okay, I'll be right there." So I got up and put my shoes on and went up on the forecastle. I don't think I had been on the forecastle more than about three minutes when a lookout hollered, "Torpedoes, starboard side!" Three fish hit the side, and shortly thereafter there were fires and major explosions. Those of us on the forecastle were isolated from the rest of the ship; we never did have communications back and forth between us.

B. J. Semmes was the senior man on the forecastle.* We stayed up there and did what we could to police the area, to try to get down into "torpedo hollow" and other areas and see whether anybody was around. We looked after the people who were there, and after a good hour we could see that people were beginning to go over the side aft. We

---

*Lieutenant Benedict J. Semmes, Jr., USN, who eventually became a vice admiral and Commander Second Fleet. Admiral Semmes's oral history is in the Naval Institute collection.

could see rafts and boats and so on drifting away. So then Lieutenant Semmes said, "Let's start evacuating people forward."

There was all sorts of burning oil around us now, and the ship was backing down, trying to get away from the pool of oil. But even so, oil was still sliding past the ship. We got the rafts and life jackets together and got all the injured off and through the fire. It wasn't very pleasant, but at least they were getting clear. Then when all of them were gone, those of us who were able started down the man-ropes and lifelines and so on. When you'd get close to the water, you'd let go and you'd drop through. If you had to come up short of the rings of fire, you always came up flailing your arms to throw the oily flame away from you and get a breath and go down again and go on. But it was a beautiful South Pacific afternoon, about 4:00 o'clock in the afternoon by now, no real waves and a lot of destroyers around depth-charging periodically, but nonetheless a pretty good rescue team. They got us all up in a couple of hours. Out of 2,200 men in the Wasp, we lost about 200.

As you know from Admiral Smedberg and from others, the Wasp was not sunk by the Japanese torpedoes, but she certainly was a fiery hulk and didn't look as if there was any chance of the fires going out.* So they had our torpedoes sink her. That way the Japanese could never get aboard and get any of the classified documents or materials that were there. They couldn't get in and see that radar plot that was so secret.

Q: It was with great difficulty that Admiral Smedberg sank her.

Admiral Weschler: Yes, but the personal point of this story is that I'm always indebted to Spiewak for calling me up and saying, "Come on up and look at the paravanes," and to Captain Forrest Sherman for having decided that he wanted to rig the paravanes if he was going into mineable waters.

Q: You think you might not have made it if you had been in your room?

Admiral Weschler: No question, no question, because others who were down there never made it. I know that that call was the thing that got me topside.

---

*Vice Admiral William R. Smedberg III, USN (Ret.), recounted the incident in "As I Recall . . . 'Sink the Wasp!'" U.S. Naval Institute Proceedings, July 1982, pages 47-49, which is an excerpt from his oral history. As skipper of the destroyer Lansdowne (DD-486), he was ordered by Admiral Noyes to sink the Wasp with his ship's torpedoes.

Q: It's amazing what little things can make such a big difference.

Admiral Weschler: It comes back to this thing of wanting to know. I like to know about things, and if it's seamanship or something new, I like to know that. It was a good thing to have that intellectual curiosity.

Q: It certainly was. That task force was perhaps the first time that a fast battleship had operated with a carrier. Did that make a difference in your formations and operations?

Admiral Weschler: We hadn't been with North Carolina all that much. She was not there with us originally, and when we first went out in connection with the Guadalcanal operations, we didn't have North Carolina right in our task group. It was only after we were held on there for these supporting ops that the carriers operated with the different supporting ships. We had different destroyers with us than we had had originally. I don't think North Carolina had been in our task group then for more than a few days, and so I have no real impression of it. We knew that the lifeline was going through here, and we were there to make sure no Japs came around and interfered with the reinforcement of Guadalcanal.

Q: You mentioned that the air patrol had just come back. Do you think the submarine deliberately stayed down until the planes were recovered?

Admiral Weschler: No. You know, this was a case in which they were able to learn from the skipper of the I-19 later on, probably his war patrol report or the like. He said that it was the luckiest thing that ever happened to them-- that the Wasp had been steaming by at high speed on a course such that he couldn't catch it. Suddenly she turned almost 135 degrees and slowed and came into perfect position for him to fire. That's why the attack happened that quickly. You recall I said it was time enough for me to get down and into the sack and hardly be there when the phone rang. I went up on deck, and in three or four minutes the torpedoes were away. We had stood on, then made the radical maneuver out of the wind, and just gone right by in a perfect position for the submarine to get a firing setup and fire. He said it was just one of those "gimmees" that you don't get very often. And he fired his spread.

I thought that article in the July issue of the Naval Institute was particularly good in which the author analyzed that the submarine got North Carolina, O'Brien,

Thomas R. Weschler #1 - 99

and <u>Wasp</u>--all with the same spread of torpedoes.* The submarine skipper really was a lucky man that particular day.

Q: You got to use your Naval Academy swimming training after you abandoned ship.

Admiral Weschler: Absolutely. And I thought of all those days on the sub squad. I had no problems at all, because I used my foolproof sidestroke, which I did beautifully--none of this crawl stuff that afternoon.

Q: How long were you in the water?

Admiral Weschler: Probably less than an hour and got picked up by the <u>Duncan</u>. Whitey Taylor was the skipper, and Lou Bryan was the exec.** As soon as I saw Lou Bryan, gee, I knew him from when my brother had been a midshipman.*** So I was delighted to see him. It didn't make any difference; he had so many people he wasn't able to do any more than say "Hi." I think there were over 400 of us aboard <u>Duncan</u>, and their main concern was topside weight. They said, "All those of you who are well enough

---

*See Captain Ben W. Blee, USN (Ret.), "Whodunnit?" <u>U.S. Naval Institute Proceedings</u>, July 1982, pages 42-47.
**Lieutenant Commander Edmund B. Taylor, USN; Lieutenant Louis A. Bryan, USN.
***Bryan and Weschler's brother Charles were in the Naval Academy class of 1932, discussed earlier in the interview.

and don't need any other care, get down in the fireroom and engine room and bilges and stay below. We'll take care of your clothes and get something to you in due course." So I spent the next six or eight hours down on the deck in the fireroom. It was nice to be warm and dry and cozy after having been there on the Wasp.

As personnel officer, my big concern was trying to remember where the rosters were and how was I going to put together who this whole crew was, and how was I going to make sure who had been lost and get word to the next of kin and all that sort of thing. I'm willing to bet you that it was two to three weeks later before I really was positive that I had everybody accounted for.

Q: How did you go about that process?

Admiral Weschler: You may recall that at that time whenever we'd get under way or whenever we had a change in personnel, we were obligated to put together immediately a list of the changes to the ship's complement in terms of actual names. We indicated where people were transferred to or where they came in from and put a copy in the mail. In addition, we distributed copies to at least two other ships in the task force.

So we had had a transfer when we had fueled the day

before. I was happy to think that I had done the right thing and made sure that before we got away from alongside I had had the new roster typed up and had put it in the mail, which had gone aboard the tanker. In addition, there had been a destroyer transfer of the mail, and I had sent one copy to North Carolina and one to somebody else who was in company. So when we started collecting in the Helena, which was the big ship to which I was transferred, I told the exec of the Helena where we had sent copies of our roster and who had copies of the master document. He called around the fleet, and by the time we got to Nouméa, things were coming in by mail.

In a week or ten days, I had copies of all the material that we had sent out. Except for one change that I hadn't received a copy of, I had enough information to make a good roster. Then the question was to get people to identify for certain that So-and-so was alive and not in a hospital ship and not over here and so on. I used to have a list.

We went aboard a Dutch passenger ship which was being used as a receiving ship in Nouméa. They didn't want anybody to know the Wasp was lost, just as they didn't want anyone to know the Lexington had been lost at Coral Sea, because we were down, at times, to one carrier operating in the Pacific. The Japanese would have had a heyday if they really knew how close to the end we were. So we were held in Nouméa for almost three weeks.

During that time, we were all living in a couple of ships, and I had a roster posted outside the personnel office door that said, "You're dead unless you cross your name off this list." It hung there, and pretty soon someone would come along and scratch his name out vigorously and come in and say, "Like hell I'm dead." But it worked. It was a good way, and gradually we got confident as to who the people were and we could identify them. A lot of people could remember when they had seen them last and what the circumstances were. From that list we were all ready to notify the next of kin, but no one was telling anyone anything, and that helped us in that interval. There wasn't a lot of pressure of worrying that some mother somewhere was worrying about her son, because they didn't know that all 2,200 of us had been in jeopardy and that 2,000 were okay.

The information on the sinking of Wasp wasn't released until that December, three months later. By that time most men were home when the news broke. They were sitting there at home with their parents, who could say, "So that's what happened, Joe. No wonder you wouldn't tell me where you were being transferred to," and so on. They'd all gone home with some cock-and-bull story that they were on leave and going to so-and-so. We were not allowed to say what was happening until it was released.

Q: I'm curious. After your ship was sunk and you had lost all your uniforms, did the Navy buy you new ones?

Admiral Weschler: You had a chance to put in for uniforms with the necessary deduction for wear and tear, so that by the time you were all done with what seemed to have cost you a fortune, you got reimbursed about $250.00 or something like that. One of the things I had to do in San Diego after Wasp was sunk was handle requests for reimbursement for all 2,000 of us who were still there. Some poor commodore who was grounded was responsible for signing all these forms and ensuring that they were valid.

Q: It was a real out-of-pocket expense if your ship was lost.

Admiral Weschler: That's right. You lost all of those goodies, and anything you had which wasn't officially required, such as pay that you had locked up in your safe or any gifts that you had from mail call were just gone, unless you had personal insurance.

Q: Well, anything more on the carrier?

Admiral Weschler: No, I think that's more than I really

should have said on the carrier.

Q: Not at all. Where did you go from there?

Admiral Weschler: I headed for a destroyer. B. J. Semmes I had liked very much when we were together in Wasp; he and I got along well. He said, "I'm going as the exec of a destroyer. How about you coming along and being my gun boss or something?"

I said, "Sure, I'd love to go." And we got two other officers from the ship. One was Ajax Tucker, who was class of '32 but had gotten out and come back in as a reserve; he came along as engineer officer of this destroyer.* And Lester Schulz from Citronella, Alabama, came along as the assistant engineer.** So the four of us from the Wasp went to join the Sigsbee (DD-502), which was then building at Federal Shipbuilding in Kearny, New Jersey.*** That gave me a wonderful chance to live in downtown New York for about two weeks, I guess, while she was fitting out before she was commissioned.

Then we had a marvelous set of operating schedules on the East Coast from probably about the first of February

---
*Lieutenant (junior grade) Augustine J. Tucker, USNR.
**Lieutenant Lester R. Schulz, USN.
***USS Sigsbee (DD-502) was commissioned 23 January 1943. She had a standard displacement of 2,050 tons, was 376 feet long, and 40 feet in the beam. She had a top speed of 35.2 knots and a main battery of five 5-inch guns. She was also outfitted with ten 40-millimeter and seven 20-millimeter guns and ten 21-inch torpedo tubes.

until the middle of July in 1943. We did all the usual, you know. There was a brief shakedown, part at Casco Bay, Maine, and part at Guantánamo. We also got help at all the appropriate schools in and out of Norfolk, and so on. But the best thing for us was the Navy working up two new carriers. In separate trips we escorted Independence and Lexington to Trinidad. They were ready just about the time we were ready.*

The island of Trinidad, in its position off Venezuela, is such that there are two entrances to the Gulf of Paria. One is called the Dragon's Mouth and the other, the Serpent's Mouth. But other than that, this Gulf of Paria is completely landlocked. They put a net over the Serpent's Mouth, and they put net tenders and a patrol at the Dragon's Mouth, so here was a huge body of water in which carriers could do complete flight workups with no risk from submarines and run through all their maneuvers in an area essentially like the open ocean.

After the training was completed, we escorted Lexington out to the Pacific. Sigsbee arrived in time for carrier raids on Marcus and Wake. From our arrival in the Pacific in August of '43, we never stopped moving in operations until following the amphibious landing in Leyte in October of '44.**

---

*The Independence (CVL-22) was commissioned on 14 January 1943, just over a week before the Sigsbee. The Lexington (CV-16) was commissioned 17 February 1943.
**The Marcus Island raid was on 1 September 1943 and that against Wake on 5 October.

Q: Did you get some antiaircraft workup at the gunnery school at Dam Neck when you were first getting ready to go to the Pacific.

Admiral Weschler: We really didn't get an awful lot of gunnery training along the Atlantic seaboard. There was too much worry about submarines, and we were too much in demand for escorting and convoys. They figured we could do that going out to the Pacific, and that was pretty well the way it worked. We got some of those gun shoots in when we were working with the carriers in Trinidad, which was another advantage of being there. They could tow sleeves for us and give us a chance to shoot.

That brings up an interesting thing that I'd like to say. Sigsbee used the Mark 4 radar system and the Mark 37 gun director, and we had really thought they were top-notch. At Wake Island we were conducting gun shoots at 31 knots when we had been sent on a patrol trying to find a downed aviator. Jap aircraft were around, and we weren't sure anyone was going to come out and support us. Everything seemed to be going very well, and we were confident we could defend ourselves.

Sometime after that we had a short yard availability at Pearl. At that time they said they wanted to put in a new Mark 12 radar on the Mark 37 director. They yanked out the one that was there, the Mark 4, put in the Mark 12, and buttoned it up. I think the whole thing took about three or four days, and then they sent us on the way.

They didn't give us a single instruction book, they didn't tell us anything about how the damn thing operated, and there were really quite a few changes. It really made me very unhappy with this philosophy of just throwing a new piece of equipment on board without the requisite training and without instruction manuals. I think I'm echoing Admiral Burke when I say that old equipment operated well is often better than new equipment operated poorly.* You shouldn't buy and install something new unless the new gear operating with a novice will be better than the old gear operated by an expert. That philosophy prevents your wasting a lot of money on incremental improvements.

Now, if you've got plenty of time to train so that you can bring your team up on the step and get past that learning plateau, okay. Otherwise, I think we are just wasting our time and money.

After those early raids, the Sigsbee participated in the landings in Gilberts and Marshalls, including Kwajalein and Eniwetok. I'd like to tell you a couple of quick sea stories about those operations. The one was how glad I was

---

*Admiral Arleigh Burke, USN, whom Weschler served as an aide, was Chief of Naval Operations from 1955 to 1961. During World War II he achieved notable acclaim as Commander Destroyer Squadron 23.

to be in the Navy versus being a Marine. You know that Tarawa was a terrible struggle for the Marines. After the first day, when there had been quite a bit of gunfire coming out to sea from 8-inch guns and the like, things settled down at sea. Although there was submarine activity around, those of us on the gunfire support line weren't worried, because we had other destroyers outboard to protect us. By the second or third day, there was no need to be at general quarters all the time as long as we had the ready mounts manned. All they were calling for was one or two guns, and we had five, so we could do the support with a condition watch.

The time came for chow, and I went down to the noon meal. It was served in the wardroom with the white tablecloth and the nice service. I remember that I was eating a chocolate sundae. The wardroom of the 2,100-tonners had a screen door at the end which was looking out toward the beach, and the door was open. There were the Marines on the beach. You could see the Japs coming up and shooting them perhaps just a mile away. And you could hear the guns and see them battling. I looked back at that wardroom table and eating an ice cream sundae, and I thought, "Are we in the same outfit? What's going on?" Well, that was one thing that I'll never forget. What a contrast!

The other story had to do with our time at Kwajalein.

As you know, when we were going up there we did not have good charts of the area, as so often happened in the Pacific. We were using 1850 maps and charts from the French Navy and just about anything we could come across. We got to Kwajalein, and one of the UDTs or a submarine found a tugboat and captured it.* This Japanese tug had a full load of charts in it. Our people managed to get them off and over to one of the AGCs, which was then able to crank out prints through the night.** Everybody had excellent charts of the area inside of about 24 hours after this capture had taken place.

Well, on the strength of those charts, they saw that the lagoon inside Kwajalein was much deeper and clearer of pinnacles than they had thought. The defenders on Kwajalein were not exposing their guns the way the Marines wanted, and the Marines were restless. The plan was to go in through an entrance, and then the landing was to be on the inside face of the lagoon. The Marines were concerned that the Japanese were really going to pick them off with crossfire, and they wanted those guns exposed. So they said, "Wonderful idea. We'll send this destroyer in there to lie off the beach about a mile and turn her searchlight on as a point of aim, and then we'll put a cruiser behind

---
*UDTs--underwater demolition teams, Navy frogmen who performed pre-invasion beach reconnaissance and clearance of obstacles to landing.
**AGC--flagship of an amphibious task force commander; ships of this type were equipped with print shops.

her. Then when the Japs shoot at the destroyer, the cruiser can shoot at the Japs." <u>Sigsbee</u>, my ship, was selected to be the target. So we steamed inside, and we anchored there. It was about 2,500 yards from the beach, and we had a big 36-inch searchlight. I said, "Captain, are you serious?"

He said, "Those are the orders." We turned that big 36-inch searchlight on the beach, and, of course, it blinded us. You couldn't see anything to shoreward with that thing on. So there we sat. We started, let's say, at about 2300. All of a sudden, about 1:00 o'clock, we saw the first salvo bracket us, and everybody hollered, "There it is!" The captain had somebody hit the TBS and tell the cruiser that the enemy had commenced firing. Meanwhile, we had the chief boatswain's mate on the forecastle. He just slipped the chain, and we were under way out of there at 25 knots.

By that time, the second salvo landed and didn't go through the hull, but we sure had water all over the forecastle from the shells coming in. If we hadn't gotten moving right when we did, they might have hit us. But by that time the cruiser was firing over us. He wasn't blinded as we were, and he had seen the crack of the shots from the beach, and he was firing in there. After about 20 minutes the word came, "Back to station," and so back we went and turned on the searchlight again. But no anchoring this time. Once was enough with the hook. We lay to, but not another round came at us, and so at first light, the landing took place. It did some good, but it was quite an experience to sit there as bait.

After that and Eniwetok we went down to New Guinea to participate in the landings at Hollandia and back later for the landings in Morotai and Halmahera. Still later in 1944 <u>Sigsbee</u> supported the landings in the Marianas and Leyte. Finally we got a break and headed for downtown San Francisco. We had an absolutely marvelous two and a half months of upkeep at Matson Line piers at the foot of Market Street in San Francisco and got out again just in time for the invasion of Iwo Jima and the first carrier raid on Tokyo.

Q: Did you conclude that you had found your niche when you got into gunnery?

Admiral Weschler: I very much liked it. There's no question I enjoyed being an ordnance PG, and I was gun boss of the <u>Macon</u> and the gunnery officer on BatCruLant staff.* Later I was aboard the <u>Canberra</u>, guided missile ship, as exec. In all those billets I had a chance to work with gunnery and to get into gunnery training and try to

---

*PG--Postgraduate; BatCruLant--Commander Battleships and Cruisers Atlantic Fleet was the type commander on whose staff Weschler served.

make a better sequence of what we were doing.

The part I enjoyed about all the experience with the amphibs was that you did so much gunfire support, so you were using your guns all the time. You really felt that you were contributing. There was none of this just being out on patrol, as so often happens with an antisubmarine mission. Here you were contributing. You could see something on the beach, the Marines would call for you to shoot, you could see the shells go into the cave or a bunker come apart or hear someone saying, "Boy, right on!" You get a tremendous amount of satisfaction in that kind of gunnery.

Q: Did your ship get to specialize in gunnery to the extent that you did become quite expert?

Admiral Weschler: I think everybody who was in gunfire support for a reasonable number of times got that way. And, yes, that was our division's role for at least three operations that I recall.

Q: You mentioned that your friend B. J. Semmes was the exec in the <u>Sigsbee</u>. He, of course, became well known later. What do you remember about him specifically?

Admiral Weschler: He's one now that's so much more a

contemporary of mine that I can be much warmer in my comments on him. When we first met in the Wasp, he was a jaygee, and I was an ensign.* He just was so capable. He knew what it was all about, and he was able to impart to you what was going on. He knew I was interested in gunnery, and so he was willing to take all sorts of time with me and tell me how the director worked and how the computer worked. He was always working with the fire controlmen when they were taking things apart. If it was something interesting, he'd say, "Come on up this afternoon, and I'll show you something we're taking apart." And he'd get me on the range finder and show me how it worked. He was a great teacher, and he knew that I was interested, and he kept pumping me up on what was going on.

He was a good "take-charge" person. You didn't have to tell him; he knew when something had to be done, as on the forecastle when he was the senior man when the Wasp was torpedoed. He was organized and knew what to do and how to get people moving in the right direction. He was low key, nicely so, about all of it.

When I went aboard Sigsbee and he was exec, we had a captain who was not our favorite. He was really like one of these fussy schoolteachers and really could get your hackles up. So B. J., as exec, was also navigator. Once we were coming into Efate, which was one of the first bases

---

*Jaygee--lieutenant (junior grade).

Thomas R. Weschler #1 - 114

that had been developed out there. It had quite a devious channel as you were coming in. As we were coming in, B. J., instead of saying, "Three hundred yards to turn," to the turning point, would say, "Five hundred yards and we'll be aground. Four hundred yards and we'll be aground."

The captain accepted that about twice, and then he said, "Executive officer, just tell me when I'm going to turn." But we all had a heckle or two with that captain. He really was a little hard to take.

Q: What was his name?

Admiral Weschler: Benjamin Van Meter Russell.* He was the only one that I ever walked off the bridge on. I was no longer a JO by then. I had made lieutenant, and I thought I was probably next to the CNO at that point. And I knew I was a good watch-stander.

The captain came on the bridge one morning, during the 4:00 to 8:00 watch. I forget what was going on--it was in some formation and wasn't anything great shakes--probably one of those screen reorientations that we had done a thousand times. He had stopped coming on the bridge through the night. He had confidence enough in all of us that if it was a Rum or Coke or any one of those, he didn't

---

*Russell was in the class of 1926 at the Naval Academy, eight classes senior to Semmes. He held the rank of commander at the time of taking command of the Sigsbee.

have to worry about it.* Something came up, and I started doing it automatically, but he gave some order to the helm. I said, "Captain, have you relieved me?"

He said, "Well, I guess so."

I said, "Aye, aye, sir," and I started below.

He said, "You get back here!" And then he said, "I think you're doing it all right." I don't remember completely now how it went, but it was just so abrupt, and it was so unnecessary that it really griped me. He was a tough one to deal with. But B. J. was good. He left before I did. He was being promoted and getting his own ship by that time. Certainly the war speeded us all along, and B. J., then a lieutenant commander, made commander and had his own ship by Okinawa.**

Q: What were your own experiences at Okinawa? That was a tough time for destroyers.

Admiral Weschler: I never got to Okinawa. I had been at Iwo Jima, and then in March '45 I got detached and went as the exec of another 2,100-tonner, the Young (DD-580).*** I

---
*Rum and Coke are names assigned to different methods of reorienting the antisubmarine screen in a carrier formation. The methods vary in the directions in which the escorts turn in order to reach their new stations when the formation axis is changed.
**Semmes commanded the destroyer Picking (DD-685) during the Okinawa operation, as he discussed in his own oral history.
***USS Young (DD-580) was commissioned 31 July 1943. Her characteristics were the same as those in the Sigsbee.

really think I was lucky, because <u>Sigsbee</u> got her stern blown off in connection with the Okinawa operation.* I used to read those dispatches, and I'd ask myself, "If you were up there, would you really be doing your job as effectively as those guys?" I really had to take my hat off to them. It must have been a terrible strain to be out there with those kamikazes coming in. That really took a lot of guts. But I guess if you were there, that most people would have done pretty much the same thing. There wasn't anything else to do; you knew you were going to be there, so you might as well dig in and make it as tough for the enemy as you possibly could.

Q: You wonder what it takes in the way of fortitude when you have no choice.

Admiral Weschler: That's right. There's nothing you're going to do except making it rough for them, and so you just have to count on yourself to function that rationally under those circumstances.

Q: So you had quite a forced-draft progression, going from a junior ensign at the beginning of the war to exec at the end.

---

*On 14 April 1945, while operating as a picket off Okinawa, the <u>Sigsbee</u> was hit aft by a Japanese kamikaze suicide plane and badly damaged.

Admiral Weschler: Yes.

Q: What were your experiences in the Young?

Admiral Weschler: We operated in the Philippines, visited Manila and Mindoro and mopped up around Davao and that area. It was part of the clean-up in the Philippines.

I was with a wonderful captain, Donald Granville Dockum, who was a great R&D type, completely different skipper from any I had been with before.* He was in the class of '36, someone I had known at the Naval Academy. He'd lived right down the passageway from me when I was a midshipman. He roomed with Norm Gillette and T. Starr King, and there was one other.** I've seen a lot of both Norm and T. Starr through the years. As a matter of fact, they both have an association with Newport, and I relieved T. Starr when he was gunnery officer of BatCruLant.

Don Dockum was just wonderful, a different kind of guy. He threw the ball to me as exec to really run the ship. I found that I had growing pains in learning to work with my peers. Previously I had been a lieutenant working with lieutenants without being in charge of them and having

---
*Dockum held the rank of commander when he was skipper of the Young; R&D--research and development.
**Midshipman Norman C. Gillette, Jr., USN, who eventually retired as a rear admiral; Midshipman Thomas Starr King, Jr., USN, who retired as a rear admiral.

Thomas R. Weschler #1 - 118

a fairly senior exec like B. J. That was one thing. But when I was exec and was about one number senior to all the rest of the lieutenants, it wasn't quite as easy, particularly when I had never seen any of them before. I got along well with, say, two-thirds of them, but there could be little frictions with some others. And there wasn't all that time to develop it. Gee, I was in <u>Young</u> March, April, May, June--four and a half, five months was the whole tour. But we were at sea the entire time and always in operations. So in terms of doing things, it was probably the equivalent of a year or two today in what you accomplished.

There was one thing I'll never forget about Don Dockum. We came into Subic and had gone to an anchorage. He said, "We've got to fuel. Find out about it." So I found out that such and such a ship over there was where we would go to fuel, and that they'd be able to take us at 4:30 or something like that. And he said, "Line me up a call on the admiral." So I found out where the flagship was that he was going to visit, and he said, "Make the call for me at 4:00 o'clock."

I said, "Fine."

Just before he was leaving, I said, "You know, Captain, we're going to fuel at 1630. We'll have to be under way by 1615 in order to be there on time."

He said, "Okay. If I'm not back, you just start moving to fuel, and I'll join you. But, in any event, I really do want to get the fuel." So off he took. But the implication was that he'd be back or catch me en route.

Well, he took off and went over there, and I could see that he was finished, and the gig started standing over in our direction. By that time, we were under way and moving towards the oiler. He stayed about two miles away from the ship and circled around and lay there so that I knew he was going to let me take it alongside and he wouldn't even be aboard. After we were alongside, he came back. I really was very grateful to him for showing that confidence in letting me take it alongside. I thought that was a marvelous thing. I've never forgotten him for it, because it was a tremendous boost to my morale.

Q: I remember the first time I was allowed to get a ship under way from anchorage, and I felt that same thing.

Admiral Weschler: These are things people can do for you, and they're absolutely fantastic. It really gave me stature in the eyes of the ship's company. I told you I was having trouble with a couple of them. At least they knew the captain trusted me enough to do that, and that they hadn't been given a chance to get it under way and take it alongside.

Q: That was a good gesture for that reason alone.

Admiral Weschler: That's right, exactly. So it was really very fine.

I'll tell you one other thing that I particularly enjoyed about that Philippine experience. I've mentioned that my brother was a prisoner of war. He had been an ED and had been stationed at Olongapo when the Japanese attacked the Philippines. Sometime before that, our Navy had moved the floating dry dock, the Dewey dry dock, which had been at Olongapo. It had been brought down to Cavite, to Mariveles Bay in Manila area right off Corregidor. Charles had taken a team of Navy and civilians to work on the Dewey dry dock, and he had been overhauling submarines and destroyers in that vicinity. He was later posthumously awarded a Distinguished Service Medal for this service.

Then, when the Japanese were closing in and things were collapsing in the area, they began to fly different people out or get them out on anything that was traveling. Charles was finally put in a group that was going to go out in a seaplane. The seaplane took off from Manila okay and landed in Davao, where it was going to fuel once more before it went on to Australia. When it landed, it tore its pontoon on something floating in the lake, and all the passengers were off-loaded in Davao except for a couple of nurses who were taken on with the crew to Australia.

So Charles was captured in Davao by the Japanese in May of '42. He stayed there until December of '44, when he began to move north. They were moving the prisoners up to Manchuria, and he was on a ship that was bombed off Olongapo. Prison ships weren't marked, so it was bombed by our forces. He got away and was free Christmas Day of '44 in the Olongapo area. Then they rounded them up and put them back aboard another Japanese prison ship. He went over to Formosa, and that was in time for some of the air raids on Formosa. The ship he was on, again unmarked, was bombed, and he was seriously wounded. He died of the wounds en route to Manchuria. We later got the story of where he was.

I got to Manila in February of '45 and went to the Japanese records center. There I found my brother's name and knew that I was less than two months behind him, that two months earlier he had been there in Manila in Santo Tomas or one of those prisons. I had the Japanese list of prisoners, because they were so thorough about all that stuff. The records indicated that he had been loaded on the ship, which we knew by that time had been bombed and were able to establish that he had been in the Olongapo area. So I felt at least close to him in the sense that I was right on the scene of where everything had taken place, and that if he had been around, I would have had a chance

Thomas R. Weschler #1 - 122

of being in on his recovery.

Q: When did you find out that he had been captured?

Admiral Weschler: Oh, almost immediately after it happened. The people on the plane reported that they had left him behind, and as they took off they could see the Japanese patrols coming through the fields towards where these men were. So they knew that they were going to be captured within a matter of a half hour of their being left behind.

Q: It was amazing--it was a little thing that saved you and a little thing that doomed him--a broken pontoon.

Admiral Weschler: Yes, isn't that something? And, interestingly, when I was in Danang as the commander of the naval support activity there, this one plane landed, and this Brigadier General Montgomery, U.S. Army, got out of the plane and came towards me, and he said, "Tom Weschler, you don't know how I've been looking forward to meeting you."

And I said, "General, I don't think we've ever met before."

He said, "I know we haven't, but I spent two years in prison camp with your brother." General Montgomery had been there in Davao and was one of those who had survived. I was thrilled to hear from him and for him to tell me firsthand how wonderful my brother had been and what a source of morale and inspiration and all sorts of good things that were wonderful to hear.

Then, about two months later, General Harold Johnson, Chief of Staff of the Army, was coming in.* I knew that General Johnson had been a prisoner of war. I also knew he was going to be busy with all sorts of calls and things that he was doing, but I wrote a note and gave it to his aide. The note said, "If General Johnson has a minute, ask him to look at the note which is asking him if I can call on him for a half hour tonight after all his activities are over, if he's up to it. I just want to talk to him a little bit about World War II as a prisoner of war because my brother was a prisoner."

I got a very nice word back from his aide that the general was looking forward to seeing me. I went over and saw him, and he said, "Now, tell me the story about your brother," and I did. He said, "It's fascinating and what a coincidence. I was in the hold forward of where your brother was. I didn't really know him by name, but I remember the wounds, and I remember the very, very little bit of medical supply that we had, and that we lost some people. The hold that your brother was in is the one that

---
*General Harold K. Johnson, USA, was Army Chief of Staff from 1964 to 1968.

had the most damage from the bombing. The hold that I was in never was touched. I can remember the agony," and so on. I thought that was remarkable years later to have those two Army officers come through and both of them to have known either Charles directly or have known of him and confirm everything that I had heard through other sources.

Q: So the question of life or death was a near thing on more than one occasion with him.

Admiral Weschler: Yes, that's right.

Q: You talked initially about the relationship between reserves and regulars in the Wasp. How was it in the Young?

Admiral Weschler: Well, by the time I got to the Young, almost all of us were reserves, except for the captain. We had a few bright new ensigns, and all the rest were reserves. I was a reserve as exec, and every head of department was a reserve officer. By that time all the lieutenants had 28 or 29 months, which we thought was an eternity, and we all felt ready for lieutenant commander. We'd had an awful lot of war experience. All of us had been in destroyers, usually had been in a number of battles, so that we were a seasoned lot, certainly in terms of shiphandling. So the reserves had made a major contribution. Really, by this time, I think they were the bulk of the force throughout destroyers.

Q: It's unfortunate that all that talent was lost in demobilization.

Admiral Weschler: That's right. I think it was most unseemly the way that we phased down after World War II. They all went out so quickly. The system of points was fatal.* As soon as you had enough points, you were eligible to get out. And so, of course, the most experienced people, whom you would have given your eyeteeth to have kept, were the ones who went home. And someone who hadn't done anything was going to stay around. To an extent, that allowed this new man to grow, but you needed a cadre, and the point system took your cadre.

Q: How did you wind up your tour in the Young?

Admiral Weschler: We got back to the States about July 20, 1945. The war wasn't over yet, but I was detached, because

---

*For the demobilization of the U.S. armed forces after World War II, the services had a point system to determine individual priorities for leaving the service. Points were awarded for length of service, overseas service, battle stars, decorations, and dependent children. Those with the highest number of points were the earliest discharged.

I had been selected for ordnance postgraduate school, which I really wanted to attend. I got to PG school in Annapolis a little before V-J Day, August '45.*

---
*V-J Day--Victory-over-Japan Day, 15 August 1945, marking the end of hostilities in the war in the Pacific. The formal Japanese surrender was on 2 September on board the battleship Missouri (BB-63) in Tokyo Bay.

Interview Number 2 with Vice Admiral Thomas R. Weschler,
U.S. Navy (Retired)

Place: Nimitz Library, U.S. Naval Academy, Annapolis, Maryland

Date: Wednesday, 23 February 1983
Interviewer: Paul Stillwell

Q: Admiral, during our first interview we talked about your sea duty experiences in the Pacific. From there you came back here to Annapolis, of all places.

Admiral Weschler: Yes, to PG school.

Q: How did that tour go?

Admiral Weschler: I thoroughly enjoyed it. First of all, I had wanted to be an ordnance PG from the beginning. My evaluation of a career was that you should have something in which you were technically qualified, other than being a good shiphandler or a good line officer at sea. So the PG school looked to me the way to get such a start. And I've indicated earlier, too, that I believe a great deal in education, and here was a chance to continue on that. As a reserve, I really didn't anticipate getting a degree, but nonetheless it was a great program.

Because of what they were offering reserves, I came to Halligan Hall and in six weeks had a chance to get brushed up on what I had had at the Naval Academy and take two or three other courses. Then I was meshed with a group of regulars who had been here for two years. So at the end of the six weeks, I meshed with the two-year group, and then we all went to MIT for the third year of their three-year fire control program. As a reserve I was going to get one year of MIT, and whether or not I'd get a degree was questionable. It really depended on whether in six weeks--instead of two years--I could catch up enough to hold onto this fast-moving educational train.

One of the best things that happened to me was that Captain Singleton, who was the head of the fire control and ordnance PG program, was a good friend of my brother Charles's.* He knew the name Weschler and had known that I did well at the Naval Academy, so he asked me if I was interested in augmenting to the regular Navy. I said I sure as heck was. That had been my dearest dream. Not only did I get augmented to the regular Navy during this period, but they moved me into the official three-year PG program, as though I had started with this other group of officers. That, in effect, guaranteed me that I'd get a master's from MIT, assuming that I passed during the one

---

*Captain Charles T. Singleton, Jr., USN.

Thomas R. Weschler #2 - 129

year that I was there. So it was a great stroke of good fortune. I did do very well in the course, which I completed at the end of '46.

Q: You were still under some pressure, though, to make up lost time, weren't you?

Admiral Weschler: Tremendous pressure. That's the only time that I took a course in differential calculus in an hour. I'd never heard of the subject, but the thing that saved me is that one of the best methods of solving differential calculus equations is what's called the heuristic method. I heard these others talking about it, and I looked up the word "heuristic," and it said, "guesswork." That's exactly what I knew how to do best, and so I used the heuristic method for everything I did in differential calculus. Fortunately, it worked.

Q: Can you comment on the relationship between the study of theory and practice in that course?

Admiral Weschler: I'd like to make two comments on that. First of all, I didn't have enough sampling of the PG school here in Annapolis to give you a solid impression as to what the caliber of education was. I saw a lot of fine profs, based on what I heard from other students, but I didn't have my own evaluation.

When I got to MIT, the thing that really made that program and that helped tie theory to practical work was the fact that one of our courses was instrumentation, taught by Dr. Draper.* Dr. Draper was the one who had used the gyroscope to develop the Mark 14 lead-computing gun sight. We used it throughout World War II, and it later was the basis for all our missile control work. Dr. Draper was really the father of every missile program we have in the United States, and he was also the genius behind the man on the moon. Almost all of our current satellite work stems from things that Dr. Draper has done.

He was an embodiment of theory and practice. He's the one who would always say, "What is it you want to find out? What's the physical analog of that?" Then, as soon as he thought of the physical analog, which was the gyro for many fire control problems, he'd say, "Now, that thing is smarter than I am. If we subject it to the forces we're talking about, then it's going to have this output. How do I quantify that output in order to have it solve the problem?"

So his whole approach to life was the marriage of theory and practice. So he was terrific to learn from. He's the only one of the profs that I really had that strong a feeling toward. I had one other professor worth

---
*Dr. C. Stark Draper, for whom the Draper Laboratory at the Massachusetts Institute of Technology is named.

noting. In 1946 we were studying what was called mathematics by mechanical methods. This was the whole birth of the computer business--not using a gyro, but using any other sort of analog. I believe his name was Dr. Dillingham, and he was the one who was developing all of these analog computers that were very similar to the fire control computers we had aboard ship. He had developed some of that theory.

I remember that course, because, as I say, I saw all of these mechanical models which Dr. Dillingham used. He had a slave computer probably as large as a 10- or 12-foot-square room to solve one fairly simple problem. Then, towards the end of the course, he led us across the hall to see the large vacuum tube computer they were designing-- ENIAC or similar to ENIAC. It was packed with vacuum tubes and was in a room as large as a small auditorium. It was being used to solve some of the gunnery ballistic tables. I cite that only to say that that was the beginning of computers and that course was introducing us to them. Here was a case where they were using devices to solve practical problems.

One other aspect of that time was my first introduction to servo mechanisms. A servo mechanism is a control mechanism to which you can provide inputs, and it will provide an output, which is a mechanical analog of some very complicated function that it might have taken three or four human beings to do. The virtue of a servo mechanism is that it is constantly in motion; it isn't something like a slide rule that solves a problem once. It keeps receiving inputs and keeps supplying outputs. You can vary the inputs, and the outputs will vary in a related and proper way.

Q: This is so you can control movement in a remote location.

Admiral Weschler: That's right. For example, this was the time when our guns had a man sitting at the pointer or the trainer side turning hand wheels to drive the mount. He would follow the pointer that provided a signal from the director. We were trying to eliminate the man and the pointer and to have a device that would make that heavy gun, through a hydraulic mechanism, follow very smoothly a changing signal and would save the manpower involved and actually do it better.

Roll and pitch aboard ship is such a major function. Whenever you are sitting there as a man, trying to match roll and pitch to keep the gun on target, you're probably off more than you're on. You really had to fire sort of on the fly. Usually when you would come down over the target, you would anticipate and fire and hope you could hold it momentarily to get the shell off. When you had a responsive servo mechanism functioning, the ship could be rolling a lot, and the gun would more or less stay level. I learned enough to know that they could be very complex devices.

I found the whole course really well suited to my needs and comprehension, so that as I moved into things like the Polaris missile program and ship design programs, I had a good engineering background to help interpret them.

Q: Admiral Hooper specialized in servo mechanisms. Did you have any contact with him?*

Admiral Weschler: I didn't at that time. I knew Admiral Hooper very well, of course. He was class of '31, right in between my cousin and my brother. And, as I say, I knew most of those classes by name if not by face. I had seen him during World War II somewhere and then saw him at MIT. He was working on a project. Much later, when I was a rear admiral in Danang, he was my boss, Commander Service Force Pacific.

Q: Did you write a thesis during this course of study?

Admiral Weschler: Yes, we were required to write a paper,

---

*Vice Admiral Edwin B. Hooper, USN (Ret.), whose oral history is in the Naval Institute collection.

and the title of ours was very complicated. It was a report on attempting to mount the tracking radar onto the gun platform in order to save cost, weight, and space. When it was actually tried later on, it was called gun and radar, or GUNAR. GUNAR was used in the Navy briefly in the period of '47 and '48. It was tested by the Operational Development Force. It was a very interesting idea, but it came right at the time when digital electronics were being born, so anything that was full of vacuum tubes and hydraulics was pretty much overtaken by events. It was the last major gasp before digital electronics and was simply too restricted in operating range and too expensive.

The paper we did analyzed the ability of a power supply to take the inputs from radar and provide some fix to the gun, with the gun also moving the radar. You had to filter out whatever motion was imparted to the incoming signal. It was a very complex arrangement, and at certain frequencies, things would go into a dither. That was one of our major problems. In correcting, the system would overreact, go too far, and then have to come back, taking too much time.

Q: How would you describe the level of instruction? That is, how did the teachers fit in with the capabilities of the students?

Admiral Weschler: I was disappointed, fundamentally, in MIT in that so few of the profs had anything to do with the students, except for the two I have mentioned: Dr. Draper and Dr. Dillingham. The rest tended to use last year's graduate student as a prof, and he would tell you the minimum that he had to in order to answer your question. So it was pretty much a self-taught course, very similar to the Naval Academy. We read the book and talked among ourselves. If one of you grasped what was involved, you'd tell the rest of the group. And then this substitute prof would sort of check it off, that he had given you classroom instruction. I really didn't find graduate school at MIT in that period all that stimulating, except for Dr. Draper.

Q: He must have loved the Navy to have worked on so many projects, and I think that would help you.

Admiral Weschler: That's right. And, as I say, he would share this excitement--the most enthusiastic prof I've ever seen. He had a blackboard that was easily 12 feet long, and he would start at one end of it and write this formula that would cover it from end to end, explaining every item as he wrote it. You were likely to be lost at the end of about the first two minutes of this dissertation. But he was so enthusiastic and would come up with a big exclamation point at the end, and you almost had to applaud this tour de force! He was marvelous.

Once you were one of his graduate students, you were part of a club. He would invite you to Locke-Ober's, which is a wonderful restaurant in Boston. About every quarter, Doc Draper would have a mid-afternoon dinner for those who were members of his class. We would go over there, and we had clams casino and lobster. It was really quite a feast, and we were his guests for this wonderful spread. He would talk about what he was doing, what his goals would be, what the possibilities were. He really was an inspiration. If ever you had wanted to be a researcher, he's the kind of person you'd follow. Many of his assistants are still there at the Draper Laboratory or are just about to retire. But they got motivated and inflamed by him.

I want to make time for one aside here. My wife didn't know Dr. Draper all that well. I wasn't married when I first met him, and later on she didn't see him too much. But once in Washington, in the early '60s, Trina was with me. We were picking up Dr. Draper to take him to a reception at Admiral Burke's quarters. He was staying at a run-down little hotel somewhere in Washington, where he had stayed since he was a student, I expect. When he went to Washington, that's where he always headed. He'd been out walking, so we intercepted him about a block from the hotel, and he climbed in. We drove on, and he wasn't taking himself at all seriously, just asking Trina questions about herself and about the children and so on. Finally, she said, "Dr. Draper, aren't you the man who's working on the moon project?"

He said, "Oh, yes, but anybody could do it." And Trina's never forgotten that--that the man didn't take himself seriously, didn't think he was one in a million. And yet, he had his picture on the cover of Time magazine--the most self-effacing genius you could imagine.

Q: Would it be fair to say that he personally saved graduate school from being a humdrum experience for you?

Admiral Weschler: No question, no question. I think that Doc Draper alone would have been complete justification for the whole period. I know that's what he was for so many.

Q: How much value was this course later on in your career?

Admiral Weschler: I think it was a key point. I know it's the only reason I went to the Polaris program. It led my career in ways it never would have gone otherwise. And it gave me confidence in a technical world. That was vital in things like the Spruance ship design. To me it was really the essential step to a successful career. I have told any number of officers since, that if you really want to have a successful career, get some sort of technical specialty, and with it, if you can, get yourself a wonderful prof to enthuse you.

Q: Some of these benefits you mention sound more like by-products rather than direct applications. Was there a direct application?

Admiral Weschler: Yes, I was the head of the fire control and guidance section of the Polaris missile project. This guidance system was being designed by the Draper Laboratory, and the fire control portion was a direct application of the course work, particularly servo mechanisms. It involved everything from conceptual design, to hardware, to how to test it. You knew how to ask the right question, and you could understand the answer enough to know if you were getting double-talk. The rule was that if you took a technical PG course, you had to have a minimum of two shore tours and one sea tour in your specialty. That was sort of the payback.

Q: More than they have now.

Admiral Weschler: A lot of people don't get that much time ashore, I guess.

Thomas R. Weschler #2 - 139

Q: Any of your fellow students in that course who were noteworthy?

Admiral Weschler: It was, I thought, a top-notch group: Admiral Tommy Rudden, Admiral Scott Goodfellow, Admiral Ben Pickett, Captain Bill Hasler, Captain Royal Joslin were the ones in that class.* Out of the first three, the admirals, all had tours in various parts of the Bureau of Ordnance along the way. Captain Bill Hasler became an ordnance ED and stayed with the Polaris project all the way through until he retired and is still working today at Lockheed. Royal Joslin--I don't know if you know him--is certainly well connected in the Navy as a descendant of Stephen B. Luce and, incidentally, is the first cousin of Rear Admiral Jack Kane.** Royal Joslin's last major command was as commanding officer of the Columbus. He was the first commanding officer of the destroyer school. So I think all five of them were wonderful people.

Q: I think the small size of the class would help you also.

Admiral Weschler: That's right. They knew they didn't

---
*As of 1946 they were as follows: Lieutenant Commander Thomas J. Rudden, Jr., USN; Lieutenant Commander Alexander Scott Goodfellow, Jr., USN; Commander Ben B. Pickett, USN; Commander William A. Hasler, Jr., USN; Lieutenant Commander Royal K. Joslin, USN.
**Rear Admiral John D. H. Kane, USN (Ret.)

Thomas R. Weschler #2 - 140

have too many billets for specialists of that type, so they kept the classes small, trying to get the right number to fill the billets.

Q: On the other hand, that makes the competition very stiff.

Admiral Weschler: And I felt that all the time that I was in that program.

Q: Well, anything more on the PG school?

Admiral Weschler: No, I can't think of anything else worthwhile on the school itself. One pleasant experience was that I became engaged to my future wife during that period.

Q: How did that come about? Where did you meet her?

Admiral Weschler: She lived next door to me in the hometown, Erie, Pennsylvania. I think I mentioned when I bought the convertible that I didn't expect to get married during World War II. So as soon as World War II was over and I was at the postgraduate school, I was seriously looking for a young lady. I wanted to get married. The time had come. I went home, and our next-door neighbor was

Katrina Quinn. She had lost a brother in World War II. He was a Marine who was killed in Okinawa. I had lost Charles, my brother, who was killed as a prisoner of war, as I mentioned earlier. So we commiserated a little about that and talked.

I had known Katrina, but she was about five years younger than I, so that when I was a college graduate, she was a senior in high school. You know how that is in that time frame. You can't even see what they look like when the current status is so different. But now she was a college graduate, getting her master's at Yale in nursing, and I was getting a master's at MIT. We seemed to hit it off pretty well, so first thing you knew, we were dating fairly regularly. It was interesting.

I always have claimed that every cent I saved from World War II was given to the New York, New Haven and Hartford Railroad. If we both were free, I'd leave from Boston, she'd get on a train in New Haven, and we'd both go to New York. If she had the duty, I'd go to New Haven. If I had the duty, she'd come to Boston. So it seemed to me we were running up and down that railroad all the time. Anyhow, it took, and we were engaged by the time I graduated from MIT, and we were married in Erie and honeymooned in a brief period.

We were married on the fourth of January of '47, and I reported to the heavy cruiser <u>Macon</u> in New Orleans the 16th of January.* So we had 12 days together, and then I didn't see her until the following April when we came back from Guantanamo. The Macon had just completed a month's overhaul, so when we went to Guantanamo, it was not an OpDevFor assignment. It was just a normal refresher training, though we had naval reserves embarked.

Q: What was the Macon doing in New Orleans?

Admiral Weschler: It was a naval reserve training cruise, and that was the port stop. We were tied up at a pier right near the St. Louis Square--the cathedral and right near the French Quarter. When you came off the brow of Macon, you were within a half block of that wonderful Morning Call, that spot where you go for French coffee and doughnuts. So liberty in New Orleans was fabulous.

Q: Probably still is.

Admiral Weschler: Probably still is. It was certainly great in '47.

Q: So did you wind up having your honeymoon in New Orleans?

---

*USS Macon (CA-132) was commissioned 26 August 1945. She had a standard displacement of 13,600 tons, was 675 feet long, and 71 feet in the beam. She had a top speed of 33 knots and a main battery of nine 8-inch guns. She was also outfitted with 12 5-inch guns.

Admiral Weschler: No. My wife's final exams were the period 12-13-14 January. So we honeymooned from the wedding up to New Haven, and then we stayed in a furnished room in New Haven while she took her final exams. When she finished her final exams, I kissed her goodbye and reported to New Orleans, and she went back to Erie. Then she joined me in Philadelphia when the ship came in from refresher training.

Q: How did you come to get orders to the Macon?

Admiral Weschler: I mentioned that you're supposed to get sea tours that jibe with your postgraduate tour, so being in the ordnance field, I was assigned as the ship's gunnery officer.

We had completed school in September, and Macon wasn't to be ready to go to sea until January. So in the meantime they gave me three months of training in the Washington, D.C.-Annapolis area. There was a gunnery officers' ordnance school at the Washington Navy Yard, and it provided a chance to get up to date on the fleet equipment. We learned all of the recent directors and radars and so on, so that we really had very good schooling about how to be gunnery officers, and then I went aboard Macon in January 1947.

Another reason for being assigned to Macon was because she was being attached to the Operational Development Force. Macon was not fully manned. We operated with about 50% of ship's company during that period when manpower was scarce. Everyone was demobilized, and since we were operating with the development force, we were not likely to have a major commitment. It made sense to put an ordnance PG there as gun boss, because they would put aboard experimental gear, or they would use the gear that we had, making a series of tests in order to develop performance specifications and improved operations procedures. I found that a very rewarding tour.

We made a midshipmen's cruise, which is always pleasant, and provided another trip to Europe. I told you I like to travel.

But I think the highlight of that tour was not gunnery in the conventional sense. It was helicopters! The yard built a helicopter platform on the stern of Macon in June of '47; we originally had catapults. So I did have a chance to give the order to launch aircraft from the ship before the catapults were removed. I think our pilot was very glad to be detached when that experience was over. We operated two helicopters on board for a trial period out of Norfolk and then went to Europe with the two helicopters embarked. We used them throughout the midshipmen's cruise.

The whole idea was to find out if a helicopter could operate effectively from aboard a ship. It proved to be a very worthwhile event. One of our pilots was Lieutenant Bill Shawcross, later Admiral Shawcross, so they sent us very good people.* Thanks to their flying skill, it all came off very successfully, and we had no major difficulties. I think it was important because in so many of these trial kinds of events, if something goes wrong, you may set the program back five years. Since this was very successful, the impetus was there for helicopters aboard ships other than carriers, as soon as their mission was clear. However, it took us about another ten years before we were really doing it regularly.

Q: What year did you make the midshipmen's cruise?

Admiral Weschler: The summer of '48.

Q: And where did you go on that cruise?

Admiral Weschler: I can't remember all the places, but I particularly recall going to the Italian Naval Academy at Livorno. It impressed me not only because it was another naval academy but also to see how that harbor was still beat up with sunken ships and damaged piers and so on, even

---

*Lieutenant William H. Shawcross, USN.

Thomas R. Weschler #2 - 146

in '48. It was a couple of years after the war, and I never thought that the Italian ports had taken all that much of a licking, but apparently they had, a lot more than I was aware of. My experience having been in the Pacific, I at that time didn't know an awful lot about the war in the Atlantic and what had gone on in the Mediterranean.

Q: The Sixth Fleet was just then in its infancy. Did you have any fleet operations, or were you largely on your own?

Admiral Weschler: At that time, yes, Sixth Fleet was in its infancy. The British CinCMed title was still there.* We hadn't developed CinCSouth, the NATO command.** None of those things had come along. My impression is that, except for seeing some of the British ships, we didn't participate in any joint operations. I don't remember seeing any flag officers in those ports. I remember the ambassadors and the Italian naval officers, but I don't recall any U.S. naval officers being around.

Q: How big a force were you in?

Admiral Weschler: We were with Missouri part of the time, but I can't give you a good recollection.

---
*CinCMed--Commander in Chief Mediterranean.
**CinCSouth--Commander in Chief Allied Forces Southern Europe; NATO--North Atlantic Treaty Organization.

Q: This was the year after the first overseas midshipman cruises following the war. There was one in 1947 that went to Northern Europe with two battleships and two carriers. The Navy was just feeling its way after being tied up for a while.

Admiral Weschler: That's right. That's right. And I remember the experience of being a gunnery officer and of having the midshipmen aboard. But except for Livorno, I don't really have a clear impression.

Q: Who was your skipper in the ship?

Admiral Weschler: The one during this period was Olin Scoggins, and I had a fantastic group of junior officers.* I couldn't have asked for better. But Olin Scoggins was a submariner, and I say that with all due respect. He was a wonderful person, but the point I'm going to make is he took every good ensign that he found and sent him to sub school. As soon as I qualified my top JOs as division officers and officers of the deck, they went to sub school. The only one who managed to survive aboard was Ed Snyder, now retired Rear Admiral Snyder, and

---

*Captain Olin Scoggins, USN, commanded the USS Macon (CA-132) from 1 May 1948 to 3 May 1949.

Thomas R. Weschler #2 - 148

skipper of the New Jersey along the way.* Ed was first division officer. He's the only one I managed to keep on board. I could rattle off a whole bunch of them, but there must have been about five or six of them who went to sub school from the ship, including Turner Joy in fourth division.**

Q: I would think the skipper was somewhat miscast in that role. It would be better to have a destroyer/surface type officer, rather than a submariner, in a ship that was doing experimental tactics.

Admiral Weschler: Oh, yes, that's right. But Captain Scoggins was the one that was available, and there he was. Before him was Captain Germany Shultz, another great person.*** He had been a surface sailor. But both of them, I think, were so happy to have a cruiser that whether it was only partially manned and working for the Operational Development Force, they were still thrilled to be in a major command.

Q: Were there any development programs you specifically

---
*Lieutenant (junior grade) J. Edward Snyder, Jr., USN. In 1968-69, as a captain, Snyder was commanding officer of the battleship New Jersey (BB-62) during her only deployment of the Vietnam War.
**Ensign C. Turner Joy, Jr., USN. His father was a noted flag officer during World War II and the Korean War.
***Captain John H. Shultz, USN, commanded the Macon from 6 June 1947 to 1 May 1948.

remember from the period?

Admiral Weschler: There weren't any that were that great shakes; that's why I mention the helicopter as the one that was the most exciting. We had the first Mark 63 director aboard. The Mark 63 was simply an adaptation of the gunfire control system with more electrical control of the gun. The Mark 63 became a dependable system. It was used a great deal through the '50s, but it wasn't that major an achievement.

Q: Who was the admiral in charge of the development force then?

Admiral Weschler: Admiral Briscoe had it.* He had relieved Admiral Lee.** Remember, Admiral Lee had died tragically of a heart attack. Our operations officer was an ordnance PG who went on to be reasonably successful afterwards, Captain Charles K. Bergin.

I enjoyed working with that group. There were a lot of other ships around that had experimental gear. I talked with their officers because so many of these ordnance PGs

---
*Rear Admiral Robert P. Briscoe, USN, was Commander Operational Development Force from September 1945 to October 1948.
**While in command of Composite Task Force Atlantic Fleet, the forerunner of the Operational Development Force, Vice Admiral Willis A. Lee, Jr., USN, died of a heart attack on 25 August 1945.

Thomas R. Weschler #2 - 150

were scattered through the force that we could get together and tell each other about developments. Technically and service-wise, it was an excellent tour of duty to learn what was going on and to have a window on the future. But Macon didn't get what I would call really big, money-making projects, things that were going to change the Navy, except the helicopter.

Q: Did you get the new 3-inch guns in place of the light antiaircraft machine guns?

Admiral Weschler: No, we had 40 millimeters, and that's what we used the Mark 63 with. We didn't really do anything experimental with our gun battery--the 5-inch or the 8-inch. The 40s were the only things we had programs with. It got us an awful lot of aircraft target services, and we did a lot of tracking.

Q: You didn't get to shoot the 8-inch at all?

Admiral Weschler: Oh, yes, we were still in competition. We insisted on that. I was happy that the captains took the stand that partially manned though we were, we were still a cruiser in the Battleship-Cruiser Force, and we wanted to be in the competition. We used the same gun crews to man the turrets and mounts. If you sounded general quarters surface warfare, they manned the turrets. If you passed the word general quarters antiair warfare, they manned the 5-inch guns and the 40s. So we had a flexible crew and could go either direction.

It was very good. I think we speeded up the orders for turret fire during that period, because, having been used to the AA battery where you'd simply say, "Action starboard," and then lock on a target and open fire, we used the same terminology with the turrets.* We would simply say, "Action starboard," and expect the turrets to swing out and be ready to go, instead of a whole series of commands about match pointers and lock and that sort of thing. So I think it was good that we had that experience with both batteries.

Q: That's interesting about the men switching back and forth between the AA battery and the main battery in the Macon. I wonder if you had any special safety precautions because of that lack of experience?

Admiral Weschler: I think the thing that made it successful--and it didn't come out in that very thumbnail idea of how we went back and forth--we still did have certain key rates who were available to each battery: for

---
*AA--antiaircraft.

example, turret captains and gunner's mates who took care of individual mounts and turrets. With those people in charge, then we could do enough training and have enough direct supervision that I wasn't really concerned about what was going to happen. If it hadn't been for having enough key petty officers, I don't think we could have done it.

We didn't use all the 5-inch mounts. We had six mounts, but we manned only four or five of them, and that depended on how many good gun captains I had available. Then the only other thing I can offer is that in those days--and this is still largely true today--you didn't fire that much live ammunition. There was no end of drill before you got around to the point where you could use live ammunition, and that helped, so that by the time live ammunition came, you were really going to get the most out of it.

Q: Actually, I think the shortage was a blessing, because you got more cross-training than you would have otherwise.

Admiral Weschler: Yes, from the standpoint of every gunner in the ship and, I guess, the crew in general. And I must say that no one had to be depressed that he didn't have a locker or a place to put his gear. Everybody had two lockers, and the hardest thing was to get those unused

Thomas R. Weschler #2 - 153

compartments clean. Everyone would always be going in there to use the extra lockers or to get away from it all, if they wanted to sneak a little extra bunk time. Those places tended to go downhill, so every so often we had to have a working party to square away those empty compartments.

Q: How was morale in that period when there were so few people?

Admiral Weschler: Very good. We had a lot of time in Norfolk, that being our home port. And working for OpDevFor, we weren't going to be taking a lot of cruises. The midshipmen's cruise was enough of a wonderful event that no one was unhappy to be gone for six weeks or two months. So it was the best of both worlds--it was a fairly relaxed schedule, yet something to do that was meaningful while you were out there, and the only cruise you had was a fairly short one. That part was very good. I was a newlywed during this period, so I was enjoying being a family man and being around the house.

Q: Were there any executive officers that stood out in your mind from the Macon?

Admiral Weschler: Well, I liked the execs very much. We

had two fine ones--Joe Costello and Robert Craven Leonard.* Both of them had known Charles very well. Bob Leonard was a classmate of Charles's. They were very good people, but I didn't find either one of them that impressive overall in terms of long-range career. As a matter of fact, much as I liked later-Captain Leonard, I felt that he didn't put out the word very well.

You know, I mentioned we were operating in Norfolk and were having a midshipmen's cruise. All the men wanted to know could they plan this, could they plan that? I went over to OpDevFor and got the CinCLantFlt operating schedule.** I also got OpDevFor's schedule of what we were to do in each quarter and what the services would be. And I got the overhaul schedule, which told when you were going to the shipyard. From those three I put together a schedule of what the ship was likely to be doing over the next 18 months. I thought the exec was going to blow his stack when he found out that I had put the information out. He said, "You know this isn't guaranteed."

I said, "I know it isn't guaranteed, Commander, but it's in all of the schedules that we're operating by and helps people to plan, gives us something reasonable." For some reason he didn't feel that this sort of thing ought to be put out--that you were likely to get everyone planning

_____
*Commander Joseph P. Costello, USN; Commander Robert C. Leonard, USN.
**CinCLantFlt--Commander in Chief Atlantic Fleet.

that they were going to be home for Christmas or going to be doing this or that. Perhaps it was a carry-over from the war, but I didn't agree with that attitude. I thought it was much more constructive to tell people where they were going and was glad it had been done before I learned the XO's position.

Q: I'm surprised you did that rather than the ops officer.

Admiral Weschler: Well, again, it's just a question of who's doing what. I guess I had a lot of curiosity. I liked to do things, and if I had a question and nobody seemed to be doing it, I didn't mind finding out. Commander Gene Rider was the ops boss, and he and I did not always see eye to eye.* I think he felt that I was crowding him and getting into his territory. But a lot of times I didn't think he was doing everything that needed to be done or that I felt might be more constructive, so I would do it. No real conflict resulted, because I was sufficiently junior to be no real threat. Commander Rider was transferred well before my tour ended.

One officer I want to mention particularly that I bumped into there and enjoyed and still see often is Vice Admiral Parker Armstrong.** Parker was the chief

---
*Commander Eugene C. Rider, USN.
**Lieutenant Commander Parker B. Armstrong, USN, at the time of his service in the Macon.

engineer. He brought order, performance, and leadership to his department and made it a first-class organization. Parker and Jean are just wonderful people and helped to make that tour so enjoyable. By this time we were all back to regulars now. The reserves were gone; everybody was a regular. So a lot of the people one met, as I did in the postgraduate school and as I did aboard the Macon, were individuals I was likely to see the rest of my professional life. Thus the contacts were very important.

Q: This was particularly a phenomenon in the prewar Navy when it was much smaller. It was more pronounced then.

Admiral Weschler: That's right. Since I was an ordnance PG, I knew I was going to be in a lot of ordnance billets, so those were gents you were seeing all the rest of your life. Simply because so many people were going into submarines and aviation, the surface community tended to be a little smaller in proportion, and so those like Parker, you did have a chance of seeing a few more times.

Nonetheless, I mentioned that I was shipmates with Mickey Weisner in '41, and through another 34 years never was in the same ship or stationed with him all the way along. So it can happen the other way too.

Q: The aviators and submariners came out of the war with

glamorous records. Were surface sailors sort of second-class citizens at that point?

Admiral Weschler: Let me say that the gun club was still fairly well recognized. I'd say that it dropped out of the ascendancy by the end of the '50s, but through the '50s the gun club still thought of itself as being pretty red hot. I don't think any of us really were wed to battleships in the sense that you could call us "battleship admirals" or battleship devotees. I think we all had enough carrier duty and had been around the carriers to know that the world had shifted and the battleship had been made an escort except for shore bombardment.

But the gun club was important enough in terms of the Bureau of Ordnance and what was coming along made you feel you were still vital. Aside from that, I feel that the surface Navy was really sort of in the doldrums. We weren't getting the ships, we weren't getting new construction, and that's why Admiral Burke coming in as CNO was so important, to give a shot in the arm to a major segment of the Navy. Otherwise, it was going downhill.

Q: Was there in that period, the late '40s, sort of an acknowledged leader of the gun club? For example, Admiral Blandy was one of those people, very senior.* Did he

---
*Admiral William H. P. Blandy, USN, formerly Chief of the Bureau of Ordnance, was Commander in Chief Atlantic Fleet.

provide any sort of leadership?

Admiral Weschler: Admiral Lynde McCormick was one who was also talked of as being an inspiration.* Admiral Blandy, I think, did more of it as CinCLantFlt. I mentioned he came over to talk with us to give us his views on where the Navy was going and what was going on. Admiral Hoke Smith, Allan E. Smith, tried to do some of that, but he wasn't a very good speaker, and he didn't have as warm a personality, so that although he wanted to imbue the force with a feeling of distinction, I don't think he did it well.**

I can't think of any others who were really big names other than Admiral Blandy.

Q: Did BuOrd reinforce any of this notion of the gun club and surface sailors?

Admiral Weschler: I think yes, and they were trying to bring out good products. I think one thing that gave the surface sailor a boost in this period was the delivery of the Salem-class heavy cruisers. The Worcester and the Roanoke, the rapid-fire 6-inch, I don't think were in the

---
*Vice Admiral Lynde D. McCormick, USN, served as Commander Battleships-Cruisers Atlantic Fleet from February 1947 to November 1948.
**Rear Admiral Allan E. Smith, Commander Cruisers Atlantic Fleet when Weschler served on that staff.

same ballpark with the Salem, Newport News, and Des Moines.* The heavy cruisers were flagships for the Sixth Fleet and had a fantastic record. That 8-inch rapid fire was one of the most beautiful pieces of ordnance ever delivered, and I know there was a lot of discussion, now that they're reactivating the battleships, about bringing back the cruisers, because they were fitted out as flagships and because those 8-inch rapid fires were so good. However, when the chips were down, all of the cruisers had been run extensively. The battleships, which had been mothballed, had so much better engineering plants and better hulls for reactivation.

But aside from those new cruisers, I don't know of anything that came along to give the destroyer force a real boost. We were continuing to operate the Fletcher-class and the Sumner-class destroyers. We were modernizing those, but all the modernizations were minor steps.

Q: There were so many of them that there wasn't room for new ships.

Admiral Weschler: That's right. There were so many of them, and the Navy was putting an awful lot of them out of

---

*Commissioning dates: Des Moines (CA-134), 16 November 1948; Salem (CA-139), 14 May 1949; Newport News (CA-148), 29 January 1949; Worcester (CL-144), 26 June 1948; Roanoke (CL-145), 4 April 1949.

commission, and they were trying to experiment with the escort role and the radar picket role and all that. We were trying to feel our way, and I think you know that during this period missilery was on its way in. The V-1 and V-2 rockets of the Germans had fired everybody's imagination. The Navy started the Terrier-Tartar-Talos program in 1947, the three-T program. As an ordnance PG during that period of September to December '46 that I was here in Washington, we were taken out and briefed on that program. A couple of PGs who were classmates got into that three-T program. All through the period of the '50s missiles were coming along. People felt that the missiles had a chance to become successful and might rejuvenate the surface Navy. That didn't quite happen.

Q: I'm curious why those three Salem-class cruisers didn't get around to Korea. Here was this fabulous gun, but it wasn't used in combat, at least not during that period.

Admiral Weschler: No. Remember we sent the Missouri out there.

Q: But the bulk of the shore bombardment came from the 8-inch bag guns.

Admiral Weschler: The only thing I can tell you is that

the Sixth Fleet was regarded as very important in those days, and I have a feeling that the Navy was trying to make a strong case for its being a vital part of the armed forces. I have a hunch that there was a certain bit of service politics in keeping a strong, effective Sixth Fleet with good flagships and that the Europeans or whoever was establishing NATO or the defense of Europe was happy to have a strong force over there in case anything went wrong.* Remember, we did have that situation in Greece, the pressure on Turkey.

Q: That's why the Missouri was sent over to the Mediterranean in '46.

Admiral Weschler: Yes. And there were enough things happening through that period that I think they didn't regard the European theater as really quiet and that the Communists were still very much on the move, and we wanted something effective there.

Q: There was an equivalent on the air side in that the three newest carriers, the Midway class, also were deploying to the Mediterranean.

Admiral Weschler: Right. Now, with the carriers, there

---
*NATO--the North Atlantic Treaty Organization began in April 1949 as a strategic counter to the Soviet Union.

was still another factor at work, and that was because we were trying to get into strategic warfare. This was the period in which the AJs, the heavy delivery aircraft, were coming along, and we were building up the view that the carrier was part of the nuclear delivery force and that we had a role in strategic warfare. I think that also was behind the carriers being over there in Europe.

Q: You mentioned Ed Snyder. I'm particularly curious about him, because he was a skipper of mine in the New Jersey.

Admiral Weschler: Oh, isn't that something? Well, Ed came aboard Macon as a jaygee. I think that's the only reason he didn't go to sub school; he'd already passed the decision point by the time he arrived. But he took first division, and I knew the day he walked aboard this was a capable gent. Ed has a way of handling himself. He just doesn't say an extra word, and he simply wants you to trust him. Then he very quickly demonstrates that he's worthy of trust. His manner turns off all sorts of fatherly advice and so on. You simply tell him what you want and then let him go. But he ran that forecastle like a dream and loved being a turret officer. He was just a natural and an excellent shiphandler--wonderful on the bridge. Never wasted a word and knew what he was about. I thought he was the very model of a naval officer.

Q: He's become much more loquacious since then.

Admiral Weschler: That's right. From having observed him in sort of a senior-junior relationship, if you're the senior, then Ed is not loquacious. If he's the senior, he has a tendency perhaps to talk more. Now that we meet in convivial circumstances, why, he's as good at chatter as anybody.

Q: When he was in the New Jersey, he very much enjoyed being a non-regulation type. Did you see this back then?

Admiral Weschler: I think he certainly liked to cut corners. He hated what looked like wasted motion and folderol. So maybe yes, I would say that he did. But non-reg in the sense of just wanting to do it a different way--no, I didn't really get that impression. Again, as a JO and so on, these were tricks that were going to be uncorked later.

Q: How much administrative work did you do in running the department?

Admiral Weschler: I'd say that the role of gunnery officer could have involved a tremendous amount of paperwork, but I was fortunate to have two or three good lieutenants as assistants. Then I had an outstanding chief turret captain named Creed who really ran the main battery for me.* I think I can give you an idea of how highly I thought of him. When I went to CruLant staff as the gunnery boss, I had a billet for a writer on the staff, and I turned in my billet as a writer to get an enlisted man who was a gunner's mate. Of course, I got this chief turret captain who came over as my right arm. With people like Chief Creed and these good assistants, the administration was very well taken care of.

Q: How did you go about getting the switch from that ship to the type commander's staff?

Admiral Weschler: It wasn't too difficult to engineer. I had told my relief when I walked off that if I could do anything about it, I was going to take Chief Creed. He was so capable that he retired ultimately as CWO-4, so he did very well in moving up in the warrant ranks.** My relief was kind enough to say, "Well, if that's all that follows you in your wake when you walk off, I can't really complain." Then the fact that I had a billet available and

---
*Chief Turret Captain Euly C. Creed, Jr., USN.
**CWO--chief warrant officer.

Thomas R. Weschler #2 - 165

was on the transferring authority, it really worked out very easily.

Q: Did CruLant control the enlisted personnel assignments?

Admiral Weschler: We couldn't go outside the type command, but for billets within the type command we had transfer authority. And so, since it was coming to the staff of CruLant, it was all within our bailiwick, so that was no problem. You couldn't get out of hand on this. ServLant, which had total control authority, would watch what was going on.* If they thought that you were inducing serious imbalances, they might call. But you could make minor adjustments.

Q: How did you get yourself moved? Was this another pay-back tour?

Admiral Weschler: No. I had done well in <u>Macon</u> apparently, and so the chief of staff talked to the skipper and said they had a billet for a gunnery officer. I relieved T. Starr King, and Captain Scoggins was a good friend of Captain Mendenhall's.** Mendenhall was the chief of staff at the time and later retired as a rear

---
*ServLant--Service Force Atlantic Fleet.
**Commander Thomas Starr King, Jr., USN; Captain William K. Mendenhall, Jr., USN.

admiral. And he asked for me. Later Roland Smoot was in there as chief of staff.*

Captain Mendenhall had talked to the skipper and decided that I'd be a good man for the billet. They knew I was an ordnance PG, and they were happy to have me come over and take that spot. You were supposed to be a PG to fill the billet, and Tommy King was. I was delighted, because it kept me in Norfolk. There wasn't any change of station involved, which also made BuPers happy, because it didn't cost money for the orders.** And it meant I would be there for another year. With midshipman cruises and a couple of other trips out, we were at sea maybe a third of the time, but that was about as much as the ships were gone.

Q: How was the housing situation in Norfolk at that time?

Admiral Weschler: We lived on the economy. I suppose there were some quarters or government housing but not very much. There was some enlisted housing and Ben Moreell housing, and some of those built during World War II.*** But officer housing was not around.

───────────
*Captain Roland N. Smoot, USN. Smoot retired as a vice admiral; his oral history is in the Naval Institute collection.
**BuPers--Bureau of Naval Personnel.
***Admiral Ben Moreell, CEC, USN, was Chief of the Bureau of Yards and Docks from 1937 to 1945.

Thomas R. Weschler #2 - 167

Q: Civilian housing was very tight after the war.

Admiral Weschler: Civilian housing was tight but not all that bad. We were just catching the wave of new construction. There must have been 10 or 15 projects just springing up in the Norfolk area, and we moved into one of those. We were the second couple, I think, to live in the house that we got, and it was one of those small things, but it was perfectly adequate and only about ten minutes from the naval base, so we felt very fortunate to be there. It was just off a golf course, which was pleasant, so we lucked out.

Q: Who was the type commander when you reported to the staff?

Admiral Weschler: My recollection is that when I joined the staff in early '49, Vice Admiral Lynde McCormick had until shortly before been ComBatCruLant, three-star.*
When he left that command, he was relieved by Rear Admiral Allan E. Smith, and it was downgraded to a two-star billet, and Admiral Smith was ComCruLant. However, we still had one battleship in commission, <u>Missouri</u>, and you know its

―――――――――
*Vice Admiral Lynde D. McCormick, USN, served as Commander Cruisers-Battleships Atlantic Fleet from February 1947 to November 1948.

Thomas R. Weschler #2 - 168

unfortunate history of running aground; that was quite an experience.* I think that's well documented in various other writeups, so I won't talk an awful lot about that experience with Missouri, except that I began to appreciate the vastness of the Navy resources and the depth of technical knowhow and what we had available, and we really had a specific challenge.

The only other time that I had that feeling of the capability of the Navy was when I was Naval Support Activity Danang and saw what we were able to move in there when it came time to support all those people on the shore in Vietnam. Each time, I began to recognize what these warrant officers and limited duty officers and skilled petty officers and all of this varied equipment scattered around--what it all meant and how it could be brought to bear, as long as you had someone in charge who knew how to coordinate it.

Q: It's ironic that all these resources and sophisticated capabilities were unleashed by a single act of incompetence.

Admiral Weschler: Yes, yes, but I must say I can't believe that anyone who was connected with that grounding of

---

*The USS Missouri (BB-63) ran aground just outside of her home port of Norfolk, Virginia, on 17 January 1950. For details, see, Dr. Malcolm Muir, Jr., "Hard Aground on Thimble Shoal," Naval History, Fall 1991, pages 30-35.

Missouri didn't learn. Admiral Smith was wonderful in the way he mobilized the team. Admiral Homer Wallin had the naval shipyard, and Admiral Smith brought him aboard as his technical expert.* I soon learned that the same pontoons with which we had helped float the Squalus and the S-4 were there to help provide buoyancy.** He brought in the ASRs, the submarine rescue ships, because they could monitor the divers who were working underneath the hull.

Then I learned there was an ARS, which is a salvage ship which is able to spud itself in with heavy anchors and then can put out a cable and exert a pull of hundreds of tons, maybe even thousands of tons, to help get a ship moving. I have never seen so many tugs. We must have had something on the order of 16 or 18 tugs on bridles, like horses out ahead of us, ready to pull that Missouri off. It was a fantastic feat. The grounding was in mid-January; I'm quite sure that was the month this occurred. There were two neap tides, and at the fullest of these neap tides, which occurred some day near the end of January. They would give us more lift than at any other time over the next six months, so that was the time we crystallized on to get the ship off.

---

*Rear Admiral Homer N. Wallin, USN, Commander Norfolk Naval Shipyard.
**The new submarine Squalus (SS-192) sank in the spring of 1939 during a test dive off the Portsmouth Navy Yard. In December 1927 the submarine S-4 (SS-109) sank off Provincetown, Massachusetts, after being rammed by the Coast destroyer Paulding.

At the preceding neap tide, which was about two inches or three inches less, is when he had his dummy run to be sure that everything worked. And then the moment of truth came at about 7:00 o'clock on the morning of February 1, when this neap tide was at its highest and everything was pulling at its maximum. Then suddenly he gave the order to the tugs to all pull, and they pulled, and using a gunner's sextant, they were checking to see whether there was any motion. At first there wasn't any, and suddenly he said, "It's moved," and then you could begin to feel the ship moving.

Suddenly, we had momentum, and then the big fear was, would it stop? These ARSs that I told you were spudded in place--suddenly, Missouri took a little bit of a sheer, and here was this ship moving, so you didn't dare stop if you wanted to get it off, sliding toward this ARS, and we carried away part of his side railing, but that was all. It didn't really do any serious damage, but suddenly this thing was in the way. And if it'd been wiped out, I'm sure Admiral Smith would have said, "So be it." He was going to get that thing off.

One feature, though, that I want to mention that might not have been reported in the history of the grounding and how it came off. Admiral Blandy was CinCLantFlt when this incident occurred, and he was having his change of command aboard a carrier at pier seven.* I mentioned we got under way about 7:00 o'clock, and so sometime then we got out, and it took two hours to get all these cables off and get a couple of tugs alongside to start moving <u>Missouri</u> towards the shipyard.

Just about 10:00 or 10:30, when the change of command was taking place, Admiral Blandy was turning the fleet over to his relief, and he was able to say, "The Atlantic Fleet is all ready for operations or will be in proper technical condition, and I am happy to say that one of that number is just going by." <u>Missouri</u> was going by at that point, and I thought that was marvelous, that Admiral Smith was able to get it off and the change of command was there. I don't know how much the two of them had dovetailed that, but it was a wonderful touch.

Q: Admiral Fechteler was relieving him at that point.

Admiral Weschler: I didn't know him at the time. I knew Admiral Blandy. He had been the head of BuOrd, and I had met him.** I think Squidge Lee was married to his daughter, so it was a name that I was very familiar with.*** As CinCLantFlt, Admiral Blandy had come and

---

*Admiral William M. Fechteler, USN, relieved Admiral William H. P. Blandy, USN, as Commander in Chief Atlantic Fleet on 1 February, the day the <u>Missouri</u> became waterborne.
**BuOrd--Bureau of Ordnance.
***Commander John M. Lee, USN, who later became a vice admiral.

talked to us in CruLant on occasion, so I was familiar with him. I left shortly thereafter and never really did get to know Admiral Fechteler until much later.

Q: Did you have any encounters with Admiral Wallin during that period?

Admiral Weschler: Every morning there was a staff conference in Admiral Smith's cabin, and Admiral Wallin always sat there with Admiral Smith. If Admiral Smith was absent, Admiral Wallin would preside. So I had a chance to see him. I thought he was one of the most impressive, technically competent, unflappable individuals that I encountered. He was really superb. He could talk any level of detail with someone who was involved.

I learned an amazing thing--this may instinctively come to you as something understandable--but here we are trying to get the <u>Missouri</u> off the beach, and we had taken off both anchor chains and the anchors as one of the first steps. Admiral Wallin one morning said, "We're going to have to put that starboard anchor back on." And I thought, "What in the world's wrong with this guy? Why are we adding all this tonnage?" But then he explained it after somebody else spoke up and questioned him.

Admiral Wallin said, "There is a fulcrum effect. The

ship has really taken the bottom somewhere aft of that point, and it's very hard aground for the width behind it, and the friction of that area aft dragging is such that if I can put this weight forward, it will tend to lift the ship. The amount of friction that I will kill by having that weight forward and the very narrow drag of the bow is a great improvement over the friction from all that weight aft the way it is now." It made perfect sense once he explained it. He was right with that sort of thing. So I had great confidence in him.

Q: He had a tremendous on-the-job training course in salvaging the battleships at Pearl Harbor, so he knew whereof he spoke.

Admiral Weschler: I hadn't realized that. I'm sure Admiral Allan Smith did, though, and that's why he would have gotten him there.

Q: He was the right man in the right place.

Admiral Weschler: Absolutely, just perfect. That was a real experience.

Q: What was the flagship when you were on the staff?

Admiral Weschler: Originally we flew our flag in a building ashore, and only when we went to sea did the flag transfer. For instance, we used Missouri the summer of '49 on a midshipmen's cruise. We used Albany by the time Admiral Holloway came to relieve as ComCruLant.* Missouri and Albany are the only two that I can remember being at sea and flying the flag in.

Q: You talked about the Newport News. Smoot got to be the first skipper. Did he engineer that?

Admiral Weschler: I feel sure that he did. Roland Smoot, as you may recall, had been captain detailer in the Bureau of Personnel before he commanded Newport News. After the command tour, he came to CruLant as our chief of staff. As a matter of fact, I remember his giving all the staff officers an excellent lecture on fitness reports: how to write them, how they were examined, and all that sort of thing. He was really an expert in Bureau of Personnel matters. He later went on to be the Assistant Chief of Personnel.

Q: What can you say about the fitness reports of the era? Now we hear that they're much inflated, and that makes ranking difficult.

---

*Rear Admiral James L. Holloway, Jr., USN, the same individual who originated the Holloway Plan for NROTC training of officers.

Admiral Weschler: The same comment was made then. We've had three or four different forms. Each one is trying to prevent having any and everybody marked over at the left side of the form. I think it's an eternal cry. If you switch forms, it takes about two fitness report cycles, and then they're back up to where they were. Captain Smoot's basic point--and I thought it was an interesting one--was that there are three things to consider in connection with fitness reports.

If you really think somebody is unsat, say so as clearly and simply as you can, and that is guaranteed to get attention and will accomplish your purpose. If you really think somebody is outstanding and ought to be promoted, then make sure that your fitness report is far enough over to the left that you are sure that he will be selected. If the guy is in between, then pretty well evaluate him as you see him, because you aren't anxious for him to be promoted, or else you would have gone all-out for him. He certainly isn't unsat, or else that would be clear. So pretty well call it as it is, and in that way you will be helping to keep the system on an even keel.

I thought that was pretty practical advice. That way you really had to make one of three decisions when you

Thomas R. Weschler #2 - 176

looked at a person--is he unsat, do you really want to get him selected, or are you going to call it even? Once you did that, then you could write the report quite easily.

Q: Did you ever sit on a selection board to judge the validity of his advice?

Admiral Weschler: I sat on any number of them as the years went by, and yes, I thought his advice was pretty good. I didn't take it all aboard that first time around. I don't want you to think I heard it, and that was it. All of us still had our own sense of moral judgment and what was right and all that sort of thing. Even though I thought a person ought to be selected, I didn't feel he was God, and I had a tendency still not to two-block him.*

That was driven home for me when I was in the Polaris program. I had a commander coming up for captain, and I thought I had given him a pretty good fitness report. Tommy Rudden, whom I've mentioned before, was then a captain and the deputy for the Polaris project. He called me up and said, "Tom, it's obvious you don't want this commander to be promoted."

I said, "What are you talking about, Tommy? I gave him a good fitness report."

---
*"Two-blocked" is a nautical term indicating that something is as far as it can go--that is, two blocks in a block-and-tackle rig have been pulled together. In this case, it means pushing performance grades to the maximum.

He said, "You didn't give him a good enough one to get him selected. If you really want him selected, I'll send it back and you can fix it up."

I said, "Well, if that's the way it is, I graded it about what I thought. And, you know, when you really tell me, do I want him selected, I'm not sure, so I'll let it stand." But he drove it home to me with that. By the time I had that conversation, there was no more doubt in my mind about what I had to do, and I pretty well followed it from then on. I moved them up when I really thought the person deserved to make the next rank.

Q: How was Captain Smoot at running the staff?

Admiral Weschler: He wasn't a great detail man. He liked to get the details off onto somebody else's desk if he possibly could. He was a wonderful idea man and a tremendous personality, wonderful working with people. But as far as details, which is an awful lot of staff work, that wasn't his cup of tea. I think he did in detail what the admiral required him to, but beyond that he was a master of delegation. And usually he had his own projects.

He was quite different from Captain Mendenhall, who had preceded him. Mendenhall was very much a detail man and was there pretty well massaging all the pieces of paper. So you had a feeling of getting more attention and being able to discuss questions of your particular area better with Captain Mendenhall and get more insight. With Captain Smoot, you had the feeling he didn't want to be bothered with those kinds of things, and so you didn't really get much advice.

Q: The advantage of the Smoot approach is that you can be your own boss to a great extent.

Admiral Weschler: That's right, and, as I say, he had his own fish to fry. He would think of things like calling us all in to tell us about fitness reports and a few other things that he felt were important. We didn't get Captain Mendenhall doing that. He would be sitting there discussing your particular problem and saying how he'd handled it in a similar position. So each had its own values. They were two quite different personalities.

Q: I think this tour of duty would have been a growth experience for you. Previously, you'd been in one ship alone. Now you had to take care of more than one.

Admiral Weschler: That's right. I found it marvelous. I'm so glad I went to the staff when I did, because, just as you say, I thought I knew all about being a ship's gunnery officer. Well, I didn't know anything about it.

I went over to see my friends in <u>Missouri</u>, and their questions were of a completely different kind. They were worrying about details of gunnery exercises that had never occurred to me to question. When I visited <u>Rochester</u> and another gunnery officer, he had a whole different outlook on how the department ought to be run. Somebody else had serious questions about the safety of an ammunition hoist that had never occurred to me. So I suddenly began to realize all the different points of view and how much there was that had been passing me by. I discovered the excellent viewpoints that certain of them had. If I had known about them before, I could have run my own department that much better. I think that that was the beginning of making me want to visit a lot of different ships and a lot of different stations. And it stayed with me through the rest of my career.

I know one of the things that I prized when I was J-4 in the Joint Staff was the chance to visit so many Air Force and Army installations and find out that they had problems that were very similar to ours. Often there were marvelous ways of handling things that would have done the Navy good if we'd have known about them three or four years before. So I know that when I was in positions of authority, I would encourage people to go visit the rest of the ships in the squadron, go talk to somebody in a cruiser or in a minesweeper, discuss your problems. You're liable to find out they've got suggestions or methods you've never thought of before.

Q: Did you try to compile these as lessons learned and distribute them in the force?

Admiral Weschler: Perhaps not quite so formally, but we did have a newsletter, and there was a visitation program. Our ships seemed to be in port often, and so I tried to get aboard each of the cruisers and the one battleship at least once a month, just to have lunch with the people and to talk about what they were doing and pass along the word about what we were doing. Gunnery exercises and other forms of competition were big things. They all wanted to know how they were coming along in that and if somebody had a new wrinkle, say, for a way to make the shore bombardment exercise more successful.

Ammunition allowances were critical, and we were always trying to find something extra for them. There were all sorts of bits and pieces of ammunition left from World War II, lot numbers that were almost extinct. We were trying to get those used up, so we'd work out a deal with them that you could let them have an extra 10 or 20 rounds of something if they would take these lots and get them fired up. That way you didn't have to account for them anymore, and you didn't have a problem of returning them for rework, both of which would cost additional money. So there was a lot of visitation and discussion, to good effect.

Q: Did you try to standardize them, or did you let them use what worked for them?

Admiral Weschler: I'm sure I didn't try to standardize them. I don't think I could have if I had wanted to. There was also quite a disparity of rank across the group, and I was probably about as junior as you could be in that particular job. They ran from a senior commander--I guess he was out of '36--down to people in '41, which was about my range, class of '41 year group. So a lot of them had more experience than I had had. Some of them had been gun bosses of other ships before this. The standardization that was implicit in standard commands and in the orders for the exercises and procedures for running computers--those things were pretty well set. But as far as running their departments, we let them do what they wanted. It was pretty much up to them, although you wouldn't hesitate to point out techniques or methods that were doing well for someone else.

Q: Were inspections as onerous for you as they often are

for ships?

Admiral Weschler: Yes, exactly. You had a schedule that had to be carried out, and it meant that you had to be around. I'm sure that there were four or five ships a quarter that had to be inspected, and the inspection always took a minimum of, let's say, two days, and sometimes three, depending on where it was, and then you had InSurv for every ship that was going in the yard.* That was crawling through every turret and every mount, base-ring inspection, and directors, and so on. It really kept you on the move. So, yes, we found the inspections just as bad on the giving side as I always did on the receiving end.

Q: I think this would be a case where Captain Smoot would probably gladly let you do that and just say a few words of benediction.

Admiral Weschler: He would come over and be the head of the inspecting party and say, "Gentlemen, here is my team," and he would depart. At the end he would be back there, and you would run over your notes of what you were going to say--good, bad, or indifferent. He'd have a private chat with the captain about things that we had been critical of that he didn't want to bring up in the wardroom. He would

_____
*InSurv--Inspection and Survey.

clear the things that you would say to everybody. It worked very well.

Q: On these inspections, did you find personnel imbalances that you could then redress through your personnel section?

Admiral Weschler: Yes, that was a possibility. I hope it wouldn't wait for an inspection, but this was the kind of thing we were trying to get on these monthly visits. This Chief Turret Captain Creed was excellent in visiting all the ships and looking at their main batteries. That was the kind of thing we were trying to keep an eye or ear open for. If someone was being hit with a lot of transfers, school quotas, and things like that, we'd try to come forward in time and anticipate and say, "Well, I've got So-and-so coming in. I'll be sure he's assigned to you."

Q: Did you have the Mississippi in your type command at that point?*

Admiral Weschler: No, Mississippi was assigned to OpDevFor, and so although she was in our competition, and I guess we probably gave her an InSurv inspection, that was about as much as we had to do with Mississippi. I would

---

*The ex-battleship Mississippi (BB-41) was converted in the late 1940s to an experimental ship, AG-128, to serve as a test platform for new equipment and weapons, including the early guided missiles.

have enjoyed doing more with her, because she was really getting some firing experience.

Q: Were there about a dozen ships in CruLant altogether?

Admiral Weschler: That's probably in the right ballpark--12 or 14 ships, and there was always one over in the Sixth Fleet, usually two, and then somebody always in the yard. So we probably had nine or ten around that we really actively administered.

Q: Ships' companies typically don't like staffs. Was that what you found?

Admiral Weschler: I know that when I went to the staff, my reaction was, "I've been ship's company. I know all the things that staffs do badly. Therefore, this one's going to be different." I really tried very hard to change that, but there simply wasn't any way to do it, because you're the one who is saying yes or no on lots of things, and you are the one conducting the inspections. Pretty soon that brush has tarred you, whether you wanted it to or not, and there's no way out of it.

Q: You were saying yes and no on money probably, too, weren't you?

Admiral Weschler: Not as much so. My areas of concern were ammunition and personnel. We had a separate man for budget, and although you could be sympathetic and put your oar in with another staff member to try to convince the supply officer who ran the money that some ship deserved a little extra allotment, he really had the final authority. The only way to get around it was for the ship's captain to see the chief of staff. When you knew that the CO was coming over to call on the chief of staff, you figured it was probably money problems or personnel. Those were the two things that brought the captains over.

Q: Who were some of the individual gunnery officers from the ships that stand out in your mind?

Admiral Weschler: Well, Missouri, I thought, had two absolutely top-notch ones. It was Otis Wesche of '38, and his fire control officer was Frank Price out of '41.* Those two were about as smart as people can possibly be. Frank Price, you know, is Vice Admiral Price, retired, who had OP-03 and worked with the FFG-7 program and so on.** Otis Wesche had been a very savvy guy in the class of '38

---
*Commander Otis A. Wesche, USN; Lieutenant Commander Frank H. Price, USN.
**OP-03--Deputy Chief of Naval Operations (Surface Warfare); FFG-7--Oliver Hazard Perry class of missile frigates.

and a gunnery PG. Dick Varley out of '40 had Rochester.* Bill Maddocks, also out of '40, had Roanoke.** Jack Beardall had Worcester.*** I can't remember the people for Salem, Newport News, and Des Moines. Much as I liked those ships, I can't remember their gunnery officers.

Q: How useful were the Worcester and Roanoke with their high-angle 6-inch batteries?

Admiral Weschler: We thought that they were pretty good, but, frankly, their machinery was not all that good. It's probably snide to say, but their gunnery equipment was built by the United Shoe Machinery Corporation, and I've always felt that it operated like a shoe machine. If I had found out that it sewed buckles on all of them, I wouldn't have been surprised. It just didn't have the reliability that the 8-inch did.

The 8-inch rapid fire gave me much more confidence. Our only regret was that it didn't have a higher angle of fire. We considered a program for using the 8-inch to fire a barrage as a defensive mechanism against incoming aircraft or missile attacks. But it couldn't get up high enough. It couldn't get the barrage up to where it ought

---

*Lieutenant Commander Richard B. Varley, USN.
**Lieutenant Commander William J. Maddocks, USN.

to be to be effective. And it wasn't any good at all against the dive-bomber. It might have been effective against a kamikaze or a torpedo plane, but that's about it.

The 6-inch we thought might be good for AA programs and so on. But the sleeves had to be streamed way aft in order to give the aircraft the safety we felt it needed for responsiveness of the battery. Those ships simply didn't get the hits that we wanted. As I recall, the 6-inch didn't have the VT fuzes and the infrared fuzes that we later had for the 5-inch at the end of the war.* So the ammunition was not up to the task that we were laying at their door. If the 6-inch had had a VT fuze, okay, but when you're using a mechanical time fuze, I think you reduced your chances tremendously.

Q: Then those two ships got wiped out subsequently when the missile age came along.

Admiral Weschler: That's right. And they weren't that great for shore bombardment, because the 6-inch shells weren't that much better than the 5-inch, and if you had a 5-inch that was really a rapid-fire gun, you not only put out an awful lot of ammunition, but in proportion you had a lot more shells in 5-inch ships, and so you could keep up

---

*VT, or variable time, was a label used for the proximity fuze that contained a small radio transmitter so a projectile would explode when it got near an air target, thus eliminating the requirement for a direct hit.

your shore bombardment for longer periods than you could with the turret guns which tended to have a smaller allowance.

Q: Beautiful ships, though, for showing the flag.

Admiral Weschler: Absolutely. <u>Worcester</u> and <u>Roanoke</u> were so impressive. A lot of people were keen on them, but my appraisal was I would have taken the 8-inch any day and felt that we were way ahead.

Q: To what extent were spit and polish, smart ship, and so forth emphasized by the admirals who commanded the force?

Admiral Weschler: It was gradually being restored. Admiral Smith was keen on it in sort of the technical sense. He wanted things to look well, and he sort of set requirements every quarterdeck had to have, but he didn't go aboard an awful lot in order to check out how the honors were given and the drill and so on.

The one who really hit the force was Admiral Holloway.* When he arrived, there was absolutely no question on two things. One was that you were going to do it the professional, old-fashioned Navy way, right down to

_____
*Subsequently he served as Chief of Naval Personnel as a vice admiral and Commander in Chief U.S. Naval Forces Eastern Atlantic and Mediterranean as a four-star.

the last seaman and pipe and so on. And the other was that we were going to be an operating force. CruLant was going to sea, and every ship was going to go to sea, and the sooner we could get to the Med, the better. When Admiral Holloway came, he became both ComCruLant and Commander Cruiser Division Six, and took his division to the Med in its regular rotation. So it really became a seagoing staff. There was no doubt Lord Jim had arrived.

Q: What was the reaction of the staff to this change in program?

Admiral Weschler: About 50-50. Fifty percent thought it was the greatest thing that ever happened, and 50% thought it was the end of the line and couldn't get transferred fast enough. The Supply Corps officer and the ED were two who felt that they had more than enough sea duty already. They were ones who objected even to going on the midshipmen's cruise, so that Lord knows what a whole deployment would have felt like. They had been relieved, so there were new ones going by that time. The enlisted, I didn't really hear that much of a gripe from. And I have to say that I was with Admiral Holloway only about three weeks, because I had my orders to the Naval War College.

I made the inspection with him aboard <u>Albany</u>, and I have never been so impressed by any individual in my life as I was by Admiral Holloway when he was checking out *Albany* for his flagship. He had asked the captain to assign him someone who knew the ship well, and it ended up being the engineer officer and the first lieutenant, both of whom walked around with him. They did the ship from bow to stern and second deck and above. The admiral wasn't interested in below-deck spaces. He was looking for every spot that might be or could be or was flag space, and he was going through the ship to see how he was going to put it together as his flagship for going to the Med.

He didn't take any notes, just made a couple of asides to the yeoman he was with. When he finished, he walked into the captain's cabin which had been made available for him, sat down, told the yeoman, "Stand by to write." Then he started the most fantastic memo you've ever heard. From top to bottom with paragraphing and numbers and the whole business: "Change this, do this, do this." When he got all done with this thing, he said, "Have this on my desk tomorrow morning." And he walked off to play tennis or something. What a man! I don't know how he had that so organized, but he knew every compartment number, just what he wanted to do, who was going to be where. Really a brain in action--a fantastic man.

Q: I interviewed him once, and he said he attributed his

success to "the gift of happy chatter."

Admiral Weschler: Well, he knew what he was doing, and he was nobody's fool. As a matter of fact, I heard an interesting story on him. He was skipper of one of the battleships, Iowa, with flag embarked, and the order had come, "Set Condition I"--preparation for battle and that sort of thing.* They were at general quarters for a long time, and nothing was going on. Captain Holloway was listening to the radio traffic. He didn't think there was anything immediately dangerous, so he passed the word to set Condition II. The admiral leaned over the bridge and said to Captain Holloway that the order had gone out to the fleet to set Condition I.

Captain Holloway said, "We have complied with that order, and the information I am getting now tells me there is opportunity for a change. If there hasn't been any reaction at the staff level, there will be at the ship level." And that was the end of it. He didn't change, and the admiral didn't push it, so that was that. He was his own man; he thought he was right.

Q: Do you have some insight into the other type commander you served under, Admiral Smith?

---

*Captain Holloway commanded the Iowa (BB-61) from November 1944 to July 1945.

Admiral Weschler: I indicated how well Admiral Hoke Smith organized the salvage of the Missouri. I feel that Admiral Smith was a man who knew what to do, but was very halting in his conveyance of his ideas to his subordinates and didn't have a very good ability to inspire you. As a matter of fact, he got a lot of people's backs up so that the last thing they wanted to do was to do what Hoke Smith wanted, which was too bad. But he came across that way. He was almost a flat or a negative personality in so much of what he did.

I got along very well with him, and I know the only reason I went to the Naval War College was directly due to him and Roland Smoot--the two of them. BuPers told me that the war college class was full when I checked. That word got to Admiral Smith, who had come from being chief of staff at the war college before he got to CruLant, and he felt I should go. He told Roland Smoot to call up and tell BuPers that ComCruLant really wanted me in that class. The next day I had a set of orders to the war college. So I was very delighted. But Admiral Smith was able to understand things, comprehended them well, and organized, but not to get them executed by others. He would drive himself--there's no question. But I think that he didn't have a tremendous growth potential. I was not surprised that he didn't go on from there.

Q: Was there any innovation in the cruiser force during that period, or was it more marking time?

Admiral Weschler: The emphasis was on trying to get these missile programs going in the ordnance community. I think that it's fair to say that the cruisers found themselves in sort of an anomalous position. They had been escorts during the war, just large destroyers, in effect. Except for shore bombardment, they didn't have that much of a role.

The flagship role was something that was very useful for them. I'd say the innovation was probably in outfitting almost all the cruisers as flagships and in administering them in that role. We probably spent more money on communications and electronics equipment than almost any other command and were fixing them up so people could use them for flagships. I know that was one place where both the chief of staff and the admiral were involved in a lot of personal correspondence and messages with the Sixth Fleet Commander, in trying to ensure that he was satisfied, hearing what was going on in the Med, and how they could do better in getting those ships ready.

Q: That part involved you not very much.

Admiral Weschler: That's right. So long as they had a reasonable gun battery and could keep up their practices, people were looking on it fairly much as a peacetime business except when they were in the Med. Those deploying ships were the ones that we particularly tried to keep up on personnel and well trained and ready to go.

Q: What about writing doctrine and tactics for the new rapid-fire guns?

Admiral Weschler: We worked on that. OpDevFor, as you know, had that as part of its charter when a ship went there for evaluation. One of the 8-inch cruisers was assigned to them for evaluation. I want to say it was the <u>Des Moines</u>, but I'm not positive about that. But one of the cruisers was assigned to them for evaluation, and by the time they finished, they put together a rapid-fire doctrine or rapid-fire turret instructions, and then we tried to adjust all of our cruiser gun-firing documents to incorporate the 6-inch and the 8-inch. Those were manuals that we kept up to date and sent out, and where we tried to be innovative and instructive as to what was going on.

Q: They strike me as ships that would have been a great deal more useful eight or ten years earlier for surface action, but you didn't face that prospect.

Admiral Weschler: No. And, you know, there was a lot of talk--Korea came along and, fortunately, helped to keep the amphibs in people's mind. If General MacArthur had not used amphibious warfare at Inchon, I think we might have lost an awful lot of our technique.* Everybody quotes General Bradley as saying, "There will never be another amphibious war."** Inchon gave the lie to that statement, and I think it was very useful that it did, because I think it's kept amphibious warfare alive today.

As we look at Vietnam, there certainly would have been a use for it if we had fought that as a real war. I think there would have been an opportunity, and you would have had to use amphibious warfare as the only vehicle to get your people in. Then the cruisers could have had a very aggressive role. But, otherwise, we didn't have enough battery for AA. It was really kind of a sad day. If we had had a major AA attack on those cruisers, except for the 5-inch--because we didn't have near the numbers of machine guns that we had had in World War II--we wouldn't have been able to defend them as well as we should.

Q: Did you also work in developing tactics for shore bombardment with the amphibs?

---
*General of the Army Douglas MacArthur, USA, commanded the brilliant landing at Inchon, Korea, in September 1950.
**General of the Army Omar N. Bradley, USA, made this statement during his tenure as Chairman of the Joint Chiefs of Staff, not long before the landing at Inchon.

Admiral Weschler: Yes. But I can't recall that we had any particular innovations.

Q: The rapid fire wouldn't make that much difference in that role.

Admiral Weschler: No, rapid fire didn't. I was trying to think of when the beacon came in. I think it was a post-World War II development. A beacon was a device that the Marines could take ashore with them and set up at some point, and then it acted like a range and bearing finder. You would tune in on this signal from the beach, and that gave you the bearing of it and also a range. And then using that as a point of aim, the Marine who was sitting next to the beacon could tell you that the target is 500 yards ahead and such and such an angle from it. And then you could set that into your computer and then open fire on this target. It really was a wonderful way of remote ranging on a target you couldn't see on the beach. So it worked out very well. That came out, I think, during that period.

Q: As long as the enemy doesn't have something similar to pick him up.

Admiral Weschler: Or jam it so that you think you're getting it, and you're over here, and then you open fire on your own troops. We were able at least to have a check bearing on what we came up with for a solution and tell the Marine where you were going to be opening fire. And then he would look on and could say, "All clear," and then you open up on that range and bearing.

Q: There was some innovation in using helicopters for spotting, was there not?

Admiral Weschler: That was one of the things that we did with the helicopters aboard *Macon*, was to try to break them in. As a matter of fact, those pilots went to aircraft spotting school so that they learned to use the same terminology--"over, short, right, left"--as the pontoon planes that we used during World War II. And, yes, the helicopter proved reasonably good at that. But he was quite a sitting duck. In those days the helicopter didn't have the speed or the agility it's got today, and so we would try to have him positioned back over friendly troops and looking down in order to call the shots.

It was fairly effective, but they were very sensitive to the fact that they could only do about 80 to 100 knots and that they were only up 2,000 or 3,000 feet, and even a rifle bullet could knock them down. That's when we began to develop armor and some of the other capabilities in the helicopters so they could operate in a more dangerous environment. Obviously Korea was what gave the helicopter in war the major boost. It was still a few years before we had helicopter platforms coming in numbers into the force, and they started out in the amphibs before they came to the cruisers.

Q: How soon did you get reports back from Korea that you were able to incorporate in what you were doing?

Admiral Weschler: We were sending ships around. I'm trying to remember who else went out. Rochester got out there and was Seventh Fleet flagship. Certainly Missouri did. I don't remember whether there were any others, but we were getting reports back just as--if you remember, in World War II, CNO used to publish, after every major battle, lessons learned from the conflict. It took about three to four months to get those out.

We would get reports from the other ships through our counterpart in the Pacific. We were always on his distribution system. There was one other thing I should comment on. I think it was Captain Smoot who started exchange visits with the Pacific Fleet, coming back to this business of making sure that you know what the rest of the players are doing.

Thomas R. Weschler #2 - 199

We would have a meeting out in the Pacific, and maybe the year after they'd come east and have a joint meeting with us. And that would be from the admiral on down. There would be a selected five or six who would make the trip. You would meet with your opposite numbers and make presentations and listen to reports. I found that very useful. What can you specifically get out of any single one, I don't know, but so often the preparation for the meeting is nine-tenths of the value. You got your own thoughts clarified; you had them all down in writing. You had to know that what you were going to say was solid. And by that time you were much improved already, and then you'd pick up a few good ideas.

Q: There must have been a sense of satisfaction in the Missouri going over there after you had worked so hard to get her off the bottom.

Admiral Weschler: I'll tell you who was surprised. You remember that Page Smith was called back to take her command.* He wanted to get her ready to operate as quickly as possible, and so as soon as she got out of the naval shipyard, she was set to go. The new skipper was

---

*Captain Harold Page Smith, USN, first commanded the Missouri from February to December 1949. He again had command from February through April 1950 to restore the crew's confidence before turning the ship over to another skipper. See Smith's memoir, "The Value of Confidence," Naval History, Fall 1991, page 36.

Duke.* Irving Duke had had Rochester; they wanted him to fleet up to Missouri.

I don't think Page Smith was all that happy to come take the Missouri, because he'd already had his command, and all he could think of was, "All I'm going to do is stub my toes like poor Brown did." Brown had had the Missouri.** I think he saw that the handwriting would be on the wall for him, but obviously it didn't. You know that Page went on to be CinCLantFlt and so forth.

Q: Was this a case, probably, where the admiral picked his top skipper from the cruisers?

Admiral Weschler: No. I know that Irving Duke had had some battleship experience, and one of the things they were concerned with was that they didn't want to have someone going to a battleship who had never served in one before. He was a top skipper in his own right, but I know that the final qualifying factor was that he had been exec or something similar in a battleship before. So they had good confidence that the Missouri would be well handled. They felt it had to cover itself with glory after the ignominy that had happened, so they didn't want any chance.

---
*Captain Irving T. Duke, USN, commanded the Missouri from April 1950 to March 1951.
**Captain William D. Brown, USN, was commanding officer at the time of the grounding in January 1950.

Thomas R. Weschler #2 - 201

Q: Anything more to wrap up on that tour?

Admiral Weschler: No, I think you've been very thorough in talking about it, but very interesting.

Q: Then you went on up to Newport.

Admiral Weschler: Yes, and I just wanted to make a couple of comments about being a student at the Naval War College. I think the first thing is that the war college was experimenting with a new command and staff course. They had had a senior and a junior course, and the two courses had tended to be mirror images of each other. The CNO and Chief of Naval Personnel decided that the junior officer really ought to be getting something more like preparation for duty aboard a staff and knowing how to function as a commander at the division commander level, something like that, whereas the senior officers ought to be looking to a major command, command of a task group, command of a task force. And so there was a difference between them. The junior course ought to be able to write op orders and the senior course to execute them. That was kind of the philosophy.

So they conceived the new course and picked about 30 students to go to it for that first go-around. The officer who ran it then was Captain E. F. McDaniel, who had done such an outstanding job in running the special PC course down at Miami.* He was putting thousands of reserve officers through there to run all of the PCs and all of the smaller ships of the Navy during World War II. Very highly thought of and a wonderful organizer and an excellent staff man. He had as his number two Captain Lot Ensey, later Vice Admiral Ensey. The two of them were a great team. What the one didn't have in pizzazz, the other one did. Between the two they really put together a top-notch course. Well, the 30 of us who went to that felt privileged, because here it was a new course, and you always feel that light of something new shining on you, and you are there, and you're experimenting with it. If it does well, it'll go on, and if it doesn't, you've helped to make or break it--whatever is the right answer.

The other thing is that I thought Admiral Conolly gave outstanding leadership to the war college.** Everybody who was there felt he was going to be selected for the next rank. The admiral didn't want people on his faculty who were "has-beens." He really was pushing. I just can name so many people--at least a third, it seems to me--of the faculty and the students who went on to flag, if you accept that as a gauge of excellence. I think it speaks well for the school that those who had tremendous records and who

---
*Captain Eugene F. McDaniel, USN; PC--patrol craft.
**Vice Admiral Richard L. Conolly, USN, was president of the Naval War College from December 1950 to November 1953.

were going places were going through the war college.

Admiral Conolly said that the Naval War College must be the apex of the Navy's educational system, and he kept it there. And he had CNO's ear. If somebody failed selection, the admiral phoned BuPers the next day saying, "What in the world is going on here? Why do you send me people who are not going to put this course to good use in years to come? It's a waste of the Navy's time." You could tell that he had the attention.

The chief of staff when I first went there with Admiral Conolly was Captain Don Felt, later Admiral Don Felt.* He was relieved by Wallace Beakley, and I've referred to Wallace Beakley before. It was that kind of people who were around.

Q: Were you challenged mentally during this period?

Admiral Weschler: Yes, I really felt I was. They had an excellent lecture program supporting what you were doing. It was the first time I had ever really heard a whole bunch of political-military thought—to become familiar with countries all over the world, to be aware of their foreign policies. And it's the first time that I had ever been put in a position to actually write op orders. I had done some on the CruLant staff in helping put together demonstrations

---
*Captain Harry D. Felt, USN, whose oral history is in the Naval Institute collection.

and minor operations and exercises. But never had really been challenged to write an amphibious op order or an op order for a major engagement and that sort of thing.

I have to comment here that one of the things that I felt, as I went through those World War II amphibious operations, was that there must be some way to put together an amphibious order that didn't require three feet of paper in order to get the operation done. If you were in a gunfire support ship, for example, you might go through two feet of paper before you came to the first page that had anything to do with your ship. There it might tell you what your ammunition allowance was, and then you'd dig through another one before you found out where you were to be on D-day at H-hour, and then something else would have the details of the plan.

Well, that gave me the determination that some day I was going to put out an amphibious op order that was on one sheet of paper, preferably on the back of the chart which showed you where your gunfire support areas were and the like. When I was Commander Amphibious Squadron Three and Commander Amphibious Ready Group Seventh Fleet, I had a chance to execute some small operations that had the title Dagger Thrust. I made sure that at least one of those was done just that way, on a single piece of paper and on the back of a chart. You couldn't do it with much of the material in a big operation, but I do think we have a tendency to use too much boilerplate in op orders and not enough getting down to specifics as to what it is you want done.

Q: It makes sense to divide it up and just give them the gunfire annex.

Admiral Weschler: Yes. And then if you want a precis of what everybody else is going to be doing so you know why this ship is in the next operating area or why somebody's cutting through your section, you've got some movement plan that is vital to this ship skipper who's off-loading all of the amphibious gear for the Marines. The average destroyer didn't need all of that. He just got confused.

I found that Naval War College course to be a good one, and then felt happy enough with it that, as you know, I got asked to stay on the faculty. Over the next two years I felt I contributed a great deal. I've always been interested in teaching. The experience confirmed it, and it gave me an interest in the war college that I still have today. I have tried to follow it pretty faithfully over the last 30 years.

Q: How much did you get into strategy in this course?

Admiral Weschler: The junior course didn't do all that much in connection with strategy. The senior course did, and they tried to have one op order in which the senior course were the admirals and we in the junior class were the staff people working for them. When you were in that role, you used to get into a lot of strategic discussions of how you ought to be employed. But most of the time our operations were at a lower level that would involve perhaps a squadron of destroyers and a couple of cruisers or maybe a small carrier task group, and that would be about as far as our course was working in our particular op order.

Q: Did you get training in planning?

Admiral Weschler: We got training in planning from these set pieces in which they would tell us the situation, and you would come up with how you thought you might go about achieving the goal--but, again, at a different level from what the senior course was. We didn't ordinarily get into what I would call the politico-military field or the broad strategy of how you picked allies or working with allies.

Q: How about logistics?

Admiral Weschler: Logistics was one of the areas that they felt had to be given more emphasis. The place, though, that it was hit well was in the amphibious op order. We had to write the ship-shore movement part of it. By the time you've written that, you really understand logistics in a local area. But it didn't bring across to us the real problem of logistics from the factory to the site. We did have a form for calculating how many replenishment ships we needed at sea and time alongside everybody and give this group an oiler and ammunition ship--how long it would take to have everybody replenished and ready to go. We did some of these exercises. But I don't think we really got a good feel for bases and the merchant marine or the support needs for the forward area.

Q: Was Commodore Bates there then doing his analyses?

Admiral Weschler: Commodore Bates was there, and he didn't address the students at the time I was there.* He had sort of fallen out of favor, I think, while Admiral Conolly was there. He was doing quite well. Then he had another admiral, and I can't think of who the name was. There were two or three sort of in rapid succession there. One of those was ready to terminate Bates's project. And so he wasn't lecturing us on what he was finding out about Midway and Coral Sea and so on. But his papers were there. We

---

*Richard W. Bates was a tombstone rear admiral on the retired list, recalled to active duty as a commodore for this study project.

used his study of the first Savo battle in one of the courses that I had while I was the "ops commander." He did some good work, but he tended to be terribly voluminous in detail, and I think that was perhaps what got him. They thought he was taking a project that should have been good for a year or two and turning it into a life's work. And they were ready to terminate it.

Q: How did you feel comparing the analysis of the battle after having experienced it yourself?

Admiral Weschler: I thought that he did a very good job. He took our area and treated it, and I think just about the way that my own thoughts had run on it. Then he knew an awful lot more about what had gone on with those individual cruisers and destroyers than I ever had known. I was horrified at the situation that he found. As I go back over it, I simply can't understand how we could have been that badly off in organization and readiness. Obviously all hands were tired from long hours at general quarters, but it was just hard to believe. Commodore Bates came out of his review with a list of some 21 or 22 major statements which I thought were a fine check-off list for task group or individual ship readiness.

Q: Were there any instructors that you particularly

remember from that period?

Admiral Weschler: Well, I've already told you Lot Ensey was superb. Henry Eccles was there and Henry Eccles still is.* I think Henry is a marvelous individual, the greatest logistician I think that we've had around. Phil Berkeley was the senior Marine there at the time, and he retired as a lieutenant general--a marvelous individual, excellent lecturer.** There were lots of others, but I can't sort them out as being that much better or worse than anybody else.

During that period, I was assigned to a speaking team to go down to the Air War College to present carrier air warfare to the student body there.*** In '51 and '52, this was still a time when the Air Force and Navy were a little sensitive with each other. The B-36 controversy was still around, and "Fancy Dan" admirals, the question of whether or not we were in or out of strategic warfare and whether a carrier could survive.**** These were the big questions, so it was sort of a sensitive role.

They put the speaking team together to go down, and I cite it only because I think it shows the excellence of the

---
*Rear Admiral Henry E. Eccles, USN (Ret.), who has been interviewed by the Naval Institute oral history program.
**Colonel James P. Berkeley, USMC.
***The Air War College is at the Maxwell Air Force Base, near Montgomery, Alabama.
****In 1949 Congress held hearings on the Air Force's proposed B-36 bomber; the hearings were marked by a great deal of controversy and inter-service acrimony.

officers of the war college. The speaking team was led by Wallace Beakley and then consisted of Frank Johnson, Draper Kauffman, and myself.* All of us went on to make flag from there. They really had some well experienced people in us. And all of us, I think, were good presenters.

I think Wallace Beakley was surprised at the strength of his team. He remembered I had been aboard Wasp, but when we were down there, we were taking questions, and he was prepared to stand up and answer the toughies. One was asked about carrier survival, and I happened to be at the podium. The question came to me, and I could have referred it to Admiral Beakley, but I gave an answer for it. Afterwards he said, "I was worried when you started, but I couldn't have added a thing to that--absolutely top-notch." So I knew he had confidence in me after that. I've always prized that compliment on what I had said.

That same team went down at least twice. We looked forward to it as one of really going into the lions' den in connection with trying to sell carriers.

Q: Anything else to add about the war college?

Admiral Weschler: I have two ideas that I think might give a perspective. The first one is about grades. We didn't

---

*Captain Frank L. Johnson, USN; Commander Draper L. Kauffman, USN. Kauffman's oral history is in the Naval Institute collection.

have grades in those days, and we were allowed to work on a graduate degree at a civilian college. There tended to be a conflict among classmates as a result of that, because some of them would buckle down and work hard on their graduate degrees, for which they received grades. On the other hand, the material at the war college was ungraded, and no one really bilged out. So when there was a push, the students tended to do what the graduate degree required and not put enough emphasis on the war college material. If you were teamed up with some of these people, you kind of got mad at them for not sticking to the basic issues and getting off on their personal stuff. I think that's always a problem that the college will face. I think today, though, with the Naval War College having grades, that there is probably some built-in protection. I'm sure that the individual would get bounced if the situation got gross enough.

The second comment is that there are a lot of people who feel that attendance at the war college ought to be recognized in the fitness report in some way, as though it were a brownie point for having attended. I've never agreed with that point of view. I've always felt that attendance at the Naval War College was a very special privilege, and if you were smart, you'd buckle down and take full advantage of the opportunity. Your own record thereafter would show that you had profited from this very special opportunity, and those who hadn't attended never had quite the same perspective or outlook or basis for an opinion. If anything, they ought to mark you lower on the fitness report if you attended here and were not really head and shoulders over your peers who hadn't attended.

Q: We know, of course, though, that there's a ticket-punching system, and people have certainly been penalized for not getting that ticket punched, in some cases.

Admiral Weschler: Yes. And it's a syndrome. I feel that it was more noticeable through the '70s. I have a feeling that perhaps we're moving away from it a little bit now, and that people are really deciding that if you do a good job in every job that you get, that that's the finest way to go. Even if you haven't had X or Y kinds of duty, you can still make promotions and still have a very successful career.

Q: Good progress today.

Admiral Weschler: Thank you for the opportunity.

Interview Number 3 with Vice Admiral Thomas R. Weschler,
U.S. Navy (Retired)

Place: Admiral Weschler's office, Naval War College,
Newport, Rhode Island

Date: Monday, 17 September 1984

Interviewer: Paul Stillwell

Q: Admiral, the last time when we left off, you covered your tour at the Naval War College in the early '50s. From there you went back to sea and got command of a destroyer at last.

Admiral Weschler: At last.

Q: It was eight years since you'd been in a destroyer, when you were exec of the Young. What kind of program did you have to go through to get back up to speed for sea duty?

Admiral Weschler: There wasn't time for much of a program like that. I got detached here and after a brief period of training flew almost immediately to the West Coast and on out to Sasebo, Japan, for the change of command. I think the change of command was one morning, and we were under way the next afternoon. So I had about 24 hours to get shaken down in the ship and then get moving again. I was heartened in that, though. I had a wonderful division commander, B. J. Semmes, who had been a shipmate aboard Wasp and aboard Sigsbee.* So I knew him well and had great confidence in him. I was in a division that had some top-notch skippers, so I felt free to go around and ask them a few questions and get myself loaded for bear for that first day under way.

Q: The present system has what's called pipeline training before taking command. Do you feel more of that would have been useful in your case?

Admiral Weschler: I would have enjoyed a greater opportunity than I had. I did have a ten-day course at Key West in sonar, because sonar had moved so fast from what it had been in World War II to what it was then. We didn't have significantly new gear, but new ranges of operating characteristics and more dovetailing of two ships working together. The instructors stressed that kind of operation for us at Key West, and that was a big help. I think it's in that technical area that you particularly need the boost in going to a new ship so you don't arrive and become shipmates with equipment you've never heard of and you have no thought of how to use.

---
*Commander Semmes was Commander Destroyer Division 302.

Q: Was the fact that you had known Commander Semmes before a factor in getting into that squadron?

Admiral Weschler: I think it might have been. Certainly, at that time, getting a destroyer command was what everyone aspired to. There were enough destroyers around that I think I could have gotten some other one, but I had particularly asked for one that would participate in the war that was then ongoing in Korea. Also, the thought that this particular division was going around the world made it even more appealing. So as soon as I heard of it, the opportunity was just what I was looking for, and the fact that it was Commodore Semmes was sort of the frosting on the cake.* I think that he took me willingly. I'm sure he would have taken others, but I was lucky that I managed to get that particular job.

Q: What do you recall about handling the ship once you reached her?

Admiral Weschler: It led to an encounter with Chick Hayward in the very truest sense of the word.** The day

---

*Even though Semmes's rank was commander, later promoted to captain, he also had the title of "commodore" because of commanding a multi-ship unit.
**Captain John T. Hayward, USN, who has been interviewed as part of the Naval Institute's oral history program.

after I took command of Clarence K. Bronson, we were assigned to fuel from Point Cruz.* The gyro failed as we were making our approach. I had a reasonably good helmsman on, but as we came up alongside Point Cruz, the ship took a sheer, and we bumped the stern of Point Cruz. We didn't do anything to him, but I sure bent the side of my bridge. Then we pulled clear and didn't fuel until the next morning. Chick Hayward was skipper of Point Cruz when I bumped into him, so that's when I first encountered him. Later on, he was a good friend of Admiral Burke's, and he brought the Franklin D. Roosevelt around Cape Horn coming from the West Coast to the East Coast after she got the angled deck.

After that, I saw a good deal of him, including the Polaris program. Admiral Hayward was in research and development, and I saw him off and on during our careers. Of course, he lives in Newport, and I see him, and he's delightful. I don't know how he knows it all, but he knows more and has wonderful recall and is up to date on everything today. He seems to know everybody.

Q: Was there any sense of disappointment that the war ended about a week after you took command?

---

*USS Clarence K. Bronson (DD-668) was commissioned 11 June 1943. She had a standard displacement of 2,050 tons, was 376 feet long, and 40 feet in the beam. She had a top speed of 35 knots and a main battery of five 5-inch guns. She was also outfitted with ten 21-inch torpedo tubes. She was a Fletcher-class sister of the USS Sigsbee and USS Young in which Weschler served during World War II.

Admiral Weschler: Not really, because I relieved in July and there was plenty of postwar activity: various patrols that had to be mounted, shaking down, getting the prisoners of war distributed, and so on. We had about four months' worth of operations in and out of Japan, and frankly, we were along the coast of Korea extensively, a lot of operations. So I didn't really have the feeling that I'd made the trip for nothing. I still managed to get in some war-related activities. By the time we set out on the cruise back to the United States in November, I felt very comfortable in the ship, and we had had a lot of time at sea.

Q: Would you describe that distribution of POWs? What did that involve?

Admiral Weschler: As far as my ship was concerned, we weren't directly involved in the distribution of POWs. The principal thing we were doing was providing patrols around the islands so that during the time that the prisoners were being distributed, no North Korean patrol boats or the like could interrupt the flow, and so that we could ensure that the coasts were secure for the distribution operations that others were handling.

Q: Where were the prisoners coming from and going to? What nationality were they?

Admiral Weschler: The bulk of the prisoners were North Koreans, and a few were Chinese on our side. On the North Korean side, prisoners were mostly South Korean and some Indian. There was a particular problem with the Indians in that the South Koreans would not allow the Indians at that time to set foot in their country again. I don't understand the politics of it, but President Syngman Rhee had determined that he wouldn't let them in-country, and so there had to be a movement of these people back and forth by helicopter so that they didn't set foot in South Korea. That added an extra dimension to what was going on. But the people were from north of the DMZ and brought back to the Panmunjom area and then being brought over to South Korea, or the other way around.*

Q: Can you describe the atmosphere in Japan at that point? World War II had been over a good while. How well were Americans received?

Admiral Weschler: My experience in Japan at that time was limited to Sasebo and one train trip to Osaka. I would

---
*DMZ--Demilitarized zone.

say, first, their outlook was very pragmatic. Most of them were looking to make money in a seaport city, and we were there and were a fine means of making money. They were very affable, as most tradesmen are, as long as there's plenty of income being provided. Underneath it, I really never felt hostility. I think every sailor felt secure as he walked the streets of Sasebo, even moving into some of the outlying areas. So that I would say that General MacArthur had done a wonderful job in defusing the situation and in trying to spread the idea of democracy and that they were moving toward a position some day as an ally rather than as a defeated enemy.* I think that the Japanese had their heads up as having done quite well and not being embarrassed to have us there.

Q: Was it a pleasant place to be based during that period?

Admiral Weschler: I found it to be very much so. There were plenty of facilities so that ships could be well accommodated; the harbor was good, very secure, lots of pleasant places to go ashore, not too expensive. So I think both officer and enlisted enjoyed it as a spot to be. I don't think anyone would have wanted to stay there longer than three to six months. I think it was that sort of

---

*General of the Army Douglas MacArthur, USA, was supreme commander of allied occupation forces in Japan, 1945-51.

thing where you recognize that there was limited entertainment. Simply there weren't the arts and crafts and sports and that sort of thing to get involved in. It was very much transient living, and it was more like a big weekend than something you could take for a steady diet.

Q: I understand there is a pretty tricky channel in and out of Sasebo. So you probably got your shiphandling experience in a hurry there.

Admiral Weschler: Yes, I did. But it wasn't that bad.

Q: Describe the satisfactions of having command of the Clarence K. Bronson.

Admiral Weschler: I really commanded only two ships, and Clarence K. Bronson was not as satisfactory a command as the later transport was. I think that was a function of the shorthandedness of the officer corps and trying to get ourselves shaken down after having World War II expansion, rapid drawdown afterward, Korean expansion, and Korean demobilization. It led to trying to do an awful lot with people who were "left over."

I don't want to demean the people with whom I worked, but there were some active duty personnel who were just sort of putting in their time until they could retire.

Then there were a lot of reserves whose focus was on getting out as quickly as possible, particularly with the Korean War over. Between those who were marking time and those who were eager to get out, it was very hard to develop a good wardroom atmosphere and to develop that sense of continuity in ship's company that I would have liked. To a certain extent, this also existed among the enlisted, but not as much. The chiefs, perhaps, had pretty much the same problems as the officer corps did.

As a result, there was this undercurrent of constant turnover and trying to find a few people whom you could treat as hard-core nucleus, to make the ship alive and keep going. In every other ship I have been aboard and served for any length of time, I have made and kept up active friendships to this day. I don't have anyone from <u>Clarence K. Bronson</u> that I can put in that category. There are a couple of casual friends but not the regular Christmas card exchange or trading visits.

Q: Were there any aspects of the ship that you particularly emphasized, such as gunnery, ASW, smartness, ship handling, what have you?

Admiral Weschler: I've always been a great believer in ASW, and I tried to build that up. Also, because of my World War II experience in gunnery and shore bombardment, I thought that was one of the strengths of the 2,100-tonners. So I'd say gunnery and ASW were where I put the bulk of my effort. The rest of it, there was a constant move to build up training because I felt we were on a steady training cycle, and except for some special achievements in gunnery at the shore bombardment range at Guantanamo later on, and some good work in ASW, we were not the most distinguished destroyer in the force.

Q: There's a sort of dichotomy there. The good leader is supposed to be able to delegate and preside over the efforts of his subordinates, but sometimes you have to run the show yourself to get it done.

Admiral Weschler: Yes. Sometimes you don't find any subordinates, or if you do, they last about six months, and just when you say, "I'll pin the rose on you," he says, "Sayonara," and you start over again. There was a lot of that. I have to say that that trip around the world was, though, one of the highlights of my naval career. I love to travel, and there's no better way to travel than in your own ship. I think the crew felt alive and always regarded it as a high-water mark in their careers. You can't visit ports like Hong Kong, Singapore, Ceylon, Bahrain, and so on, and not have them stamped indelibly on your memory.

As a matter of fact, as sort of proof of what I've

Thomas R. Weschler #3 - 223

just said, having not heard anything from <u>Clarence K. Bronson</u> personnel for 30 years, the fourth of May this year we had our 30th reunion of the around-the-world trip, the first time that we'd ever gotten together. A bunch of the enlisted men decided that, gee, this trip around the world deserves some sort of a celebration, so we had our first get-together, and it really was a good one, thoroughly enjoyable.

Q: Maybe you can relate some of these memories that have been indelibly stamped from that trip. What highlights stand out?

Admiral Weschler: I picked up a feeling about Singapore then, which I hold to this day, that if I were a young man starting over again, not in the Navy, I would go to Singapore. Because I felt it was the crossroads of the Pacific, that it was replacing Hong Kong as the most vital spot out there, and it's just a natural bridge between all of the nations around the Pacific basin, and the wealth of oil and minerals and commerce is all flowing through it. I think if you see Singapore today, you'd be impressed with that and feel that that's true.

Hong Kong is one of the most beautiful harbors in the world. It was not the first time I'd seen it, but it was the first time I'd ever seen it with enough time that I

Thomas R. Weschler #3 - 224

could develop what Hong Kong looked like, and I still feel that it's one of the magic spots on the surface of the earth.

I don't think I appreciated the Middle East as much until in retrospect. Today I'm so glad that I know where Bahrain is, that I've been through the Strait of Hormuz, that I've been through the Suez Canal and the Red Sea, and that I know how all of this fits together and have some idea of the time and space factors involved. If I had a recommendation for our Navy and for our naval officers, it would be that they take a trip around the world at least some part of their career, just so that they know what the rest of the world and the other ports look like.

Navy ships tend to follow a fairly set pattern of deployments, so that you get into a few ports. But unless you sort of break out, such as a trip like this provided, you're likely to end up a career never having seen a lot of places that, if a war came, you would suddenly be challenged to visit. I think it's useful to have as many ports as possible in your kit bag.

Q: Was it the end of the war that permitted this trip--that you weren't needed off the coast of Korea?

Admiral Weschler: No. It was the fact that the Korean War, as with Vietnam, demanded so many ships that it wasn't possible to sustain all of the operations with just the destroyers available in the Pacific. And so they had to draw on the East Coast. As long as they did, and geography being what it is, it was just as easy to send a ship around the world, having had it visit Korea or Vietnam, as it was to require it to come home by the same route that it went out. I think that the powers that be were sympathetic enough to adventure and travel that they said, "Go on out one way and then keep on going and come back the other." It was really necessity that started it, but imagination that let it be as rich an experience as it was.

Q: Was this a single-ship operation, or did you go as a division?

Admiral Weschler: We went as a division. There were some who went as a squadron, and the same was true with Vietnam, that there were divisions and squadrons who made those trips around the world.

Q: How much division training did you get en route from port to port?

Admiral Weschler: A lot of station-keeping! We tried to get training services so that we could do something else.

Thomas R. Weschler #3 - 226

The British were helpful as we came through various of the areas. I think it was near Ceylon that we got a target sled and were able to do some firing with our guns. We met a submarine somewhere on the approaches to Singapore and had a little sonar ping time. But there weren't that many services. We came back through the Mediterranean; we were able to get a little help in the Mediterranean. Otherwise, it was just the things that destroyers could do with each other, so we were imaginative and did some things. But it wasn't as great an experience, from that point of view, as you might have liked.

Q: You mention that there were some other good skippers in that division. Whom do you recall?

Admiral Weschler: Art Johnson, out of '38, was skipper of <u>Daly</u>.* Walt Rountree was skipper of <u>Cotten</u>, and Jack Collingwood was the skipper of <u>Smalley</u>.** Those were my running mates, and each of them, I thought, was excellent. I'd say that Collingwood was the best ship handler of the lot, and I know that all of them went on to make captain. That was the last I saw of them professionally, was somewhere along in their captaincies. One of them is dead now, and I haven't seen the other two in years.

---
*Commander Arthur F. Johnson, USN.
**Commander Walter J. Rountree, Jr., USN, commissioned in May 1939; Commander John F. Collingwood, USN, commissioned in May 1941.

Q: You mentioned one was out of '38. You'd been running with '41, so it sounds as if you caught up.

Admiral Weschler: Yes, I'd say these others were all about that same vintage.

Q: How do you remember the Persian Gulf-Indian Ocean area compared to the way it is today?

Admiral Weschler: I think the big thing I remember about it, of course, was that if you were putting colors on it, it was all painted Great Britain pink. Bahrain, although it was the U.S. area--you know, we had our Middle East Force there--it was still really the British who were powerful ashore, and we went to visit the British senior naval officer in the port. Arabian-American Oil had a lot of British background to it in having acceptance with the various sheikdoms in the area.

We went into Aden, which was a British port, and, of course, now that's the capital of Communist Yemen, and we haven't had a ship in there in years. Coming through the Suez Canal at that time, it was still being run by whatever the Suez Canal company was, which was British and French owned. They hadn't been ousted yet, so that this was very much a world that still felt the spirit of British colonialism and was just in the process of changing over. I don't think any of us had any idea how far it would go when the changes took place.

Q: Did you have any interchange with the U.S. Middle East Force that was out there?

Admiral Weschler: Yes. When we were in Bahrain, which was their home port, the Commander Middle East Force was Wallace Beakley, who was ex-CAG from the USS Wasp, and his chief of staff was Dave Bill, who had been my roommate aboard the Wasp when I was there.* And, of course, B. J. Semmes had been a shipmate there, so the four of us had a Wasp reunion when we arrived in Bahrain. It was a marvelous experience. We couldn't have been more welcome.

Q: Bill was the fellow that swiped Douglas Fairbanks's pants.

Admiral Weschler: Exactly. You've got an excellent memory, Paul. I have to tell you one quick story. You've probably heard these sorts of things from others, but I was so grateful--I think all four skippers were grateful--that Commodore Semmes was along. Because at Bahrain we were

---
*Beakley was by this time a rear admiral, and Bill was a commander.

invited to this wonderful dinner, and it was really run by the Arabs the way that they run their dinners. Going in there was the washing of hands before you were seated, and then the host scoops the rice and tears off a piece of lamb and puts it on your plate all the way around. Then at the end, he reached forward and took the eye and put the eye on Commodore Semmes's plate and motioned for him to eat. B. J. had been schooled that this was likely to happen, and he manfully took it and took a bite of that eye and chewed away. I don't know whether he had any trouble swallowing, but he didn't let it be apparent. Then, as only B. J. can do, he passed the eye to the skipper who was on his right-- I forget which one it was, probably Art Johnson, and said, "I mustn't eat it all." So anyhow, that was cute. I was glad I was a little farther down the table and didn't have to get involved.

Q: What do you remember about Semmes's leadership of the division in that period?

Admiral Weschler: I just thought he was great. I know I've reflected that thought before. He didn't bother you about a lot of details. He gave you good general direction; he loved initiative and was open to suggestions. If one of you had a bright idea that afternoon and would pick up the voice radio or send over a message saying, "Why don't we have flag hoist drill?" Or, "Why don't we do this or that?" he was all ready for it. He thought that was fine. But he didn't want to set out a plan of the week in which every hour was taken. He'd much rather let you do what you thought your ship needed and then come forward if you thought there was something where you could all work together fruitfully.

He did another thing that I appreciated and that I think was good for me. He received queries about use of destroyers or new designs or new features which he, as commodore, was being asked to comment on. When you were in port, he'd give you a copy of the letter and say, "If any of you have any ideas on this, I'd be happy to have your thoughts so I can incorporate them in the reply and send them back." Two or three times I wrote up something that he thought was particularly good, and I know he used it in sending it forward.

That gave you a chance to show if you had any originality or thoughts of your own, and I know that he felt that I did pretty well on thinking of things like this and giving him these thoughts. So that's nice; you like the feeling that the boss is coming to you and giving you a chance to shine if it's an area where you feel you're competent.

Q: Do you remember any specifics of things that you did pass on to him?

Admiral Weschler: No, frankly, I don't. I'd say one other thing, and that is that B. J. was an excellent inspector. He didn't inspect often, but when he did, you knew it was going to be a good one. He had a nice sense of humor, so that in inspecting the men, he would frequently stop and ask some sort of a question that could catch a guy off guard, and he would do it deliberately just to see what sort of a response he would get. When he went around the ship, he certainly had the naval experience to know what was what, and you didn't pull the wool over his eyes. There wasn't any of this having covered up something that was lousy, and thinking that B. J. wouldn't be aware of it. He knew what was going on, and he impressed you that way.

Q: Did he impress the enlisted men that way too?

Admiral Weschler: I know particularly that he impressed the chief petty officers. They're the ones that I think spoke most highly of him. They just liked the way he handled himself and that he didn't bother them with all sorts of details. He let the ships be reasonably run on their own. And he was disposed to try to give the chiefs every break on liberty, so that they were highly regarded and treated as part of the team.

Q: That was a time, wasn't it, when there was more attempt to give chiefs that role?

Admiral Weschler: That's right, and I think he felt that. It would come up in a place like Athens. We were there just before Christmas and through Christmas. I don't remember the circumstances, but I think there had been some to-do in Greece, so that normal liberty ended at either 2300 or 2400. Men were allowed to stay ashore until the next morning only if they had some authorization from the CO. Well, B. J.'s guidance to us was that as long as the chief petty officer had a good record, go ahead and sign them all out for overnights if they wanted. Well, they were very appreciative of that, because there were a lot of ships in a lot of divisions where they were much more hard-nosed about this kind of thing. But he figured they'd been a long time at sea, that they were as old as he was or older, there certainly wasn't any need to hold them back like a bunch of children, and I think they appreciated that kind of attitude.

Q: What about the younger sailors? What kind of a rein was kept on them to prevent the ugly American image?

Admiral Weschler: I don't remember any real limitations as we came through the Asian ports and up to Bahrain. In the Middle East ports, liberty was terribly restricted because there were so few places to go; there was practically no liquor available. I think you're aware that most of those Muslim countries are dry. We had organized sports events for the crew. There were certain compounds they could visit like the Aramco area, where they could be given a beer or two, which we provided, and then came back to the ship.* So that stretch from Bahrain through the Suez Canal was pretty restricted as far as enlisted were concerned. And for the officers, except if you went to somebody's club or somebody's home, there wasn't really very much you could do.

When we got to the Med, of course, we were officially part of the Sixth Fleet, and so the regular Sixth Fleet rules applied. As I recall them, the enlisted men were pretty well all supposed to be back by midnight. Overnight liberty, where they could really get in trouble and create the unfavorable image, was the thing the fleet commander was trying to stay away from.

This was still soon enough after World War II that all of the rebuilding hadn't taken place. It took Europe longer than six or seven years to get really back on its feet. Greece, as you recall, had that war right up until

---
*Aramco--Arabian-American Oil Company.

Thomas R. Weschler #3 - 234

'49 or '50, when we had been preventing a Communist takeover. So I think in '54 it was still feeling some of those ravages and still some restlessness in the country.

Q: What other liberty ports did you hit in the Mediterranean?

Admiral Weschler: We got to Nice and Gibraltar. Nice was wonderful, and the local people there were so used to the Sixth Fleet, and so used to everybody having a good time, that I don't think a sailor gave any problem. They had plenty of facilities, the casinos, everything that you can imagine, so that the sailors were well taken care of. Gibraltar, pretty much the same. Although it's not a big town, there were plenty of naval facilities for recreation, and our men were welcomed with open arms. I would say in Gibraltar, more than any place else, that they pretty well could come and go. We were tied up alongside, to boot, so that it was a very welcome and wonderful jumping-off spot before we headed back across the Atlantic.

Q: Did you get involved in any Sixth Fleet operations or just pass through?

Admiral Weschler: No, because it was all through the holidays, except for the transit from Athens to Nice, when, as I recall it, we had a gun shoot at a towed sleeve. I think that was the only AA exercise we fired as we made the trip. We were in Athens before Christmas, in Nice by New Year's, and sailed from Gibraltar about the fifth or sixth of January. So those were probably the two or three weeks that were the quietest in the Sixth Fleet life.

Q: Did you see much British influence in the Mediterranean? You mentioned it in the Indian Ocean area.

Admiral Weschler: We certainly were aware of it in Gibraltar. I think that the continuity of the British presence in Gibraltar came across to us, when we read the dates. I can't remember when they really first took that rock, but certainly it seemed like a couple of centuries. And to see how well dug in they were, that there just wasn't anything about it that wasn't British, gave every aspect of lasting forever. Having come through Hong Kong and Singapore and Ceylon and then all that in the Middle East, and then Gibraltar, the British Empire was still very much evident, even though the dissolution of it was then in progress. You certainly knew what a big force they had been, and then you saw the few ships they had at Gibraltar. You could see how much the British Navy had shrunk and that it was probably not going to come back to what it had been before.

Q: How capable was your ship in AA gunnery?

Admiral Weschler: I'd say just fair. There's hardly anything that you shot at with time fuzes that was tougher than a towed sleeve. We weren't using the VT fuzes, the proximity fuzes, at the time. I don't remember whether they were in short supply or whether just too expensive, but anyhow, for a typical exercise, unless you really had a good radar sleeve, you just fired time fuzes, and time fuzes at a sleeve, even if it's pretty slow, are never very good for a lot of hits. The three-dimensional aspect can get you. You might be right on in bearing and elevation, but you can still be off in range, and you wouldn't have gotten any hits.

Q: It was really a matter of guesswork in that case.

Admiral Weschler: That's right, and a need for a rocking range ladder. You know, in those days we were using the stereo range finder, and some people were really good at seeing stereo and others weren't. But I know I had a good stereo range finder operator, because it showed up in shore bombardment, where he did very well.

Q: You came back to the United States. How did you spend

your time here?

Admiral Weschler: Came by way of Bermuda, which was also fun, the only time I'd ever taken a ship into Bermuda, and then on back to Newport. When we arrived home, as was done typically for these ships coming home, they had cleared the side of ComDesLant's flagship and the four destroyers returning would be brought right alongside.* The families had all been collected, and they all came trooping aboard as soon as we were all tied up. Captains were notified that calls were considered made and returned for the day; the next day would be ample time to see the admiral. Somebody from the staff would have come aboard and given us the admiral's compliments, and told us what was going on and so on, but you had that day free and clear, which I thought was a very nice gesture.

Q: Who was the ComDesLant then?

Admiral Weschler: Admiral Hartman.** He felt very strongly on the place of the family--that as close as possible, the family ought to be number one. He recognized the ship had to come first, but he didn't really like to make that distinction any more than he had to. He wanted

---
*ComDesLant--Commander Destroyer Force Atlantic Fleet. The cruise ended at Newport on 15 January 1954.
**Rear Admiral Charles C. Hartman, USN.

that family to be right in there pitching.

Q: Probably fairly soon thereafter, you were out to a buoy.

Admiral Weschler: Absolutely. This was January, and if there's anything colder than picking up a mooring buoy in Narragansett Bay in the middle of January, I'd like to know what it is.

Q: How long did you spend here in Newport before you went south again?

Admiral Weschler: We had been gone for a long time, so we stayed around here several months. We had an overhaul between the tender and Boston, and along about August of '54, we went down to Guantanamo for refresher training. I think by that time we had a new commodore. Commodore Ed Carlson had relieved B. J., and the biggest thing, I think, about that trip south was again the fun of having our own division together.*

The first ship of the new Dealey class, DE-1006, was in Newport and was heading to Guantanamo for shakedown training.** Since she was the first and not yet assigned

---
*Captain Edward B. Carlson, USN.
**The USS Dealey was commissioned 3 June 1954. She was the first of the post-World War II destroyer escorts.

to a division, she was added to our division and went down with us. What we enjoyed was seeing the capabilities of this new destroyer escort class and watching her perform against the submarines as compared to our destroyers, and learning what the new Navy was going to be like. She was very impressive.

I think the biggest thing I recall about the DE-1006 over and above a fairly well laid out ship and an awful lot packed into a reasonably small hull, was her maneuverability. We destroyers would be on a submarine that would make a tight turn, and we could come around in about 300 to 500 yards. It seemed to me that DE would snap around in about 150 or 200 yards, and so the submarine had a very tough time getting away from the Dealey class, whereas it was a fairly easy tactic for the submarine to double back through a knuckle and shake us, because the destroyers couldn't turn fast enough to stay with him all the time.

Q: The drawback, though, was that she couldn't keep up with the fleet.

Admiral Weschler: Yes, but she was designed for a different purpose. I'm very much aware of that because of my Spruance experience. The Spruance was designed as an ASW ship to operate with the carriers. The Dealey class was designed as an ASW ship to operate with the amphibious forces and the mobile logistic support forces. So they had already accepted the fact that she wasn't going to operate with the carriers. Now, having said that, we're faced with the practicum that if you have only so many escorts and you have so many ships to be escorted, you're going to use whatever escort you have, and just because it wasn't designed to operate with the carrier doesn't mean that it won't. The same thing applies to the 1052s.* We've used our new frigates any number of times to screen carriers, and we used them that way in Vietnam because they were the only ships available. I think we have to recognize that.

Q: That's happening also with the FFG-7s.

Admiral Weschler: Exactly. Yes. The FFG-7s, same thing.** Designed as an AAW ship for the less fast forces, but because she's an AAW ship and we need all we can get, they're operating with the carriers. So we have to know that's going to happen.

Q: What were the operations like out of Guantanamo?

---
*The destroyer escorts of the Knox (DE-1052) class entered the fleet between 1969 and 1974; they have a top speed 27 knots. In 1975 the ships of this class were reclassified as frigates, the FF-1052 class.
**The frigates of the Oliver Hazard Perry (FFG-7) class entered the fleet between 1977 and 1989; they have a top speed right around 30 knots.

Admiral Weschler: I thought they were pretty good. The best thing about Guantanamo is that it gives you a standard by which to judge yourself. If every skipper becomes his own setter of levels, it's likely to be good for one or two things, where the skipper is really experienced. But there are going to be a lot of other areas which he doesn't know all that much about, and the training could end up not being stringent enough or detailed enough to really make the crew come alive.

The advantage of Guantanamo is that they have gotten the fruits of hundreds of ships coming through there, and they have inspected the same sorts of things over and over again. They can recognize the errors as soon as you start to make them, and they know how to get you out of them, or they can really crack the whip on you. If you're recalcitrant and decide you're not going to come around, they'll show you the error of your ways very quickly in a more complicated situation. So I like what they are.

I think the fleet training group was a distinct asset, and it was for the school of the ship. It was your ship learning things internal to the hull almost all the time. The only place that we really got into external exercises was in the two-ship operations in antisubmarine warfare. And Guantanamo always had submarines, so you could get more submarine service at Guantanamo and more training for your sonar operators there than any place else you operated.

Q: Had you had a fair amount of crew turnover during that overhaul period?

Admiral Weschler: Yes, and I'd say that we were finally beginning to settle down by the time we went down for this refresher training. We had been given a full crew when we started on the around-the-world trip, and most attrition was either for illness or for people whose enlistments expired. Those who wanted to ship over in some other place would opt to come home, be separated, and then ship over to wherever they wanted to be in order to get their new duty station.* Because we were so far away and because they knew we were coming home and the war was over, the tendency was not to send out replacements.

So the whole cruise was one of attrition as we went around the world, ending up, perhaps, with between 80% and 90% by the time we got back to Newport. Those had been replaced in those first couple of months, and then during the yard period, they again worked on us to bring us up. So we had pretty good numbers by the time we went to Gitmo, and they tended to stay with us at least for the further year that I was on board.**

---
*Ship over--to reenlist for another period of service.
**Gitmo--Guantanamo Bay.

Thomas R. Weschler #3 - 243

Q: What was your shore bombardment experience like in that area?

Admiral Weschler: They had a fine range. I'm trying to think how to describe it. They had one course for 40-millimeters and another for the 5-inch, and one of the things I particularly enjoyed for the 5-inch was that they had an exercise which was called the moving tank. Although they didn't actually run a tank across the field for you, they had a series of points that you had to have your battery transit through as you fired, as though enemy tanks were running across the field. That was one of the more advanced exercises. It took some skill at getting yourself set up, but it was really a good challenge for the whole battery by the time you could fire that one successfully.

Q: Was this at Culebra?

Admiral Weschler: Yes, this was at Culebra where we did our firing. We also had a range at Vieques, but we didn't use that one at the time. It was faster to get to Culebra, and so that's the one that we went to.

Q: For the moving tank exercise, was this a direct fire thing, using the ship's director?

Admiral Weschler: Yes, that was direct fire, and you had a point of aim for the initial salvo. From then on, the observer could see the marks on the ground, the track of the tank that you were to move along. You just had coordinates for what it was doing, and you would set it up in the computer to track along with that. You had to have a good initial fire control solution if you wanted to be able to stay with it as you went along.

One other thing that we fired was the reverse slope, in which you put the shell on the far side of a hill. This meant that you were using an extra angle of elevation in order to have it come in and drop behind the peak of the hill. That was always a good exercise and required your computer operator to be pretty skilled in order to get it set up and to fire it. That's where the people from Guantanamo were so useful. They would have a whole set of procedures, and you could have your own school of the ship running through this before you got on the range, making sure that everything was right. Then, when you got there, it was really easy; your operator felt comfortable about going through the procedure and doing the job.

Q: Did you deploy after that training period?

Admiral Weschler: No. When we finished at Guantanamo, we

came back to Newport and for some reason our division got a "bye" on that deployment. Maybe it was because we had already had a year's trip away and had only been back about a year by then. Whatever it was, we didn't have to deploy, and we continued to operate out of Newport and participated in fleet exercises. I think there was an amphibious exercise down off North Carolina, and we went down to Springboard. I think we were just beginning the Springboard exercises in February of '55. So that kind of thing is what kept us busy.

Q: Did you work with any of the carriers out of Quonset, for example?

Admiral Weschler: Yes, but not very much. In those days, there was still a task group designation, and there were divisions that were assigned to the carriers pretty much. As long as those divisions were available, they wouldn't get any extra destroyers. But there were times when one or two of those would be down or that they wanted to augment the screen and they would assign us. But it was not a terrifically active period. It was fairly slow, thank heavens. It was sort of a nice time to be back, because with that Gitmo deployment and so on, we'd had quite a bit of time away, and this was a chance to catch up.

Thomas R. Weschler #3 - 246

Q: You talked briefly about the families. Did many of the enlisted men have families?

Admiral Weschler: I would say probably on the order of 30% of them. Because of the Korean War, the draft, and the recruiting for that, we had an awful lot of young people aboard, and as soon as their enlistments were up, they went home. So you had a constant turnover of these 17-, 18-, 19-year-olds, who were not married. About the only ones who were married were your senior petty officers and chief petty officers.

I had occasion to contrast this. I've already mentioned that there was this <u>Bronson</u> 30th reunion in '84. I also go to USS <u>Wasp</u> (CV-7) reunions. And how different they are. When you go to the <u>Wasp</u> reunion, almost everybody there is a retired naval person, officer or enlisted, who had put in his 30 years with the tour aboard the <u>Wasp</u> just having been one that had come along. After the <u>Wasp</u> was sunk, almost all of them went on to complete their Navy careers, wherever they were. When we see them now, 40 years later, we all see each other as sort of Navy types together, who have really continued that close Navy association.

When I went to the <u>Bronson</u> reunion, there were only about four people there who were retired Navy or who were still active in the reserve. All the rest were straight civilian. That time they'd had aboard the Bronson was the only Navy time or military time they'd ever had. They had no intention of keeping on with it, but they looked back on it as a very interesting and happy part of their lives, so this was a civilian reunion. Everybody there was a police officer, an architect, a businessman, or whatever, completely different environment. I commented on it to my wife as being one of the most amazing things, that I had no idea how different two reunions could be until I went to those two, and then puzzled through what the difference was. In World War II, I was dealing with a regular Navy or at least long-term Navy crew, and in the Bronson, nearly everybody was a reservist or a short-timer, or whatever, sort of pumping through.

Q: I would guess also that at the Wasp reunion you were treated as a vice admiral, and at the Bronson one, as a commander.

Admiral Weschler: Yes, reasonably so. Reasonably so. As a matter of fact, I was quite surprised at how much the Bronson people insisted that I play the role of being their captain. Although they hadn't thought much about it, that was the only association they had for me, and they really didn't know an awful lot about what was different about a vice admiral and a commander. At the Wasp reunion, since I had been an ensign and a jaygee with them, if they knew me at all on a personal basis, they knew me in that association. They were much more familiar with my eventual rank, and I was the speaker the first occasion with the Wasp people. They were looking forward to my remarks as a vice admiral, and not as just Lieutenant (j.g.) Weschler, who had been aboard.

Q: Anything else to wrap up that tour in the destroyer?

Admiral Weschler: Yes, and I'm going to use it as a lead-in to my next duty. I indicated that we did some operating in and around Newport during that period of January to late May 1955. In the course of that time, Admiral Burke was aboard the flagship, which was in Melville, and Melville is about six or eight miles north of the fleet landing.* An awful lot of the activities of the destroyer force required sailors to go back and forth from the fleet landing or from Coddington Cove, where the supply center was, out to Melville, where the flagship was.

Admiral Burke apparently was in the habit of picking up sailors as he drove back and forth. Whenever they'd get into the car, he'd ask them what ship they were from and what was going on and what did they think about this, that, and the next thing. I wasn't aware of this, but,

---
*In January 1955 Rear Admiral Arleigh A. Burke, USN, became Commander Destroyer Force Atlantic Fleet.

nonetheless, it was the case. So in the Decoration Day weekend of May '55, I took leave. I really hadn't had that much leave, so I took a week off, and my wife and I were just picnicking near the house. We had two children and we were taking the kids off on weekends and so on. One day we were on the picnic, and only a close friend really knew where I was. Suddenly he showed up and said, "The chief of staff of DesLant wants you to give him a call as quickly as possible. It's no emergency, but you're going to be needed on a personal basis."

So we came back home from our picnic area, and I phoned Captain Caufield, the chief of staff.* He said, "Admiral Burke has been named the Chief of Naval Operations designate, and he wants you to be his personal aide. He has just departed for Norfolk, and we want you to get down to Norfolk as quickly as possible."

I said, "Gee, Captain, it's about 4:00 o'clock in the afternoon now. I'm on leave. I don't really have the laundry, I don't have all my uniforms together, and I'm broke. It's the end of the month. I'll have to really do some digging to see what I can do."

He said, "Oh, I wouldn't worry about it. As long as you're under way before 6:00 o'clock tomorrow morning, I don't think anyone will care. Count on us for full assistance."

---
*Captain Cecil T. Caufield, USN.

I said, "Thanks, Captain. I've got the general idea. Now I've got to think through the details." With the staff's help, I just made it!

Now I'll jump to the point when later on I checked in with Admiral Burke, and I met him for the first time other than his change of command in taking over DesLant. I said, "Admiral, I know that I met you once officially, but I have no idea how I was selected as your aide."

He said, "Well, obviously some people on the staff spoke highly of you." B. J. Semmes was operations officer by this time, and a classmate of mine, Lee Savidge, was assistant operations officer.* But he said, "When I drove back and forth in my car, picking up sailors, I used to keep a black book and would make notes in it of people who seemed to be doing well with their commands. After people had given me various ideas of whom I might pick for my aide, I looked through my black book and, lo and behold, you were the winner. They simply corroborated what I already knew, and so even though I didn't know you personally, I felt I knew everything about you professionally that I wanted to know, and I picked you as my aide." So that time around Newport paid off for me in ways that I hadn't expected.

Q: Did you find that he did indeed know your record pretty well?

---

*Commander William L. Savidge, USN.

Admiral Weschler: Yes. I always felt that he didn't know it as well as he thought he did, but I wasn't about to tell him so. If he thought I was the greatest thing that happened, why, that was fine with me, and I was thrilled to have it that way.

Q: I think Admiral Burke prides himself on knowing everything.

Admiral Weschler: Yes. So that fit into it.

Q: Did you have much chance to get your family moved?

Admiral Weschler: No. That's interesting. After some fast action, obviously, that night, I was under way the next morning, and I did get down to Norfolk and joined him. As a matter of fact, again just a funny thing, Admiral Burke was in Admiral Wright's office when I checked in.* Captain George Miller, later Rear Admiral Miller, was there, and I checked with him and said, "Here I am.** I just want you to know that I'm around. I've got my gear in the BOQ room over here, and I'm ready to do whatever I can."***

---
*Admiral Jerauld Wright, USN, Commander in Chief Atlantic Fleet/Supreme Allied Commander Atlantic from 1954 to 1960.
**Captain George H. Miller, USN, whose oral history is in the Naval Institute collection.
***BOQ--bachelor officers' quarters.

He said, "You better get that gear out of that BOQ room. I think he's leaving in five minutes for Washington, and he expects you to be aboard."

So I managed to get a car and ran over and got my gear, and I told Captain Miller, "I'll meet you at the flight line."

He said, "You better, and try to beat the admiral."

I got out there about two seconds before Admiral Burke arrived, and that was sort of the way my first two months with Admiral Burke went. It was constant scrambling to stay ahead of him, to have some idea what he was doing and not to be a drag, but to really be an assist in what he was accomplishing. Nothing was worse than those first 48 hours, when I didn't know the players, didn't know where I was, didn't know what town I was going to be in next, and still trying to do something for him.

After I had been his aide for about two weeks, I reminded him that I was commanding officer of a destroyer and that if he would find it convenient, I'd either like to get back to the bridge or locate a relief. He said, "Oh. Well, go ahead, just call the bureau and tell them that you need a relief, and then I can give you six hours off any time you want to get relieved."* Well, he actually gave me 12 when the time came. They did find someone who was destined for another destroyer and they rerouted him. We

---
*He was speaking of the Bureau of Naval Personnel, which controlled officer assignments.

had a change of command some time in early June, and I was relieved as commanding officer of CKB, and stayed full-time, then, on Admiral Burke's staff.

Admiral Burke stayed here in Newport officially until about July. In that time, we had done a very thorough trip of the Western Pacific. We'd gone all over the Pacific, and he made his visits as CNO designate. When he came back from that, he and Mrs. Burke moved down to the Westchester Apartment in Washington. Knowing that he was going to do that, I had scouted around and found a summer rental in Washington, which wasn't too far from where he was going to live. My wife had very dutifully gotten everything packed and ready to go, and we put everything in storage and moved down to this summer rental.

After Admiral Burke took over in August and had moved into quarters and we were sure that everything was firm and locked in, then I located a house in Alexandria and bought it.* I had learned enough about him by that time that the house was five minutes from the Mall entrance to the Pentagon, so that I could work as late as he worked, which was phenomenally late. When the time came to go home, I could give my wife a call, and she could be there in five minutes, grab me, and get me home again in very short order, and that was sort of the way life went.

---

*At that time the CNO occupied quarters on the grounds of the Naval Observatory in Washington, D.C. The house is now the official residence of the Vice President.

Q: You didn't rate too good a parking spot at the Pentagon?

Admiral Weschler: I don't think the aide had any, frankly, and I couldn't afford two cars, so this was the right compromise. The five-minute drive was useful to me, in that I didn't have any long-distance commute, and also we didn't have to get a sitter. For ten minutes we would leave them unguarded or just notify the neighbor that Trina was racing out and coming back, and all was well.

Q: I have heard that the purpose of Admiral Burke's meeting with Admiral Wright was to let him know that he had been picked, because Wright would have probably been a logical candidate.

Admiral Weschler: As a matter of fact, Admiral Wright was one for whom Admiral Burke had pushed substantially to be the CNO. He had told Secretary Thomas that before the official announcement was made, he personally wanted to go down and tell Admiral Wright that he, Admiral Burke, had been selected, that it was not Admiral Burke's choice.* He felt Admiral Wright really was the gentleman it should

---

*Secretary of the Navy Charles S. Thomas selected Burke to be Chief of Naval Operations. Burke was in the Naval Academy class of 1923, and Wright was in the class of 1918.

have been, and he wanted to be there to tell him firsthand about it. He said he would appreciate being in Admiral Wright's headquarters when the announcement was made, and wanted Admiral Wright to share in the announcement.

Q: Did you get any reaction on Admiral Carney's part from leaving after only a two-year term?*

Admiral Weschler: Nothing adverse, no. I think Admiral Carney had been around official Washington sufficiently and had watched Admiral Fechteler and Admiral Denfeld come and go, that I think he wasn't the least bit surprised to go at the end of two years.**

Q: Describe, then, the routine as you moved into it under Admiral Burke.

Admiral Weschler: Well, I tried to give you a feeling of the franticness in that first bit of it. A lot of that continued. First of all, I was terrifically naive about how Washington was put together. Although I had had the war college course and knew the names of the offices, I really didn't have a feeling of how Washington functioned,

---
*Admiral Robert B. Carney, USN, Burke's predecessor, served as Chief of Naval Operations from 1953 to 1955.
**Admiral William M. Fechteler was CNO from 1951 to 1953; Admiral Louis E. Denfeld was CNO from 1947 to 1949.

wasn't well aware of the budget cycle and a lot of the things that I feel our years of peace have made us more aware of. My years had been pretty active with war or the war college, and I think every sailor today in 1984 is much more aware of the bureaucracy and how Washington works than was true in '55.

The second thing was that Admiral Burke was much junior to so many other flag officers that he didn't feel free to call on many of them to come in and brief him. He might have felt free were he in fact a three-star making four stars, someone who was highly accepted in that role. And sharing some of this position that he was in, there weren't very many of the aides who were forthcoming to tell me everything that was going on. Even though as a commander, I was closer in rank to the aides than Admiral Burke was to their bosses. So there was a certain element of this.

As a matter of fact, people were not going overboard to give Admiral Burke an office of his own in Washington to allow him to function as the CNO designate. There was a visiting flag office at the Pentagon, which was available for any flag officer who came to Washington, and that was the one we used. The only difference was that we were in the office a little longer than most. Even then we had to watch for who else was coming in, so that we could be sure there were spots for a visiting fleet commander or a three-star to come into Washington to be accommodated.

After the first couple of weeks, it got to be a little easier, but initially it was two-star Admiral Burke, and that took some getting around. On Admiral Burke's WestPac trip, I'll comment that as he went around, even though the messages said "CNO designate is coming," there were some of the two-stars and three-stars who were a little reluctant to give place.* I won't say anyone was stuffy about receiving him, but there certainly were many who would make sure they sat in the right-hand seat and Admiral Burke would sit on the left, as they drove around on inspection tours and that sort of thing. That by-play was sort of interesting to watch.

One who went out of his way to receive him and make him feel warm and welcome was Admiral Stump, and I think Admiral Burke was eternally grateful for that.** Admiral Stump was an aviator and a gentleman who had strong opinions and was perfectly capable of expressing them. Had he taken any sort of a dislike or shown any personal animosity to Admiral Burke, he could have made his job much more difficult. But as it was, he went out of his way to be receptive and to be helpful and to be courteous. I think the two of them developed a marvelous rapport, and it was one of the strengths of Admiral Burke's whole tour to

---
*WestPac--Western Pacific.
**Admiral Felix B. Stump, USN, Commander in Chief Pacific and Commander in Chief Pacific Fleet, 1953-58.

have Admiral Stump as supportive as he was.

Q: Maybe that's why Admiral Stump stayed out there so long.

Admiral Weschler: I'm sure it didn't hurt, but it was a wonderful thing to see.

Q: Did you detect that this coolness grew out of resentment in any cases?

Admiral Weschler: Let me put that in context. I don't think it was ever resentment of Admiral Burke himself. I think it was a resentment to some extent of the Secretary of the Navy for visiting this kind of thing on a military system. They didn't like the military system being abrogated. I think that was at the heart of it. Secretary Thomas, in discussions with Admiral Burke that I became aware of, said that he had conducted a poll of all the three- and four-star admirals in the Navy and many of the two-stars whom he'd come to know, when he was trying to decide who the next CNO was going to be. He knew it had to be a younger man, someone who would be more receptive to new ideas and who could get the Navy back on the step. Secretary Thomas felt that the Navy needed a good kick in the tail, and that the Navy wasn't getting it, and it had to be brought together as a unit.

Secretary Thomas said, "The thing that impressed me, from all those lists, was that there wasn't a one that didn't have Admiral Burke's name on it as a CNO in due course." So the only difference between Admiral Burke's being CNO then and Admiral Burke's being CNO a few years later was that time compression that Secretary Thomas had imposed. But as a result of Admiral Burke's unique reputation, and the fact that he had worked with everybody--aviation, surface sailors, Marines, submariners--meant that he was highly accepted as an individual, and his professional stature was of the highest. So that was really it. They wanted him, they respected him, but they just didn't feel that all those other good people should have been pushed aside, and that took time to weather.

During his first two years in office, Admiral Burke was particularly sensitive to all these aspects. In every appointment that was made, everything that he did, he thought of what this would mean to those others who were being passed over or excluded. He would take pains to send for them or to visit them or to talk with them. He really couldn't have been more careful and thoughtful as he handled that phase of this jumping about 90 numbers to become CNO.

I was going to mention that we finished the WestPac

trip, and we came back to Washington, and by this time Admiral Burke was taking residence at the Westchester Apartments. Secretary of Defense Wilson had a conference down at Quantico each summer, and he notified Admiral Burke, as CNO designate, that he wanted him to attend.* Admiral Burke went off by himself with the driver and arrived at the conference. That afternoon the phone rang, and it was Admiral Burke. He said, "Tom, I want a set of four-star shoulder boards down here by tomorrow morning." He was in khakis. He said, "Secretary Wilson has told me I'm out of uniform, and he'll give me until tomorrow morning to get in uniform." So that's when he got his four stars, at that Quantico conference, and we sent them down by car. From then on he was four-star Admiral Burke. His trip through Europe was with four stars, and everything went swimmingly. The military can understand that, happily.

Q: Any memories of the trip to Europe that are worth mentioning?

Admiral Weschler: In connection with the trip to Europe, I think of two highlights. Number one, Lieutenant General Pate, who was then the Commandant Marine Corps designate,

---

*Charles E. Wilson served as Secretary of Defense from 28 January 1953 to 8 October 1957.

Thomas R. Weschler #3 - 261

teamed up with Admiral Burke.* It was impressive to me, as a young commander, that Admiral Burke knew Marines as thoroughly as he did and was as accepted by them as he was. There was no question that General Shepherd, General Pate, and so on, really knew him and appreciated his outlook.** I think that was one of Admiral Burke's strengths, which came across, that he really knew so much of the Navy and Marine Corps family that he could pull it together through this personal friendship over and above his own capabilities.

Q: Was there at that time still a thought that the Marine Corps was part of the Navy rather than a completely separate service?

Admiral Weschler: I feel sure that the attitude was that they were a team. Secretary Thomas was a challenge to both CNO and the Commandant, because Secretary Thomas wanted to be a "strong man." Both the CNO and the Commandant worked for him, and I think they used to get together to talk about the Secretary, as to how they were going to handle some of his demands that they weren't prepared to go along with, and how they could finesse him without looking as

---
*General Randolph McC. Pate, USMC, was Commandant of the Marine Corps, 1956-59.
**General Lemuel C. Shepherd, Jr., USMC, was Commandant of the Marine Corps, 1952-55.

though they were being disobedient.

Q: Do you have any examples of that?

Admiral Weschler: No, I don't. I just know this was an attitude, and I know the teamwork that developed between Admiral Burke and General Pate. Certainly that trip, the two of them having had a chance to be together for a couple of weeks, was a wonderful time to develop some mutual understandings.

A second thing that I was going to point out was that when we were in Europe, one of the things that Admiral Burke had said right away was, "Well, I want to go visit my good friend in the U.S. Army, General Hodes," who was Commanding General Seventh Army.* So when we got near Seventh Army headquarters, we made a special stop there, and, boy, General Hodes was right out there to meet Admiral Burke and General Pate. He gave them a very full lunch and afternoon at the headquarters before we got back on our Navy tour. Again, I was impressed to think that this three-star Army general knew Admiral Burke so well. Well, it developed that the two of them had been on the Korean truce team together, and this was just following up on a friendship where the two of them had been battered around by the North Koreans and had shared the experience.

---
*Lieutenant General Henry I. Hodes, USA.

Thomas R. Weschler #3 - 263

When we visited there at Seventh Army headquarters, and then when we came to a couple of other places, one other feature of the Marine Corps impressed me, and I think Admiral Burke noticed it also. When General Pate landed, the senior Marine in the area always was there to greet him, and it didn't make any difference whether it was a staff sergeant or a sergeant major or a colonel or a general. Whoever the senior Marine was, they knew he was coming, and even if the individual had to travel 30 to 50 miles, there was some Marine on the tarmac there to say hello when he stepped off the plane. To me, it gave real impetus to our recognizing the master chief of the command and making some designation of the enlisted, whoever was senior, as being a responsible party and sort of carrying the flag for his unit and his service, more than had been the custom in the Navy before.

Q: Where else did you go on that tour? Did you visit CinCSouth headquarters?

Admiral Weschler: Yes, we did. We got to CinCSouth's headquarters, but that was not a long stay. Naples was important, but CinCSouth was not the major part. Admiral Burke had a feeling that he could do NATO later on when he was CNO. What he was now trying to visit was as much of the fleet as possible, and he didn't stay there long, because his last sea tour had been as a cruiser division commander in the Sixth Fleet.* He knew the Sixth Fleet, so he thought he'd better get around and see some of the other areas. For instance, I know we were in Greece, because he wanted to see what the MAAGs were doing over there.** There was a Rhine River patrol at that time; Admiral Rodgers had command of it.*** That was still an ongoing unit from the end of World War II. Then we spent some time in London. Also, although I said he wasn't seeing that much of NATO, we did come through Paris, because he at least wanted to make his number with the senior commanders there, as we came through.

Q: General Gruenther at that point?

Admiral Weschler: General Gruenther, but he actually wasn't aboard.**** I think General Norstad was acting when we came through, but he called on the senior admiral, who

---

*During most of 1954, Burke served as Commander Cruiser Division Six. His flagship was the cruiser Macon, in which Weschler had served several years earlier.
**MAAGs--military assistance advisory groups, the organizations that administered the distribution of U.S. military assistance to other nations. General Alfred M. Gruenther, USA, Supreme Commander Allied Powers Europe and Commander in Chief U.S. European Command. General Lauris Norstad, USAF, was air deputy to Gruenther.
***Rear Admiral Bertram J. Rodgers, USN, Commander U.S. Naval Forces Germany.
****General Alfred M. Gruenther, USA, Supreme Commander Allied Powers Europe and Commander in Chief U.S. European Command.

was a French admiral, as I recall.*

I recall quite well that visit, because Admiral Burke was always playing tricks on aides. He sort of enjoyed it. When he went into the admiral's office, he had left me in an anteroom, and the admiral's office was more than just an individual office. It also had some sort of a sitting room and then an office where he had an aide and secretary different from what was in the anteroom. So Admiral Burke got in there and went out by another door, and then had the aide come back and tell me, saying, "The admiral went to lunch about ten minutes ago. If you're interested, come with me." He did that deliberately, I know full well. I was really stewing about that time, too, because I knew he was overdue for this luncheon, and I had been around poking heads in various doors and couldn't find anybody, which is what he wanted me to do. So anyhow, the European tour was not nearly as long as the Pacific one, where we really were covering a lot more countries and an awful lot more Navy, and because of his most recent experience.

Q: Was there an emphasis in the Pacific tour on the Formosa situation?

Admiral Weschler: He was certainly very aware of that and

---

*General Lauris Norstad, USAF, was air deputy to Gruenther.

included that. I'm trying to think where he really put a lot of emphasis. He had been in Japan and Korea during the Korean War a great deal, so that wasn't as big, although he did visit a lot in Japan. Taiwan, just one touch-down. He did call on Chiang Kai-shek, though, while we were there, and the Philippines.* I'm trying to think. You can get an idea, again, of Admiral Burke's prescience in knowing who was good and Admiral Stump's support. When he came through Pearl, he had asked Admiral Stump to give him a good team to guide him on what was going on in the Pacific and to organize the tour for him. The people who accompanied him from the staff were Charlie Duncan and Oley Sharp.** The person assigned to come from Naval Intelligence at Washington was Bush Bringle.*** So you can see that he was really getting some top-notch people to go with him, and that was typical of Admiral Stump, in putting this together.

Q: All future four-star admirals.

Admiral Weschler: Exactly. They were assigned to go with Admiral Burke, so you can see their seniors thought they were comers, and CinCPacFlt wanted the CNO designate to get

---
*Chiang Kai-shek was President of the Republic of China (Taiwan).
**Captain Charles K. Duncan, USN; Captain U.S. Grant Sharp, USN. Both later became four-star admirals. Their oral histories are in the Naval Institute collection.
***Captain William F. Bringle, USN.

the best earful. I would say that the Philippines, Vietnam, Indonesia were more in his mind on that trip than Taiwan, although Taiwan was certainly very important, and he made the right calls there. But I don't have the same impression of interest as I gathered that he had in the others.

Q: What about Seventh Fleet per se?

Admiral Weschler: Seventh Fleet per se, yes. We saw them in Yokosuka. That's where we picked up Seventh Fleet. One good friend of Admiral Burke's that we saw on that trip was Fitzhugh Lee, who was then Commander Fleet Air, Western Pacific, stationed at Atsugi.* I remember I didn't know Fitzhugh Lee at all, but when Admiral Burke was selected for CNO, Fitzhugh Lee just sent him a, "Dear Arleigh," and there was this face smiling, "Signed, Fitz." And Admiral Burke sent back a note which was a face smiling and, "Me, too, Arleigh." It was a nice exchange. So I knew the two of them knew each other and had a lot of rapport. I don't recall where they had gotten to know each other so well, but they obviously had gained a great respect for each other.

These are just a couple of little stories of either

---

*Rear Admiral Fitzhugh Lee, USN, whose oral history is in the Naval Institute collection.

the Admiral or Mrs. Burke that I thought might sort of set the tone, primarily for me finding out who they were and what they were like. I have to say that I knew Admiral Burke professionally and was aware from his talks and so on, how interested he was in people. But Mrs. Burke came on so thoughtful of you as an individual and so self-effacing that I couldn't believe it was genuine. I really thought, "Well, come on, Mrs. Burke, get off it. Just relax and be yourself and let us do something for you."

Well, it's now just about 30 years later, and she's exactly as serious about that today as she was then. She is thoughtful of you absolutely, thinks nothing of herself. That's just the way she is. And she just is so wonderful to work with, as a result, and you have to assert yourself to even get a chair for her, or else she'll be seating you. Anyhow, I'm sure she contributed a great deal to Admiral Burke's career, and I think Admiral Burke would be the first to tell you that that was true.

The first DesLant party that Trina and I were able to go to when Admiral Burke was the type commander was a Valentine's Day party in 1955. It was being put on at the officers' club. All of the officers and wives of the force had been invited, and Admiral and Mrs. Burke came. Of course, the chief of staff, or whoever was acting master of ceremonies, asked Admiral Burke to make some remarks. He took advantage of that opportunity to say how important he thought families--and particularly wives--were to the Navy, and that the bulk of the career decisions were made because the wives said, "Let it be so." If a wife was dead set against it, there would be no career decision in its favor. He was so persuasive and so wonderful in the way that he addressed the wives and the families, that it went down in my mind as one of those things that I never wanted to forget.

I feel that Mrs. Burke helped sensitize him to that, but I think Admiral Burke was well aware of that as the way that things should be. I think today our whole Navy is a lot more sensitive of wives and families than they were before, and I would give Admiral and Mrs. Burke, on that CNO tour, probably nine-tenths of the credit of giving that kind of emphasis to that aspect of our career lives.

Mrs. Burke said that when she was leaving Newport to go down to that Westchester Apartment, that they had been living in a very nice place here in Newport called the Clock Tower Apartment on Dixon Street. It was really a very lovely spot, and it belonged to one of the big Bellevue Avenue names. They were very happy to be living there. As so often happens, when it came time to leave, she had gotten rid of everything and cleaned everything up thoroughly, but she had these two steaks that looked so beautiful. She didn't have anybody to give them to at the time, because the car was at the door and they were ready to go. So she left the two steaks in the refrigerator for whomever was coming next, and she put a little note on them saying, "Hope you enjoy these."

About two years later she was talking to some friend here in Newport who said, "Oh, Mrs. Burke, I just don't know what went wrong, but I have heard that when you left the apartment, you didn't even clean out the refrigerator."

Mrs. Burke said, "You know, I haven't ever looked that lady in the eye who rented me the apartment. I don't know what she thinks of me at this point." But I thought that was marvelous.

Another one was something that Admiral Burke told me and that I saw demonstrated. Admiral Burke does have a pretty good temper if he lets it get going. If Mrs. Burke felt there was a sensitive point, something where he might lose his temper or where he might be insensitive in his dealing with somebody, she would put a note in the pocket of his uniform. He would be going merrily along, and all of a sudden maybe he'd be bawling you out for something or other, and he'd reach in his pocket and pull out the note, and it would say, "Don't be too hard on him. Remember, you were a JO once," or something like that, and then he would change and be that much more affable. But she knew him well enough, and he would know that she probably had done it, so he'd search his pocket if he felt himself getting mad, to see if she had a note for him on the subject, which

Thomas R. Weschler #3 - 271

I thought was great.

You asked about getting myself indoctrinated and the schedule. I was very unaware in Washington of civil service hours. At 4:30 suddenly the corridors were full of people all dashing to the parking lots. Then all the streets were jammed for an hour or an hour and a half before they opened up again. Well, while we were in this visiting flag office, the admiral wasn't keeping regular hours. Suddenly one afternoon about 4:20, he walked out of the office with his briefcase, ready to go, and I had stuff spread all over the office, and we had a yeoman who was riding with us also, and the yeoman was sitting at the typewriter typing. Admiral Burke said, "I'm ready to go."

I said, "Oh, gee, Admiral, you caught me unawares. I'll be ready in a couple of minutes."

So he said, "I'll give you ten seconds." He walked back in his door and I don't think he gave me more than a minute. We ripped stuff out of typewriters, slammed it into briefcases and we were ready by the time he came out the second time. Well, he really was kind of whizzed about that, and he said, "I want you to know that when I'm ready to go, I want to go. I don't expect to wait for you. Just that one minute, at this crucial time, can cost me 15 minutes or a half hour in the car, and I want to make sure that the aide is assisting me, and me not assisting the aide."

Well, I really learned from then on that whenever I thought he might be ready to go, I sat there with one piece of paper out of the briefcase working on it, and could slam it in when the time came. But he was very used to civil service hours and what was going to happen, and I wasn't even thinking along those lines. There was nothing going on in his particular office at that moment, so he thought, "Let's get home early for a change." He didn't want to see it sandbagged by someone who wasn't ready. So I learned, and from then on, I was ready.

Q: I got the impression, though, that it was much more likely to be the opposite, that he would stay later.

Admiral Weschler: That's right. And he had, up until this one day that he finished early. That's why I stressed this was while he was in the visiting flag office and not in his normal job. Once he became CNO, the hours went on forever and ever.

There is one other story I wanted to tell you about, relayed to me from his driver, Chief Hamilton. It had to do with Quantico again. It was not the '55 one where he got his four stars, but a couple of years later. With the job, there was a huge Chrysler Imperial that was available to the CNO. Usually you went down to Quantico on a Saturday morning, and he didn't want to have the car kicking around there unnecessarily. This day he got the driver and said, "We're going down to Quantico, but it's such a nice day, I want to drive." So Admiral Burke climbed in the front seat, and he said to Hamilton, his chief, "You get in the rear seat. I'll give you the ride down." So down they went and arrived at the gate. The sentry saluted, and Chief Hamilton returned the salute from the back seat. Then they pulled up to the building where the conference was, and a Marine sergeant opened the door and the chief climbed out. Meanwhile, Admiral Burke, who was in shirt sleeves up front, climbed out, put on his four-star uniform, and walked around the car. He said it was worth the price of admission to see the expression. He loved that. Then he sent the car off and had it back later. I thought that was classic Burke.

One other story, just to show personality. Early on, Admiral Burke was always trying to get people to use their initiative and to do things on their own. So he told the captains with whom he was working regularly that he was going to create an award for the fellow who first exercised his initiative or went beyond his authority to such an extent that it was necessary to reprimand him. After he had said this, everyone sort of forgot about it. Then one day he said to me, "Put together a citation. I've got a winner."

I said, "Do I know who it is?"

He said, "It's young Jack McCain. Admiral Duncan has just had him in his office and has bawled him out for grossly exceeding his authority. I think it's appropriate that tomorrow morning I have him here and give him his citation."*

Q: This is Admiral Wu Duncan, the VCNO?

Admiral Weschler: Admiral Wu Duncan, the VCNO, had chewed out Junior McCain, who was then Admiral Burke's Navy propagandist.** He had a special office, whose job was to dramatize the Navy and sell it to the Navy itself and to the Navy League and to congressional committees. So that unlike Chinfo going external, this person was really internal and was getting all the word back and forth with Admiral Burke in order to sell the Navy to itself, and I think the biggest target was Congress.*** Anyhow, that was Jack McCain's job.

The next morning Admiral Burke had his usual meeting of the deputy chiefs and the vice chief after he had met with his aides. When they were all assembled and they'd had the intelligence brief and discussion, then I was

---
*Captain John S. McCain, Jr., USN, was then officially director of the Progress Analysis Group in OpNav. He was also instrumental in developing sea power presentations for public audiences.
**Admiral Donald B. Duncan, USN, Vice Chief of Naval Personnel. Admiral Duncan's oral history is in the Columbia University collection.
***Chinfo--Chief of Information.

called in to read the citation. Jack McCain had been alerted, and he was waiting on the other side of the office. The aide over there, who was Captain Thurston Clark, sent Junior McCain in.* He saw this four- and three-star group sitting there, and then I came in and read the citation, which congratulated him for being the first to have so grossly exceeded authority that he had to be personally upbraided by the Vice Chief. I said that Admiral Burke wanted to shake his hand and let him know we needed more like that. Well, it was wonderful. Wu Duncan was kind of flabbergasted, and all the deputies just really thought it was funny, after they kind of figured out what was going on. Anyhow, it was a lot of fun.

Q: It was kind of a joke on the VCNO more than anybody.

Admiral Weschler: That's right. But, by the same token, it got across the point of what he was trying to do, and all of the captains knew that he was watching. As long as what you were doing was for the good of the Navy, if you stepped on a few toes, that wasn't going to bother Admiral Burke too much. This reminds me of a favorite Burke quote: "You only get your toes stepped on when you're sitting still."

---

*Captain Thurston B. Clark, USN.

Q: How would you characterize the working relationship between Burke and Duncan?

Admiral Weschler: I was just coming to that, because I wanted to mention two other points from these stories. Number one, I really think that it was six months to a year after Admiral Burke became CNO before he stopped standing up every time Admiral Duncan walked into the office. If Admiral Duncan came in, Admiral Burke rose and talked with him until they both sat down to have a cup of coffee or to go over the papers, or Wu would shove him down and hold the papers there and go through what was going on. But that's the way he treated him.

Admiral Duncan had had enough experience around there that he was wonderful for Admiral Burke in those years. He had the rank.* There wasn't any question that he could call up anybody he wanted to, three- or four-star. He had many more years on them, so he was a wonderful bridge to say a lot of things to people that needed saying that Admiral Burke might have been uncomfortable saying. Admiral Duncan was sensitive enough to be able to fill that kind of a role for him.

Also, you know, in Washington, there are an awful lot of ideas that every time you get a new boss, all these old

---
*Duncan was in the class of 1917 at the Naval Academy, six years ahead of Burke. He had been a four-star admiral since 1951, four years earlier than Burke.

papers surface and come sailing up to the front office. "Why don't you turn the Pentagon 90 degrees on its axis?" kind of thing. Wu had a drawer and when one of those arrived, it would go down in Wu Duncan's drawer, and it stayed there unless Admiral Burke himself asked to see the piece of paper. Then Wu would reach down and bring it out. Otherwise, he just sat on more dumb ideas, or old ideas, or controversial ideas, that he thought were going to interfere with getting on with the Navy. So he was a wonderful counterpoint, and I think the two of them developed a very fine relationship and got along very well in the job.

Q: Do you have any more stories?

Admiral Weschler: Let me see if I have any more. Yes, this is, again, educating young aides, which was for me. Shortly after Admiral Burke was CNO, I got a call from a flag officer. I'm not sure who it was, but I think it was Admiral Will, who was deputy commander of the Military Sea Transportation Service.* He was very highly thought of by Admiral Burke, and Admiral Burke had been asking some questions. Admiral Will was coming through with some step in the process of answering what Admiral Burke wanted. I got the call from Admiral Will, and it implied that certain

---

*Rear Admiral John M. Will, USN.

things still had to be done. I held the message for Admiral Burke. When Admiral Burke came in, I told him that I had talked with Admiral Will and that this was the situation, and now what did he, Admiral Burke, want to do?

He said, "Tom, that's the only time I'm going to take a message like that from you. You know as well as I do that I would go to X." (Who X was, it doesn't matter at this point, but he would have gone to one of his deputies) and would have said, "Follow up on this for me." Then that deputy might very well have come up with some sort of an answer, which might have been sufficient for Admiral Burke or might have implied that he had to do something and he could get back to me. He said, "Now, you're perfectly capable of doing things like that. That's what you're sitting out there for, is to save my time. Now, let's just make sure you get the word, and that this is the only time I ever mention it."

So I tell you, I got the word. From then on, I didn't hesitate to call anybody that I thought that Admiral Burke would have called, regardless of rank. I told them that Admiral Burke was busy but needed this kind of information, this is what we had to date, and I'd appreciate a memo or something in a reasonable time frame, usually defined, so that he could take action on it and finish it when he got back from wherever he was. That was great.

Q: Would it be fair to say that your job was mainly managing the flow of paper and the visitors?

Admiral Weschler: No. I want to separate it. Admiral Burke always had two aides as CNO. The one was the senior aide, who handled the professional side of the office, what we now call an executive assistant. Then the junior aide handled the personal, social, and the travel side of the office. After he had been in the office a bit, in addition to myself as a personal aide, he also had a Marine Corps aide, a lieutenant colonel. The lieutenant colonel and the commander alternated in going on trips, and both helped out with the social affairs that were going on, ran the mess, and took care of the quarters and those sorts of things. So that was really the split. But even though we were on the personal side, he included us in many of his discussions and relationships with people. He wanted us never to forget that we were professionals first and involved in personal dealings second. Those personal dealings were supposed to be professional in nature, and he didn't want to treat us as though we were flunkies who would do really personal service for him. He was quite careful on that kind of a distinction.

Q: Who did take care of the personal services, then? There are bound to be the flunky-type jobs.

Admiral Weschler: Yes, there are. He tried to prevent them being done for him, but he had a remarkable chief yeoman, who later became warrant officer, Madeline Corsiglia.* She had been in the CNO's office, I would say, for probably four or five years before Admiral Burke came to the job, and she stayed in the office certainly through his six years. I don't remember whether she stayed on after that or not, but she has since retired in Washington. Admiral Burke thought most highly of her, and I think she retired as a W-3, after her tour there. But Madeleine was one who enjoyed getting a cup of coffee for the boss. She knew that Admiral Burke had a fondness for these little candies called "turtles." They're a sort of a chocolate and caramel and nut kind of thing, and she would keep a couple of those in the drawer. He limited her to one a day, and he said, "Find the blackest point of the day," and then she'd walk in to give him the turtle. She'd say at least she got one smile out of him, something like that. She helped.

He also had a wonderful chief steward, who was directly across the passageway, connected with the CNO mess, and he would come in to do some things. But he was not one who was demanding in personal relationships and tried to keep you out of personal care. But yes, everybody

---
*Chief Yeoman Madeline F. Corsiglia, USN.

could get in the act if necessary.

I have two quick stories, if I may, on that subject. In April of 1956, Admiral Burke had become a great friend of Commodore Robins, who was the head of the Belgian Navy.* In connection with the swing to visit NATO in Europe in '56, Commodore Robins said, "You've got to give me a week. I want to get you down to the Belgian Congo, because I think that the Belgian Congo is vital. I think that Belgium may need some help in connection with antisubmarine warfare and mine warfare, so you ought to be familiar with our facilities."

So Admiral Burke said that sounded wonderful, and he would see if he couldn't make it so. So yes, we did. We did the trip over there. We went to Belgium, we picked up Commodore Robins and his wife, and we flew down to the Belgian Congo, and we visited in Leopoldville. In connection with the visit, there was this outlying Belgian Air Force base, in Katanga Province. I think the base was called Katadi, which is about as remote in Africa as you can get. We arrived about 4:00 o'clock, and it had been a terribly hot day. Admiral and Mrs. Burke went to their quarters, and we were going to give them about a 15-minute rest before they had to go to a reception at 4:30. When Admiral Burke got there, he hauled out a pair of white service trousers, and there was this servant assigned to do

---
*Commodore L. J. J. Robins, Chief of Naval Staff, Belgian Navy.

any touch-up with an iron that might be needed. So he took Admiral Burke's trousers and disappeared. Well, I didn't know any of this. I was somewhere else waiting for Admiral and Mrs. Burke to show up at the appointed hour at this reception, and I had scouted where the reception was and knew what was to go on. It was about five minutes to go when I saw Mrs. Burke running around. I said, "Mrs. Burke, can I help you?"

She said, "You won't believe it, but we've lost Arleigh's pants." There just aren't that many more pair of white service pants that would fit him that were available up in Katadi, with a reception in five minutes. I found another man and I asked him where this fellow might have taken the pants to press them. He pointed me to a room, and I got over there, and the gentleman in question hadn't realized the urgency. As soon as I said it, he got up and did a press job, and I got them back to Admiral Burke within a few minutes. But it's just one of those memories of seeing Mrs. Burke scurrying around saying, "Arleigh's lost his pants."

The other one that I wanted to mention occurred after I had left the aide job, but Colonel Walt Cornnell, who was the second Marine aide in Admiral Burke's tour, was with him in Yokosuka.* Admiral Burke was preparing to call on the Emperor, and so they had left Yokosuka and had driven

---

*Colonel Walter F. Cornnell, USMC.

up to the Sanno Hotel in Tokyo, the one that the armed forces had. Admiral Burke had a room assigned him, so he and Mrs. Burke could freshen up just before they went to call on the Emperor. They'd had the drive up in khakis and he shifted to whites while he was there in the room. Everything was set. Let's say it was 1425, and at 1430 the entourage was going to head off for the palace. At 1425, Walt Cornnell walked in to see the admiral and said, "Is everything set? We're due to leave in five minutes."

Admiral Burke said, "Yes." He reached for his hat and as he did so, they saw that it had a khaki cap cover and he didn't have a white cap cover, with him.

The only other person along was Vice Admiral Ralph Wilson, who was OP-04, so Walt ran down there and knocked on the door. There was Admiral Wilson all set to go. He said, "Admiral Wilson, what size hat do you wear?"

Admiral Wilson said, "Seven and a quarter."

Walt said, "Admiral Burke's cap only has a khaki cap cover on it. Can I borrow yours?"

Admiral Wilson said, "I plan on calling on the Emperor, but watch this." He opened his case, and he had a brand-new cap in there with a white cap cover in size seven and a quarter, which was exactly what Admiral Burke needed.

Walt ran back to him and handed it to him as though planned, and they went off in the car. Admiral Burke heard about the story as he drove out in the limousine, and when he came back, he said, "Walt, I'm half-serious. I want you to send out a message to the fleet that says that from now on the only people promoted to admiral will have head size seven and a quarter." Anyhow, they avoided that catastrophe. Admiral Wilson said he'd done that all of his professional life, that he had always carried a spare cap with him. Can you believe it? Maybe he means when he was selected for flag, but, boy, it sure put out the fire then.

Q: What other kinds of social events did you get involved in where you had an active role?

Admiral Weschler: There was practically nothing that went on in the quarters that didn't involve us. Admiral and Mrs. Burke were busy enough, just going to all the things they got invited to, so they had very little time for planning things themselves. So I usually would have to reach Mrs. Burke in the morning early to get her ideas for a party, what she wanted, and then I'd take over to get all of the tables set and paraphernalia. Initially, they didn't know what was available at the quarters, and if they wanted to have a seated dinner for a large number, I had to arrange to borrow or bring in the materials to do it.

I learned a great deal about protocol from Admiral Burke. I don't think he enjoyed teaching me, but I needed it. He said to me early on, "Now, the first thing I really want to do is have a party for the secretariat, for the Secretary of the Navy and the assistants. The only time I can see available is either this day or that day."

Well, I got back and I doped off on it. I didn't do anything for, say, a week after he told me he wanted it. Suddenly I realized that I'd lost a week and that I really better get on the step. So I called around. I couldn't get any immediate answers from any of the secretariat or the assistants. I got the word out to all the aides, but I couldn't get an immediate answer, and the only one who came back and said that he could come for sure was the general counsel. So Admiral Burke then, sure enough, that afternoon, asked me what was going on, and I said I had gotten each of the aides notified but I was late in doing so, and the only positive answer I had is that the general counsel could come.

He said, "Tom, I don't care if the general counsel never comes. He's not one of the assistant secretaries; he is not one of the principals of what we are doing. I want you to know that when I'm talking about the secretariat, it starts with the Secretary and certainly includes the Under Secretary, then as many of the assistants as can make it. But I don't care about some of the professionals who are helping them out in their job." I learned that. I began to develop. He then introduced me to the <u>Washington Green</u>

Book. I don't know if you're familiar with that, but it's like the New York Social Register, and in the Green Book it has everybody listed by hierarchy--precedence within the government, and then an interlacing of religious and foreign and social for seating purposes. I got very familiar with the Green Book. That solved a lot of problems for an outlander who suddenly had been brought into the Washington scene.

Q: You talked briefly about his relationship with Secretary Thomas. Anything more on that to discuss?

Admiral Weschler: Yes. I think that was interesting to watch. Now, some of this I learned later on. I don't know exactly when Admiral Burke told me or shared with me some of his views, but Secretary Thomas, as I say, was determined to have Admiral Burke as the CNO once he had made his selection. So Admiral Burke had been to see him before the announcement, and even before Admiral Carney, perhaps, had been aware that Admiral Burke was going to be in the running. Admiral Burke told the Secretary that since he had just had a cruiser division and then the type command, that he was missing some of the most rewarding and professionally enhancing experiences that an officer could have in order to be a good CNO. He said that he would like to take his turn at being Sixth Fleet Commander and an ocean fleet commander, if that were in the cards, before he became CNO, because he thought he'd be that much better as CNO.

Secretary Thomas was adamant. He said, "I know what the Navy needs. You have to trust my judgment. You're going to be the one I nominate, and unless you turn me down cold and say you won't serve, you're going to be the one I put up for it."

So Admiral Burke said, "I hope that you will approve my talking this over now with Admiral Carney so that I have Admiral Carney's awareness and support if this is the way it's going to be."

Secretary Thomas said, "Okay, if that's what you feel you should do, by all means, go talk with him."

So he did go down then and see Admiral Carney and tell him about it. He was the only one, really, that Admiral Burke had discussed it with before things moved along to where he talked with Admiral Wright just before the announcement.

Then as he worked with Secretary Thomas, I think one of the greatest challenges that he had was to respond to Secretary Thomas's desire for initiatives and still preserve the initiatives as coming from the uniformed forces. In other words, he didn't want the Secretary to be telling him, "This is my initiative, Arleigh. Now you do it." It had to be an initiative that Arleigh thought was good for the Navy and that then he could spearhead with Secretary Thomas's approval.

That became particularly touchy in connection with flag assignments. Secretary Thomas was frequently pushing for such and such an officer to be given this job, and Admiral Burke would say, "It's up to me, the uniformed Navy, to nominate to you, Mr. Secretary, whom we think would be good in a particular job. If possible, I'll give you a range of choices so you can take your pick of the range of choices that I offer. But the picks have to come from me to you, and then you can take your choice. But I don't want to have you making the selections. I think that would ruin the whole hierarchy and the authority of the CNO if someone else would be making the appointments." He found that one a very sticky and continuing problem in his relationships with the Secretary, and I think this is one where he probably worked hardest to keep his cool and to be persuasive and try to get his point of view across.

That reminds me of another thing about Admiral Burke that I think you would enjoy. In addition to the Secretary and Under Secretary and, let's say, the three assistant secretaries of the Navy--there might have been more--there was also SecDef and Deputy SecDef and all those assistant SecDefs, and every one of them has a flag.*

So Admiral Burke had this absentee board made up that

_____
*SecDef--Secretary of Defense.

had the flags of the Secretary and all of the assistant secretaries of the Navy and the Secretary and all of the assistant secretaries of Defense. He put it on the console directly across from his desk. When he looked up across the office, he could see the console and then this ream of flags. It was up to the aide to keep the flags turned for whether they were in town or out of town. Now, he really didn't give a damn about their presence or absence after a couple of days, but the big reason for that being there was to remind himself that there were 17 people who could say no for no reason at all, and it took all 17 people saying yes before anything could get done. He said, "It just helps me keep my perspective about how much authority I really have and what it takes to get things accomplished in Washington." So he passed those along with suitable fanfare when he got relieved: "There's an education over there for you, and pay attention to it."

Q: What about his relationship with Secretary Gates?*

Admiral Weschler: I'm going to divert for one other story while I'm at this point, because it's, I think, more on the human side of Admiral Burke.

When he took over the office, I forget what was

---

*Thomas S. Gates, Jr., was Secretary of the Navy from April 1957 to June 1959. A naval reservist In World War II, he served at sea as an air combat intelligence officer.

hanging on the wall behind him, but in the office was a wonderful portrait of what looked like a burly petty officer from the old Navy, probably the early 19th century. When he looked at this picture, he said, "Tom, I think that sailor would chew me out without hesitation if ever he thought I was wrong. Put him over here right behind me so that I'll know that he is looking over my shoulder all the time. I think it'll make me do a little better job." And so he did. For the whole time he was there, he had this burly sailor, a fine painting, looking down at him at his desk.

I think his relationship with Secretary Gates was marvelous. First of all, Secretary Thomas was a short man and, as is often the case with some short men, he was a little sensitive. He was also quick-tempered and strong-willed. When you put those words together, you've got a person that's a little hard to deal with, and yet Admiral Burke was his choice, so he really had to put up with him. Well, the two of them developed a lot of mutual respect, and they got along despite some pushing and hauling. With Tom Gates, I think there was a lot more spontaneous respect. Secretary Gates had been in the armed forces, had been in the Navy at one time. He was a big, tall man, very easy-going, very secure in his own person, and very interested in hearing other points of view; I think he found it stimulating. As a result, the relationship was just night and day between Secretary Thomas and Secretary Gates.

Then a personal rapport developed between the two. I think they both enjoyed each other's company, and then you may recall that Mr. Gates had that terrible tragedy in which his son was lost in a ski lodge fire. I think Admiral Burke was one who was most helpful to him during that period, and after that, I think, the two of them could have been inseparable, they got along that well. They could tell each other anything that had to be done professionally or whatever. It was rare the way that their relationship developed.

Q: I've gathered that Secretary Gates really did his homework. He knew a lot more substantively about the Navy than most Secretaries.

Admiral Weschler: No question. I think this is where Admiral Burke would have been good with him, because he really wanted to know. He wasn't trying to tell him how to do it. He really wanted to know so that he could represent it fairly, and so that when he said yes to a decision, that he intellectually was satisfied that he understood it. When he went forward as Secretary of Defense, I think he took a wonderful understanding of the Navy with him. This is why I think the Navy was more willing to go along with

Mr. Gates as SecDef when he began to consolidate some things than they might have been with somebody else. They knew Mr. Gates knew where he was coming from, whereas some of the others, like Mr. Wilson, they would have been up in arms about it, thinking he didn't know what was going on.

Q: How much of an operational role did Admiral Burke have up until 1958 when the new Defense Reorganization Act came in?

Admiral Weschler: Admiral Burke had been really the Chief of Naval Operations up until that time in the old sense of the word, with the fleet commanders meeting with him regularly and getting all of their instructions and war planning going on and all that sort of thing. The role of the unified commanders was a lot less well understood and not as thoroughly supported in those years as it is now, when they report directly to SecDef. So the contingencies of the world really came right to CNO's desk, and it was necessary for him to be available, to have his intelligence briefings frequently, to keep up to date with a lot of message traffic around the world. Now, that's where the professional side of the office was a lot more involved than the personal. Nonetheless, a lot of our trips were planned with the idea of getting him to the right place at the right time so that he could be influential in helping the fleet commanders and seeing their subordinates when they were assembled for various fleet conferences.

Q: Who was running that professional side of the office?

Admiral Weschler: It was Thurston Clark, Ralph Shifley, Bill Martin.* I think that's the order in which they came in, all three aviators. It was sort of understood that the senior aide would be an aviator, so that the aviation side of the house was satisfied that their point of view was getting across to the CNO, who was a blackshoe. And, of course, Wu Duncan was an aviator, which was also part of the pattern that we're seeing today.

Q: Did you get involved in those operations at all? Were you called in for your point of view?

Admiral Weschler: Not professionally, no. I got in on things, simply because I might be around when things were happening. I have the feeling that Admiral Burke, after I had been with him for about a year or a year and a half, used me as a sounding board or would tell me things that he didn't tell others. I was with him a great deal. If he stayed late, he might secure the other side of the office,

---
*Captain Thurston B. Clark, USN; Captain Ralph L. Shifley, USN; Captain William I. Martin, USN. Martin has been interviewed as part of the Naval Institute's oral history program.

but Madeline Corsiglia and I were usually there until midnight or 1:00 o'clock, whatever it was. If he was around, we were there. So I think he used to tell me things that would be on his mind and speculate on certain things. But no, I was not in on things in any sort of a regular way unless I just by happenstance was in the conference when the item came up and might have a point of view to offer.

Q: How typical was midnight or 1:00 o'clock in the morning?

Admiral Weschler: We used to pray for big parties, because then he'd go home at 7:00. Mrs. Burke insisted that there be two nights a week when he could come home "early," which meant he'd go home at 10:00. Once in a while he would work until midnight or 1:00 o'clock. I'd say that the 10:00 o'clock was routine, at least once or twice a week, but something approaching midnight or later was about once in six months or a year, just enough that you could say it.

Q: How early did these days start?

Admiral Weschler: He always came in the office between 7:15 and 7:30. The aides were always there by 7:00, so that we had a chance to get the message traffic, have skimmed it, learn if there were any emergencies, anything that was going to upset the basic beginning of the day. The traffic had been put together earlier by one of the night duty officers into a folder which went out in the car to Admiral Burke at the quarters. That meant he could leaf through the principal traffic and read the notes from the duty officer through the night, as he came to the Pentagon. When he hit there, if there was no real emergency, then he had another half hour, let's say, before his day began.

At usually a few minutes before 8:00, he'd brief the aides on what was on his mind, anything to change the order of the day or the week, or a trip that he thought he'd better now decide to do or to cancel as a result of something, and then he'd finish with us in about ten minutes. By that time the deputies and the Vice Chief came in, and he had a regular formal briefing and ran over with them what was hot. And then the day was on. Usually he had appointments that went continuously until about 5:00 o'clock. Maybe there would be a half hour unscheduled in the course of a day--so much of it JCS and visits to the Secretary or to the secretariat all over the building. Then by 5:00 o'clock he could settle down and do what he had to do, and that's where the aide got into the act again. I was responding to the leadership of the day as to what was red hot, burning through on his desk that he had to get to right away, for whatever reason, and then just let him work at his desk until he was done.

Q: Was it up to you to keep that flow of visitors moving?

Admiral Weschler: Yes. The visitors were pretty much ours. You had to exercise your own judgment in that to some extent, although we had developed a sort of by-play. If someone was in there, he would buzz me and say, "Did the Secretary send for me yet?"

Then I'd say, "Yes, Admiral, I was just coming in to tell you that the Secretary wanted to see you."

He'd say, "Thank you very much. Well, I have to break off." He'd walk out and go into the head on the other side of his office. The visitor would come out, then Admiral Burke would come back in again when the coast was clear.

If I thought a visitor was going overly long and the admiral hadn't done it, but I still thought there were some golden moments slipping away, I used to go in and just say, "Admiral, I wanted to remind you that so and so had asked you to call."

"Oh, yes, I'd forgotten about that." Then he'd know I was putting the heat on him to get moving and that he'd better not have that other cup of coffee or tell that other story. So that was sort of interesting. There were a couple who really he would develop a heave-ho technique for. When I got a bunch of rapid buzzers, I knew that I'd better invent something like an earthquake had just happened in order to move this gent along, because Admiral Burke was going to lose his temper if I didn't get the guest out of there in a few seconds. There were a few like that that required some delicate handling.

Pretty soon you knew that certain ones would never get in the office if you could possibly maneuver it. I'd clear that with him, saying, "Admiral, I have a hunch that so and so is coming by today. This is what my plan of action for him is."

He'd say, "Sounds great. Sounds great. I'll be away until after that happens," or something like that. Then I could steer whoever it was out and take him over to see somebody else, and say, "The admiral asked me particularly to have you visit so and so." I had lined it up with that individual to say the admiral was busy, but he was happy to fill in for him. That sort of thing.

Q: On the other hand, were there people that he would drop everything to see if they wanted to see him?

Admiral Weschler: That's right. He really felt that way about the staff. As a matter of fact, that was one of the things that I had to watch. I had to make sure that some of these people who were working hard for him didn't sort of share all their troubles with him. I had to make sure they got in and got out, so I gave them the word before they went in, "Five minutes. That's all. You've got to get in and get out." If they didn't, I didn't hesitate to walk in and say, "Admiral, your next appointment is here." And they knew. Because now I had perhaps six guys lined up, each with a crash mission. Then the other side of the office would be having some crashes of its own, so that's when we really used to pump people through there, and we'd try to keep each other coordinated and move it along. He responded pretty well to this kind of control which we were exercising. He knew it was for his own good, but every so often he'd really blow up. You could see it coming. You could just feel him tensing in the chair, and then you knew you were going to get it for having just given a little too much steer on a particular thing.

Q: Admiral Peet said he was a difficult man to work for because sometimes he'd lash out at you. You wouldn't really deserve it, but you were just there.

Admiral Weschler: You were the one. You were the one. At the end of the day, he'd be tired and there wasn't anybody else around but you to take it. He didn't mind opening up and telling you. The next morning he might say, "I hope that didn't bother you too much last night."

I could say, "No, I knew how tired you were. I sort of felt it coming," or something like that. But, as I say, I thoroughly enjoyed working with him because he was such a brain, and I don't know how he did all he did. He knew everybody in the Pentagon in some official way, so that his relationships came from a matter of depth. He was not surprised by what people were doing or where they were coming from. On those things like the Joint Staff reorganization, he had done so much work back there in the days of the B-36 controversy on how the JCS ought to be organized, that he had a breadth of feel for it. I think very few in Washington were his equal. He could vocalize it. Admiral Burke was not a good speaker, as you know, but in a man-to-man situation, talking directly to people around the conference table, he was so persuasive and so on the ball, that it was just wonderful to really share things with him.

Q: How much of a life of your own could you have under those circumstances?

Admiral Weschler: Not an awful lot. I was out by 7:00 A.M. and would get home at 7:00 at night or later, so my wife and I would often have a couple of hours after dinner. Sometimes we went to the parties. Sometimes leaving the office at 7:00 was because we'd all be on deck at the quarters for two or three hours for the reception that was coming up. But he really wanted you to take leave if you felt you wanted to go. I have to tell you, that November of '55, that first year I was with him, I put in for leave over Thanksgiving.

My wife and I are both from Erie, Pennsylvania. My mother had been down visiting, so we drove my mother home and had my wife and the two children in the car. As we started towards Erie, it began to snow, and as we drove closer and closer, the snow increased. I realized how bad it was because about 15 miles from Erie, I couldn't see the edges of the road, and there weren't any other cars around. I just had the car in the center of the road, keeping it centered by the telegraph poles on either side, and driving as though through a field of snow. I got within about a block of my wife's house, where we were going to stay. As I turned a corner, the car slid into the curb, and it stayed there for about a week.

That was the first that my mother, who ordinarily is scared to death in a car, realized that we were in a blizzard. We were the last car, as far as I could tell, to get to Erie, and we got to my wife's folks' house, and there were about 40 of us assembled for Thanksgiving dinner. The last person left there that Sunday night. I was due to start back to Washington on Monday. I wired back Sunday that I didn't anticipate being able to get out of town before Tuesday, and Admiral Burke sent back a message, something to the effect of, "We miss you in Washington, but we recognize a clever maneuver when we hear of one. Let us know when the ice breaks. Good luck." Or something like that. So he really wasn't fussed about it at all.

The Marine aide was backing me up while I was gone, and fortunately it was Thanksgiving, and the Army-Navy game was that same weekend, which usually tended to be a relaxed Washington weekend. So until that Monday or Tuesday, it hadn't been too bad. The long answer is that there wasn't much family life, but you could get leave, and on the leaves you could sort of make up for it and relax.

Q: Did you ever go along with him when he went on JCS business?

Admiral Weschler: No. Never. He had an aide particularly for JCS matters, Johnny Ferriter, out of '38.* And Vice Admiral Ruthven Libby was his OP-06 and was lead shop on JCS.** I'll tell you, that Admiral Libby was sharp; if Admiral Burke didn't know it, Admiral Libby did. Between the two of them, no one was putting anything over on the Navy in those days.

---
*Commander John B. Ferriter, USN.
**Vice Admiral Ruthven E. Libby, USN, Deputy Chief of Naval Operations (Plans and Policies). Admiral Libby's oral history is in the Naval Institute collection.

Thomas R. Weschler #3 - 302

I did have one comment here when we were talking about JCS. You may recall that Admiral Radford was chairman when Admiral Burke took over.* Admiral Burke used to buzz me once in a while when he was fed up with what was going on. The Chairman of the JCS has a phone which goes to each of the chiefs of service, and I would hear the phone buzz and see Admiral Burke whip around and answer it and talk to Raddy. This would go on for five minutes or so, and often he'd slam that thing down and buzz for me, and he would say, "I just don't know what to do. Admiral Radford's my own service. He leans over so far backwards, I think he's lost his balance." Admiral Radford did want to be even-handed, but that was sort of the perception that Admiral Burke would get. It really used to bug him.

Q: Did you see his relationship with President Eisenhower at all?

Admiral Weschler: No. I did make one comment there that I had also jotted down. I did go over to the White House twice with Admiral Burke when he was going over for some White House ceremonies when they were going to present something. So I did have a chance to meet President Eisenhower in the White House.** In fact, I almost

---
*Admiral Arthur W. Radford, USN, Chairman of the Joint Chiefs of Staff, 1953-57.
**Dwight D. Eisenhower was President from 1953 to 1961.

slammed the door on him one time! You know how that can happen with a lot of people moving around, and suddenly there was the President coming through the door that I had started to close. But you know President Eisenhower asked Admiral Burke to stay on for his third term as CNO--his fifth and sixth years--so that President Eisenhower wouldn't have a new CNO break in on his watch. When I had heard the speculation, I thought, well, Admiral Burke isn't going to accept it, but he did. Perhaps 10 or 15 years later, I said to him, "I really was surprised at that, Admiral, that you accepted. My reading was that you were going to say no."

He said, "Tom, you simply can't say no to the President of the United States if he asks you to do something. In retrospect, of all the decisions of my six years in office, the one basic decision that I would change if I were offered the opportunity now, would be that one. I would not have served those additional two years. I think four is plenty, and I think the task of leadership in the Navy is so great and the demands of the office are so much, that I think in four years a person has contributed everything he's going to contribute, and after that, it's time for somebody new." And he said, "I still feel that way." I think of that when we talk about Admiral Gorshkov and his 20-some years in command of the Soviet Navy, and

Admiral Burke's perception that there is strength in diversity.*

Q: I heard exactly an opposing point of view. Someone said that our Navy would be in much better shape if Admiral Burke had been CNO as long as Gorshkov was of the Soviet Navy.

Admiral Weschler: I think I would share a little bit more of that point of view because of my respect and admiration for him, but I have quoted Admiral Burke, which is what I think is more important.

A couple of things also that I think of. You asked if I had been in on some of his major decisions, JCS and otherwise, and I indicated basically it was personal. But there are two events that I was aware of that might be of interest. One was in July of '55, when he was still CNO designate. There was a commander, and I can't think of the young man's name, somebody who was a great friend of Admiral Burke's. He was a guiding light and stimulant and full of ideas, not George Miller, but somebody else, a young aviator. He came to Admiral Burke and said, "Admiral, you've got to get time to get up to GE, Syracuse, New York. They've got a great idea that you've got to hear."

---
*Admiral of the Fleet of the Soviet Union Sergei G. Gorshkov served as head of the Soviet Navy from the 1950s to the early 1980s.

So he came with us, and Admiral Burke and myself and X--and I wish I could tell you who he is--flew up to Syracuse and went to GE Heavy Military. When we got there, there was quite an assemblage of GE personalities, the senior of whom was the head of this military electronics department. They told him, "Admiral Burke, we have you here because we want to present to you the idea of the fleet ballistic missile. We think this is so fundamental, you have to think in terms of this vein. Carrier aviation is wonderful, but there are other ways of delivering a major punch, and we think that the fleet ballistic missile is the way to go. It can be launched from a ship, a carrier deck to supplement the air group, or it can be launched in a cruiser. We frankly haven't studied the submarine, but perhaps it can be launched from a submarine."

That was the first time I had ever heard of the fleet ballistic missile. I couldn't tell whether Admiral Burke had ever heard about it before, but, of course, the missile business was being talked up at that time. The big thing was that they were talking in terms of a solid fueled missile, whereas all the other work was being done with the liquid fuel missiles, and most of the Navy's overtures up till then had been in this area. The possibilities of accuracy had not been addressed, and GE had a good feel for that, talked about the inertial guidance systems and the things that were possible in that area. They considered an idea of payload, if nonnuclear, what it could have done, and the accuracy and some general parameters. Well, I thought that was very interesting, because Admiral Burke really was looking for a new initiative.

One other thing that Admiral Burke said very early on when he became CNO was, "Tom, I've been around Washington enough to know that if I don't start everything that I want to do in the first six months, it'll never be accomplished on my watch." In those days he was thinking of a two-year tour, which is all the CNOs were appointed for, and having looked back at Admiral Carney, etc., two years looked like all that he could reasonably hope to get, particularly when he was having all these strains with Secretary Thomas. So he said, "If I don't start it in six months, it'll never be done." So he was thinking nuclear-powered submarines, he was thinking the fleet ballistic missile, and he was determined to get more aircraft carriers. You remember that we had lost the United States, and he was determined to get a program going.* So that's where his efforts were directed, the Forrestal class, the whole Polaris program push, the fleet ballistic missile, and nuclear submarines. Then he was working very hard on missiles in

---

*In a real blow to postwar naval aviation, Johnson directed the end of construction of the super carrier United States (CVA-58) on 23 April 1949, five days after her keel-laying.

addition. You remember Canberra and Boston, the first of our guided missile cruisers, came on his watch, and he had Admiral Savvy Sides there working in this area.*

Early on, he was looking for some sort of a souvenir to give away when he made these trips as the CNO designate. He felt badly that he didn't have anything to leave behind, but as CNO designate, people could understand that he wasn't yet in the driver's seat. He said, "I'm not going to make another trip without it." So he said, "I want you to get me something that will show continuity but also let them know of the new things that are coming."

One of Admiral Burke's treasures was a capstan-shaped 1898 tobacco humidor from the Spanish-American War. You know he smoked a pipe and used this humidor constantly. I looked at that and said, "Admiral, there's what I'm going to get you. I'll get you some capstan-shaped humidors, and we'll put on the sides of it the new Navy that you're working on."

He said, "Sounds like a good idea." So I worked with Fitz Lee over in Japan, and we had these humidors made up that had the four stars, an anchor in blue and gold on the top, and then had the Polaris submarine and the Forrestal aircraft carrier. It had the carrier on one side and the submarine on the other, and then it was capstan-shaped to show continuity, done in blue and gold. Well, he liked

---
*Rear Admiral John H. Sides, USN.

that, so that typified his first months in office, and he was happy to have it.

Q: Where did Regulus fit in with all that?

Admiral Weschler: That's, I think, one of the toughest decisions of his watch, and I would say, in retrospect, was probably an unfortunate decision on his watch. Admiral Sides was working hard on the three T's, on Regulus I and II, and then on a new missile they called Triton.* Triton was going to be a longer range, heavier warhead missile, more reminiscent of Tomahawk than Regulus.** One of the prices of the Navy getting the Polaris missile and the whole submarine program was that we had to take the cost out of the Navy's hide.

Admiral Burke didn't like that, and he tried hard to get some additional appropriations, but he felt that it was essential that the Navy be in the strategic missile program, and so if he had to put up Navy money in order to do it, he was willing to. So we bought the Polaris program out of the Navy budget. As that squeeze came on in '57 and '58, Admiral Sides's big question was, "What do I drop in order to keep some program going and not drive all ships

---
*The three T's were ship-launched surface-to-air missiles: Tartar, Talos, and Terrier. Regulus I and Regulus II were ship-launched cruise missiles.
**Tomahawk is a long-range cruise missile for use against either land or sea targets. It entered the fleet in the early 1980s.

out of the Navy budget?" So Regulus got canceled as part of the squeeze, as being duplicative of what the new attack aircraft were able to do. The reasoning was that people would rather have a smart aircraft with a dumb bomb than to have a smart missile. At that time we still had quite a few aircraft carriers and quite a few aircraft. We were getting a lot of missiles in the Polaris program and we just didn't seem to have funds for Regulus.

As you recall, we were still working on the AJ aircraft in those days in order to have a strategic attack capability from the carrier. We simply had so many programs, something had to go, and the Regulus was it. We kept the emphasis on the air defense aspect of the three T's, because we didn't have anything that could duplicate that. That was absolutely essential. Triton, which was still in, fell of its own weight. It just got too expensive and not productive. It didn't have enough warhead to be worth all the expense that was going into it. And so with Regulus canceled and Triton becoming too expensive and pricing itself out of the market, we lost almost ten years in the ship-to-ship or cruise missile business.

Q: Another casualty of that crunch was the jet-powered seaplane.

Admiral Weschler: To an extent. Did you know that Admiral Burke was behind the P6M all the way?* There were two things which he and Admiral Mountbatten did.** (Incidentally, that was a wonderful marriage. To have Admiral Mountbatten as First Sea Lord at the same time Admiral Burke was CNO, was a remarkable coincidence. The two couples got along remarkably well.) I went with Admirals Burke and Mountbatten when they went down to Key West and rode the Albacore.*** The Albacore was the first of the whale-shaped submarines, and to see Admiral Burke and Admiral Mountbatten at the diving planes, steering this thing and diving, they were just like two kids with a roller coaster. It was a wonderful concept and got Admiral Mountbatten's attention.

The P6M was the second item and something they were both very keen on. They had been to Baltimore the week before that aircraft's fatal crash, had been there and had been taken on a high-speed taxi.**** They had a very good

---

*Prototypes of the P6M Seamaster jet-powered seaplane were developed and tested by the Glenn L. Martin Company, but the aircraft was never put into mass production.
**Admiral of the Fleet Lord Louis Mountbatten, RN.
***The USS Albacore (AGSS-569) was a conventionally powered submarine commissioned in December 1953 to test the feasibility of a submarine hull designed primarily for underwater operation. Until then the hulls for submarines were designed for optimum operation on the surface. The Albacore-type hull shape was subsequently used in U.S. nuclear-powered submarines.
****During a test on 7 December 1955 a P6M prototype exploded at an altitude of 5,000 feet and crashed in the Chesapeake Bay near the Potomac River mouth.

impression of the plane and were very strong on it. Then, you know, a week later the plane had that tail flutter and crashed. Since the plane had already been running way over budget and over schedule, the program was canceled as just being too expensive.

I think it's significant that one of the pushes at that time--and this is Junior McCain as much as anybody, but I think Admirals Burke and Mountbatten shared it--was that with the British pulling out of the Middle East, there had to be some sort of a presence in the Indian Ocean. The presence that seemed most compatible with the dollars and the time frame and the sensitivity of the area was to put a seaplane tender there with some sea-based aircraft. The P6M was being developed with that concept of a fleet in the Indian Ocean in mind. I think Admiral Burke hated to see it disappear, because it was a strategic deployment that he felt was essential and we didn't really have anything to take its place.

Q: Do you have any other memories of Mountbatten and Burke together?

Admiral Weschler: I'll try to think of any. That was the one trip I took with them. I was privileged to be Admiral Mountbatten's guest at dinner one time. Admiral Burke had gone over to England. To give you an idea of how Admiral Mountbatten really wanted to have him well received, he had arranged that he was received by the Queen. He also called at Number 10 Downing Street, and he had a lot of briefings at Whitehall. Then Admiral Mountbatten had a wonderful dinner party for him, a stag dinner at his townhouse. I got in on that because one of the guests at the last minute dropped out, and Admiral Mountbatten said, "Aides are lucky people on occasion. And you, young man, if you'd like to, I'd be happy to have you on my left." So I sat on Admiral Mountbatten's left for the dinner party that evening. I think Admiral Mountbatten shared the belief that Admiral Burke was a great man, and that's why he made sure he saw all of the hierarchy in London and sort of personally lined up everything for him to be sure he was well received.

Q: Was CinCNELM included in this gathering?*

Admiral Weschler: No, he was not. It was not that Mountbatten didn't see him, but I think, again, that he was more interested in having all the Brits possible have a look at Admiral Burke, and so the Secretary of Defense equivalent and the Secretary of the Navy equivalent, and a couple of others were included in the party. But the only Americans were Admiral Burke and myself.

*CinCNELM--Commander in Chief U.S. Naval Forces Eastern Atlantic and Mediterranean.

Q: Speaking of Burke getting along with people, what was his relationship with Admiral Rickover?*

Admiral Weschler: Let me see. I'm trying to think if there was any time when it was not one of the absolute warmest respect. Admiral Burke included Admiral Rickover just like other flag officers at his receptions, and Admiral Rickover and Mrs. Rickover came to the receptions. He used to tell me to make sure that people talked with Admiral Rickover because he didn't want him to have any feeling of being an outsider. I know that I, on a couple of occasions, went over to talk with Admiral Rickover and took somebody over to say hello or to meet Mrs. Rickover.

Early on in Admiral Burke's time as CNO, Admiral Rickover came in to the office to tell me that he thought it was absolutely vital that Admiral Burke get up to the Bettis plant in Shippingport, Pennsylvania, so that he became familiar with the nuclear power plants, would recognize their dimensions and some of the discussions that were going on about the plants, what kinds of ships they could be used in. He asked me to come up with two or three alternatives, because I knew Admiral Burke's schedule, and bounce them off Admiral Rickover and see if they would fit

---

*Rear Admiral Hyman G. Rickover, USN, was the head of the Navy's nuclear power program.

with him, then present them to Admiral Burke and see what he would say. So I did that for Admiral Rickover and got Admiral Burke lined up very early on, probably September or October of '55, to go up to Shippingport.

Admiral Rickover was up there ahead of time and met us at the airport and drove with Admiral Burke to the plant, took him through everything, was talking to him personally all the way about everything that was going on. I was able to attend everything that happened there. Then it just so happened that there was a weekend outing in the Pittsburgh area that Admiral Burke was going to, so when he finished at the Bettis plant, he climbed in his limousine, and the entourage that had been around suddenly disappeared. Admiral Burke had gone off for this weekend. The only two people left there were Admiral Rickover and myself. Admiral Rickover looked at me and he said, "Where are you going?"

I said, "Well, Admiral, I have to get to the Pittsburgh airport and I think I'm a long way from there, and I don't know how I'm going to get there."

Then Admiral Rickover said, "I'll drive you." He drove me to the airport, which I thought was the nicest possible thing.

I can still remember some of the conversation that we had in the car. One of the things I asked him was, "Admiral, could you give me an idea of your thoughts on safety? Because I know that's the thing that everybody is talking about on nuclear power."

He said, "Really I have a very simple rule. I say to myself, 'I have a son. I love my son. I want everything that I do to be so safe that I would be happy to have my son operating it.' That's my fundamental rule."

I said, "You can't have anything more straightforward than that." And then I said, "Admiral, the first time I ever heard you speak was when I was a student at the Naval War College in 1950, and I can remember you standing on that platform telling us about the Nautilus and how wonderful it was, and that you really didn't have an awful lot of spare gear on it, that you just had the ship itself. What were you driving at in that connection?"

He said, "Oh, it's very easy. The second you get a new project here in Washington, you're going to find out you have a million helpers. Every one of them wants to help your program get through because it's going to be a platform for their gadgets. I learned early, no helpers, no gadgets. I was building a nuclear submarine, and that's what it was going to be, and I didn't need all these other people who would have sunk my ship or the project."

I remembered that, because later on, you may recall that Admiral Burke brought along a destroyer program. The only building program that Admiral Burke ever lost completely was his destroyer building program, when he was trying to build the program called Typhon. He said, "I could just watch that thing gradually sinking. It started out being a destroyer, and then it became a light cruiser, and then it became a heavy cruiser, and then it became a battleship, all on a destroyer hull. It just couldn't carry the weight of gear nor the dollars that were attendant to it, and it just disappeared, and I didn't have the heart to rescue it."

I think that's part of why he says that he shouldn't have stayed on for his last two years. I think he feels that he lost his initiative or his fight, or that too many people knew how to get around him by that time, whereas if he'd been new and articulate and fresh on the job, he might not have lost it. That's surmise, but that's sort of the way that I read it, because it's the only one he ever lost.

Q: Admiral Roy Benson had a phrase from Rickover that described the same syndrome. He said, "You've got to repel boarders and keep them from trying to stick things in your ship."*

Admiral Weschler: Nicely put.

---

*The oral history of Rear Admiral Roy S. Benson, USN (Ret.), a submariner, is in the Naval Institute collection.

Interview Number 4 with Vice Admiral Thomas R. Weschler,
U.S. Navy (Retired)

Place: Naval War College, Newport, Rhode Island

Date: Tuesday, 18 September 1984

Interviewer: Paul Stillwell

Q: Admiral, yesterday we went into some detail about Admiral Burke and your relationship with him. We touched briefly on the Polaris program. Why was that limited to submarines and not put into surface ships?

Admiral Weschler: I think there were two reasons, Paul, why that occurred. I made note of the first one, that although the Polaris missile was part of our strategic warfare capability, it wasn't funded from some general pool of money, so the Navy had to take the cost out of its hide. Therefore, the tendency was to buy only those missiles and have that capability which was really unique and for which there was no substitute, and that certainly applied to the Polaris submarine program.

When it came to putting the missiles in cruisers, they were very expensive, for one thing, and the second thing was the question of vulnerability. Although we could tell ourselves that moving around on the surface of the ocean they wouldn't be too readily apparent to an enemy and that the enemy would have difficulty zeroing in, people were thinking more and more about overhead surveillance and capabilities like that. The idea of having them in surface ships, running around on the ocean, just didn't have enough attraction to merit a strategic investment. It was one of those concepts that gradually wore itself out.

You may be aware that in today's world, in which we've been talking about the MX and some means of getting a capability separate from the MX and separate from the Trident program, that we have again considered putting missiles into surface ships.* I remember this discussion in Washington, and as with so many things there, they used to call it the "Crocus" program because it came up every spring. I think this is just another one of those. I don't think the Navy's ever convinced itself that very large missiles in ships is the way to go. We did come close. <u>Albany</u> was fitted to take Polaris missiles, but none was ever put in her.

Q: To go back to some of the events of that time you were with Admiral Burke, the Red Chinese were shelling the offshore islands from time to time, stirring up the Taiwanese. What was the involvement at your level with that?

---

*MX was a proposed U.S. strategic missile system much debated in the 1970s and 1980s.

Admiral Weschler: I have to say that on that one, I had no experience, that I had left Admiral Burke before that really came up, and so I don't have any comment for you.

I do have one area, though, that I wanted to come back to, and that was the fall of Cuba, the Castro takeover.* Admiral Burke had gone down to visit President Batista, and the admiral believed strongly in holding onto Guantanamo and felt that Cuba was a valuable ally. He wanted to do his best to make sure that our relationship stayed good. He developed a reasonable friendship with President Batista and kept close to him. As the upswing of Castro's power became evident so that President Batista might fall, Admiral Burke assured President Batista that if something were to happen to him, that the U.S. Navy would do its best to take care of his family.

Before Havana really was taken over by Castro forces, President Batista's family was flown to Spain, courtesy of the U.S. Navy. That got them away from there so that at least they were safe at the time that the downfall of the Batista regime took place. I cite that as an example of some of the little things that are done on a personal basis that may mean a great deal later on. Had Batista come back to power, I'm sure that he would have had a feeling for the

---

*Fidel Castro Ruz and the 26th of July movement seized power by force on 1 January 1959 from President Fulgencio Batista y Zaldivar, who fled the country. Although Castro at first promised elections he established himself as a dictator during 1960 and remains in power to this day.

U.S. and for the U.S. Navy that couldn't have been substituted for.

Q: What do you recall about the Suez Crisis in 1956?

Admiral Weschler: I think certainly the admiral was restless on that one. He and Admiral Mountbatten had quite a few exchanges, because obviously we were on opposite sides of the fence on that particular issue.* I think the crux of it all was explained, really, by Admiral Cat Brown.** Maybe you've heard this story, but in any event, Admiral Brown was Commander Sixth Fleet, and he was out there in the Eastern Mediterranean. As things were getting more and more tense, Admiral Burke sent word to him to be particularly alert and to be ready to take action if anything happened. Admiral Brown sent back, "I'm alert. I'm standing on the tips of my toes. Just tell me, who's the enemy?"

I think that was really the situation in which so many people found themselves, that it was hard to think of the

---

*On 26 July 1956 President Gamal Nasser of Egypt announced that his country was nationalizing the Suez Canal Company. Israeli forces invaded Egypt's Sinai Peninsula on 29 October 1956. Britain and France then intervened militarily on behalf of Israel in an unsuccessful attempt to secure the Suez Canal, which was damaged and closed to traffic. Rather than support the British and French, the United States asked for a United Nations resolution to end the fighting. A cease-fire took effect on 6 November.
**Vice Admiral Charles R. Brown, USN, Commander Sixth Fleet.

British and French as somebody that you would ever shoot at. Even though the circumstance was very difficult, you hoped you could have said, "Don't do it that way, fellows," and you would have been able to find some other way to go. I think Admiral Burke was very happy that that situation sort of collapsed of its own weight, that Great Britain dithered at a time when it ought to have moved quickly, and the opportunity for success had passed, and there wasn't going to be any further shooting. I think President Eisenhower and the whole administration breathed a big sigh of relief that it had gone by.

Q: The Navy still had some involvement in moving civilians, did it not?

Admiral Weschler: Yes. I think that was one of the first times that we had used our forces to evacuate civilians from Alexandria, which was the collection port. We sent an amphibious squadron, part of the Sixth Fleet, in there to pick up those people and get them out. That operation went very smoothly and very successfully. That was one of the efforts that was instituted.*

---

*For details see Thomas A. Bryson, "Mission of Mercy," U.S. Naval Institute Proceedings, Special History Supplement, March 1985, pages 88-96.

Q: What do you recall about the relationship between Admiral Brown and Admiral Burke?

Admiral Weschler: Just one of great friendship and sort of laughing admiration for each other. I think that Cat Brown had enough of a peppery nature, and at the same time a great sense of humor, so that there were some classic exchanges between the two. I can't remember anything other than the one I cited, but I think Admiral Burke thought he had a great person there in Cat Brown in Sixth Fleet. He used to enjoy hearing from him. If Admiral Brown came back to the States for any reason, you could be sure that was going to be one of the appointments that Admiral Burke would keep without any fail, just to hear what he had to tell him.

I was going to come back to one other story about the quarters, that I just wanted to throw in, because it's a side of Admiral Burke that wasn't particularly well known. All the time that Admiral Burke had been in Washington before, I think as a commander and certainly as a captain and a new rear admiral, when he didn't have quarters and other places to relax, he and Mrs. Burke used to go out to a place in Virginia called Difficult Run. It was just a little cabin down on this stream, not that far off Old Dominion Drive in McLean, but you'd think you were deep in the country when you got to this site. It was just a little cabin, except that it must have had a 15-foot destroyer painted on a board up there over the porch that looked out on the little stream.

The thing that distinguished the grounds was a lot of the natural Virginia dogwood. Well, if there's one plant or tree that the Burkes enjoy, it's dogwood. So when Admiral Burke became CNO and got out there, he was trying to think what he could do to add his contribution to the quarters. There was Admiral Carney's table and somebody else's mirror, and somebody else's decorating scheme for a room. Admiral and Mrs. Burke didn't think they would do anything like that, but he said, "I'm going to plant dogwood." If you go by the CNO's quarters today--or the Vice President's quarters today--you will see that the entire area is ringed with dogwoods, and all those dogwoods came from Admiral Burke's place, Difficult Run, and they were all planted by Admiral Burke.

On succeeding Sundays, he'd get out there in a set of white coveralls and be busy working and planting. He really used to enjoy people coming up and saying, "We're not used to seeing federal personnel working on weekends and on Sundays, and you're to be commended, my good man," and so on. He'd be out there planting away, having a wonderful time. So I always enjoyed that as his contribution.

Q: For the most part, I've gathered, though, that the Burkes were very thrifty in the maintenance and upkeep of the official quarters, because Admiral Anderson then came in for a very thorough renovation when he took over.*

Admiral Weschler: Yes. That's a good point to make also about Admiral Burke. He had been around Washington enough to know that it was easy to have slush funds or to have a lot of your people who were doing things that if you really probed, you wouldn't have been happy about. So as a personal aide, I was told right from the beginning, "I want every cent accounted for that comes from the public treasury. If there's ever any doubt in your mind as to whether it should be public money or private money, I want you to have it charged to Burke." He always used to check with us and say, "Do you have enough money? You better take some money. Just keep it in the drawer, so if you need it, you'll have the money to do this." Even down to the business of what kind of a postage stamp went on a letter. "Did you mail that with my stamps, or did you mail that with the government's stamps?"

He would query you on that sort of thing. He really wanted it to be 100%. That's his natural bent anyhow, but I think the fact that he had been connected with things

---

*Admiral George W. Anderson, Jr., USN, was Chief of Naval Operations from 1961 to 1963. In his Naval Institute oral history he discussed renovation of the CNO's residence.

like OP-23 and these other circumstances where he had been in positions where other services might challenge, that he didn't ever want to have any silly little thing trip him up in a major event by having done something stupid which they could then play against him and spoil his credibility. In any event, that was very, very strong in his mind.

His concern extended to the greenhouse, where you worked with the gentleman there about what plants he had and where they were all coming from, or into the drivers, the car pools, everything. We really cleaned house when we came in, in terms of getting new people in if we had any feeling that there were holdovers of cadres who were too used to working together, and therefore you weren't absolutely sure of what was going on in their area.

I can remember, as a matter of fact, I had been in the job about six months when Admiral George Russell came in to see me, and he said, "Tom, break out your books and talk to me about what you're doing as the aide to run the admiral's mess and to run the quarters."* The quarters were primarily the Marine aide. I got the Marine aide in. Admiral George Russell had been Admiral King's aide, and Admiral Burke knew that, and he figured that Admiral Russell, as an ex-aide, would really know what we were doing and could make sure that what we were undertaking was

---

*Vice Admiral George L. Russell, USN, Deputy Chief of Naval Operations (Administration). As a rear admiral, Russell served as the Navy's Judge Advocate General, 1948-52.

all above board and absolutely no questions.*

Q: As a former JAG, he would know the legalities of it.

Admiral Weschler: Exactly. Yes. But that's the way Admiral Burke was. He didn't want any questions, and so he did nothing to the quarters that didn't absolutely have to be done, except to paint and have them fresh and attractive that way, but he wouldn't undertake any major renovations or things like that if he could possibly get along without it.

I think one other thing I'll just stick in here, I don't know what the relevance of it is, but it always impressed me. One day, again, the admiral had probably been in the job six to nine months, and he came back into the office. I don't know what sort of a meeting he had been attending, but anyhow, he came into the office and buzzed, and I walked in. He said, "Tom, I just want to tell you. If anything should happen to me so that I weren't around to give you the answer, I want you to know that the relief I would nominate today to be the CNO is Admiral Jim Russell.** I haven't told anybody else that,

---

*Before and during World War II, Russell served on the staff of Admiral Ernest J. King, USN.
**Rear Admiral James S. Russell, USN, was then Chief of the Bureau of Aeronautics. As a four-star admiral he later served as Vice Chief of Naval Operations from August 1958 to November 1961. Admiral Russell's oral history is in the Naval Institute collection.

and I don't want you to tell anybody, but I just want you to know that if I were going to do it today, it would be Admiral Jim Russell. So if anything happens, you make sure the Secretary knows that." Of course, I didn't forget it. Much later, I mentioned it to Admiral Jim Russell, and he said, yes, he became aware of it about a year after the admiral told me. He was delighted that Admiral Burke thought that highly of him.

Q: Admiral Jim Russell came in as VCNO under Admiral Burke. Were you there during the time they were together?

Admiral Weschler: No. The one who had come in there before was Don Felt, and there was an interesting team.* They got along quite well. Don Felt was not an easy person to work with. I had known him at the Naval War College when I was here as a faculty member. Don Felt had preceded Wallace Beakley as the chief of staff at the war college in 1950. Don Felt was very close-mouthed, and, as you may know, the expression was, "Have you been Felt today?"

A good friend of mine, Ebby Bell, was his aide.** He said it took a special pair of britches to get through a day with him because you were blow-torched all the time for not moving faster or for doing something wrong. But they

---
*Admiral Harry D. Felt, USN, was Vice Chief of Naval Operations from September 1956 to July 1958.
**Commander C. Edwin Bell, USN.

were a remarkable team, because Don Felt was intensely loyal to Admiral Burke but at the same time had an awful lot of moxie and ideas of his own. He wasn't afraid to assume the responsibility for doing things and not "bothering" the CNO about a lot of things that were coming around. So he would say, "That's the final decision. Now get going. Don't bother me with going over there or are we going to brief him. I'm not going to brief him. This is the end of it. I'll take the responsibility. Now get going," which was good most of the time.

Q: One thing we sort of touched on yesterday was Admiral Burke's ability to absorb great quantities of information and retain it. I gather he had that ability.

Admiral Weschler: Yes, he really did, and he was a voluminous reader. If you put material on his desk, nine times out of ten he would have read every word of it. That was particularly true of JCS documents or controversial issues. He was perfectly willing to read all of the material before he reached his decision. In addition, he schooled himself to record everything that he did. He said, "What I am doing is of historic significance to the Navy, and one of the problems in Washington is lack of continuity, so I want to make sure [it was not applied to the social side near as much, but to the official side] that the memos that I send out and the key memos which I receive, on which I make notations, that we have copies of those in the file." Whenever he came back from a chairman's meeting, he would buzz for people to debrief him. The yeoman would come in and he'd make a transcript of what was done, which Admiral Burke would sign off the next morning. If there were important conversations or that sort of thing, he debriefed on them as well.

He was very, very thorough, and he almost always would send for somebody to sit in there while he talked to the yeoman so that he got dual action out of it. If it wasn't clear, they could interrupt and say, "Admiral, put a note in there about what you meant by so and so." By the time he was done debriefing, he now had the aide charged with what had gone on so he could now go off and start doing some of the things, one, two, three, that the yeoman had recorded. The aide had taken his own notes and could go out and implement things. So he was very efficient, very effective that way. I think you'll probably find that the Burke CNO years are as thoroughly documented as any could be.

Q: Was he a fast reader?

Admiral Weschler: Yes. I don't know that as a matter of fact; I only can tell you by inference. When I saw the

Thomas R. Weschler #4 - 330

stacks of material that he went through and what he did, he had to be a fast reader.

Q: Some top-ranking officers have a hatchet man to do their unpleasant duties for them. Did Admiral Burke have one, or did he do that kind of thing himself?

Admiral Weschler: I have two comments. I'd say, first of all, that he didn't mind being his own hatchet man, if it came to that. By and large, he didn't like that way of operating. He would feel that most people who had reached reasonable seniority, whether captain or admiral, in order to be in Washington in these senior positions, he would figure they probably had a lot of good in them that he hadn't seen, even though they had done something that he thought was doltish. So he preferred to let them know that he felt they had let him down, and then would move them somewhere else, but it wouldn't be a big blot on their records. However, I do remember one captain, no name, who did something, and I think he was out of Washington in less than 12 hours. There wasn't any question as to who told him what he should do and where he should do it.

There is one other angle I want to bring up. He was in no way a cliquish man. I think you are aware that certain CNOs, in coming in, brought in a whole entourage who were really their group and their kitchen cabinet.

Admiral Burke almost leaned over backward to prevent that. He said, "The Navy has a system which produces competent people; I will accept it and let the system work." The exceptions would be people like the aides when he made a personal choice, perhaps. But you see, with me, he didn't know me from Adam. He let the system tell him I was someone he would like. He preferred that kind of an approach, and as a result, when you don't have a clique around you, then you can begin to let the system work, and if people aren't good, you can move them out just as easily as you could move them in. If they're your own men, then you kind of have to ax them, because you're the one who brought them and therefore you're the only one who can get rid of them.

Q: And you might tend to keep somebody longer just out of a defensive mechanism if he was your man.

Admiral Weschler: That's right. He didn't do that. So I think those things go together in the fact that he didn't really have a lot of hatchet men. But as I've indicated, with Don Felt, whether he knew it or not, there was a lot of hatchet work going on next door, so that he was spared the necessity to be one, and it was like that good captain-exec combination. I think Don Felt said, "I'll do the job whether he asks me to or not."

Q: I gather from what you say that when Admiral Burke did do it, it was more a sense of disappointment than rancor.

Admiral Weschler: That's right. He tried to keep himself that way and I indicate that on one or two occasions he would really blow up. Then Mrs. Burke's note in the pocket would get to him, and he'd simmer down and decide it wasn't as bad as he thought it was, most times.

Q: One thing that Admiral Peet felt onerous about the job was Admiral Burke's fetish about answering correspondence right away. Did this cause you any problems?

Admiral Weschler: Yes, it did. I'll tell you, the biggest problem about answering correspondence was when I would let one slide. I don't care, you can be as faithful as you want to be, and suddenly there's one piece of paper that you look at and you say, "Oh, my golly, it's a month old." I probably had more conniptions over getting an answer in there for Admiral Burke to sign for a letter that was a month old than anything else that I did in that whole job. You know, there really wasn't any basic excuse. You'd been getting information and suddenly it got to the bottom.

You knew he was going to see it, and you'd get some remark. If you didn't get it right then, the next time you were sitting in the car with him going somewhere, he'd say, "You're not keeping up the paperwork like you used to," or something like that. You'd know full well that he had noticed that this thing had come through. So it kept you on your toes, and it was amazing the number of bits of information you had to collect, and it had to be good. Particularly, he was very concerned about widows, and early in his tenure, there were still a lot of widows left over from World War I and a few from the in-between years, who didn't have the support of our current retirement benefit law. He worked to get the law extended in order to include them. That was one of the pieces of legislation he really worked hard on, a widows' benefit bill. He felt keenly on that.

Q: In his dealings with the material bureaus, which supposedly reported to SecNav during that time, how much did Admiral Burke involve himself in those relationships?

Admiral Weschler: A great deal, and he had two ways in which he worked with the bureaus. First of all, being an ordnance PG himself and the heads of the Bureau of Ordnance being old and very warm friends, there was never any concern that he felt out of touch with what was going on in the Bureau of Ordnance. With the other bureaus, I mentioned already that he was having the deputy chiefs in.

He decided that perhaps once a week or once every two weeks he ought to have the bureau chiefs in, and so they began to come over to meetings. So he was hearing from them on a fairly regular basis as to what they were doing. The fact that they were coming over and talking and telling people what was going on was in itself a tremendous bridge. It showed his interest, and they were perfectly happy to keep him up to date on what was going on.

In BuShips Admiral Mumma was the bureau chief during the time that I was there.* He was in Admiral Burke's office, it seemed to me, a couple of times a week, often on matters that Mumma thought were urgent and that Admiral Burke ought to be aware of because his prestige and interest would help in getting some points across. Or if Admiral Mumma came in to see the Secretary, he was likely to drop down and see Admiral Burke and just tell him what was going on.

So I think it was that he either knew a lot of the people well, or evinced the interest, and as a result, he got a lot of cooperation and information. He was not averse to the amalgamation of Ordnance and Aeronautics when they became the Bureau of Weapons.** P. D. Stroop, who

---
*Rear Admiral Alfred G. Mumma, USN, was Chief of the Bureau of Ships from 1955 to 1959. He has been interviewed as part of the Naval Institute oral history program.
**In December 1959 the Bureau of Ordnance and Bureau of Aeronautics were merged to form the Bureau of Naval Weapons. The first chief of the new bureau was Rear Admiral Paul D. Stroop, USN, whose oral history is in the Naval Institute collection.

got the job, was an old friend of Admiral Burke's and an ordnance PG, and I think Admiral Burke felt that if it was going to take place, that this was as fine a person to try it with as anybody who was coming along. I don't think he minded efficiency _if_ it really was going to achieve that end.

Q: I talked to Admiral Pride and he thought that was a bad idea.* He said instead of efficiency, what you're going to have is a person with one function that had it in Aeronautics, one that had it in Ordnance; now they'll both still be there and you'll have a guy over top of those two in weapons.

Admiral Weschler: Yes. Well, I think Admiral Pride proved to be prescient, because that certainly is what happened in the Chief of Naval Material's office. We will probably be commenting on that later, but when I had the <u>Spruance</u> program, I was working for both the CNO and CNM at the time that CNM was created. And to watch that CNM grow, it was exactly as you've commented. The people who had been there before now stayed put or advanced to the senior positions in CNM, and new people all floated up. You really had the entire establishment as before, a layer on top, and

---

*Rear Admiral Alfred M. Pride, USN, was Chief of the Bureau of Aeronautics from 1947 to 1951. His oral history is in the Naval Institute collection.

everybody one job senior to what they had been before. So it was a very high-priced proposition.

Q: You describe Admiral Burke seemingly as a man constantly in motion--trips, lots of meetings, lots of reading, and I've heard of him also as a man whose work was his hobby. What, if anything, did he do to relax, to get a break from this pressure?

Admiral Weschler: I cited the one real thing that he liked, which was gardening, and I don't mean gardening, I meant like that Difficult Run or planting dogwood or working around the quarters. He could do that. He enjoyed being outside and doing that kind of work where his mind didn't have to be involved and he could just sort of do some chores. He had no family to speak of, and so work really became his all. There was a time when they had a dog, but I think when that first dog went, they never got another. I think they found that in moving around, it just got to be too much of a bother. You took a trip, what did you do with the dog? There was just too much of that.

So he didn't have hobbies. He formed friendships with so many people that he worked with, and then these people would be coming back to visit and to see him. So whenever he wasn't busy in the office or busy doing all his work at home, he was likely having friends come by, particularly foreign, who would be there to keep up contacts. The Japanese, I think you're aware, were a great love of his. In that post-World War II era, they really became attached to Admiral Burke, and it continues to this day. The house that he had on Hawthorne Street had some cherry trees planted in its front yard that were a gift of some of the Japanese who came to visit. I think it's at the Japanese Naval Academy that they have a little shrine where they have busts of the principal heroes of the Japanese Navy; Admiral Yamamoto and some of these others are around.* The only foreign officer that I understand is memorialized there is Admiral Burke, and that's sort of a wonderful thing for the Japanese to remember him the way that they do. In years past he often went to speak at their Naval Academy or at their Naval War College. So that might have been a hobby or an outlet of something aside from his regular work.

Q: He was there from early in the morning until late at night. Did he take time off for meals, or did he grab those on the run?

Admiral Weschler: He would grab lunch in the office 60% of the time. The other times he felt that he really ought to

---
*Admiral Isoroku Yamamoto, IJN, was Commander in Chief Combined Fleet in World War II.

get over and talk with the people, so that his going to lunch, when he did go, was as much dictated by a desire to be with the Vice Chief and the other chiefs and tell them what was going on and listen to what they were doing as it was for the food. It was not unusual for him, when there was a fleet commander around, to invite him in for a sandwich. When I say that, I mean, literally that's what it was. It wasn't a little table set up and everybody sitting around and taking a lot of time at it; they'd be at the desk and there would be a sandwich and a cup of coffee. When that was finished, that was lunch, and then he went on to the next thing. A lot of that. On those evenings when he would stay late, there was very likely to be a hamburger which he ate at the desk, and that was as much as there was, and that was probably dinner for the day.

Q: Did he exercise beyond the gardening?

Admiral Weschler: No, that was one of the things that concerned SecNav. Admiral Burke had a doctor assigned to him. This was Secretary of the Navy's doing, not Admiral Burke's doing. The Secretary of the Navy said, "Arleigh, you're not getting enough exercise. I want to make sure that you have a physician who's checking you regularly. I don't want any heart attacks or any difficulties that way.

And whatever that doctor tells you, you better do." So Dr. George Hyatt was assigned as Admiral Burke's physician, and I think he also looked after Admiral Radford.* George Hyatt would come in about once every two weeks; he'd come in with the aides and with his blood pressure gear and so on, and when the aides were finished, he'd sit down and give the admiral some sort of a thump and a check just to see how he was doing.

He tried to encourage Admiral Burke to go for walks on the weekends and in the evenings, if he could get him to do it out at the quarters. He also suggested massage, saying that if he didn't like anything else, maybe he could at least have that, which could give some stimulation to circulation and could be worked into the day without getting him into a sweat and having to have a whole clothes change and so on, which could be a problem.

There were times when he would do that, but it never sold. You knew it was being imposed on him by a system that he didn't really endorse, and as soon as things got tight one way or another, that would be the first thing to go by the board, and then the doctor would have to work hard to get it back into the schedule. He'd say, "Now, you're not doing your job, aide. I told you mark him down for it, get it on the calendar, and I don't want to see it erased." Dutifully, we'd put it there for a couple of

---

*Lieutenant Commander George W. Hyatt, Medical Corps, USN.

weeks, and you'd see Admiral Burke crossing through it.

So yes, in a way, he tried to do some things for his health, but nothing that lasted overly long. By the end of my two years with him, only the physical checks remained. He did go out for the annual physical or a special check if he had a cold, but he had no difficulties during the time I was there. As you know, he's still getting around pretty well today, even with the artificial hips.

Q: Did he like to get out and visit the fleet?

Admiral Weschler: He was marvelous at visiting the fleet, and he particularly liked to visit the people of the fleet; that's what he wanted more than anything else. When you scheduled him for a ship visit, he was willing to let the captain have a few minutes to show him what he really wanted, but then after that, he wanted to talk to the officers in the wardroom. He wanted to visit with the chiefs. He wanted to talk with the crew. He wanted to get all the officers assembled on a tender or in an auditorium or someplace. He liked to be with the people, to talk to the people, to explain what he was doing, and then to have some informal breaks when they could tell him what was on their minds.

I think that he was, to that extent, in the '50s, well ahead of the time in his relationships with people. He was not an informal man in the sense that he dismissed a lot of the courtesies and routines that the seniors were accorded, but he didn't want any barriers between himself and the people he was talking with. If the chiefs, when he was finished, wanted to come up and ask him a question or sit with him at a table in the chiefs' mess or wherever, that was fine with him. He really wanted that kind of rapport, and he liked to talk with the families and get them included in things that were going on. So I felt that he was much more in tune with the Seventies than a lot of other people were back in the Fifties.

Q: Did you go with him when he testified in Congress?

Admiral Weschler: No. I simply drove with him. I was in the car going up and in the car coming back, but no, he didn't really want us, the aides, to get involved in that. He said, "I know my lesson, and if anybody's with me, I want somebody who is current on the subject I'm going to be testifying on." So you often would turn him over to somebody else who would look after him and would have a phone number to call or, using the congressional liaison, would get word back to us of what was going on and what we should be prepped for.

Q: Did you sit in on any murder boards to prepare him for

testimony?*

Admiral Weschler: I sat in on some murder boards for certain of the JCS items. That was about the only thing that I got in on as a personal aide. I'd line up those things for him, but unless I really didn't have anything else to do and would go in and sit in a corner, I didn't get in on that sort of material.

Q: It sounds as if in many things you almost had to be a mind-reader to figure out one step ahead what he was going to want and be ready.

Admiral Weschler: Yes. He didn't want to waste your time. He knew that he kept farming out jobs a mile a minute. I never knew him to be embarrassed about the number of things he'd ask to have done, but he knew that he fired out an awful lot of things, and as a result, he didn't want you to do things that weren't specifically your requirement. He could understand that occasionally you were that interested professionally that you'd want to know what was going on, and he wouldn't turn you off when the occasion was right. But he knew that you had enough else to do that if you declined to stay in the room and went out, it was because

---

*A "murder board" is a group of people who throw tough questions at the boss ahead of time so he will be able to think through his answers before the testimony itself.

you felt your desk was loaded enough with all that correspondence he shot out or the tapes that he'd handed you, or the notes about what he wanted to do. There was plenty.

Q: What do you mean by the tapes?

Admiral Weschler: He would take a bunch of personal correspondence home in the evening, if he hadn't been able to get to it in the office, and if he felt that he wanted to put his own little touch on it, he might take a wad of 15 or 20 letters home, particularly on a weekend, and then he'd just turn on the tape recorder and he'd say, "On letter so and so to Mrs. Umptyump, make sure there's something in it to this effect." And then he'd go on to the next one. So the guidance on 20 letters would be on the tape, and the yeoman would come to it and would simply type out what the admiral had said about it, and then you'd have that plus the letters in order to write out what Admiral Burke's response was.

That was very helpful because that's when you really got a lot of projects, to turn to the Bureau of Personnel and get complete data, or if he thought you could finesse something, he would indicate it, "Let's not get into this. Just give her a nice brush-off," something like that. And that gave you what you needed. Part of this morning routine when we came in was that he'd empty everything that he had accumulated in his briefcase and pass out his treasures. Then you'd march off with what you had to do.

Q: Didn't he also tape office conversations?

Admiral Weschler: Yes, he did. He sometimes taped them. He used to have some of them recorded longhand, because tape recorders were really just coming in in that period. They weren't near as effective as they are now, but he would have Madeline Corsiglia, whom I've spoken of, take down in shorthand what was going on on an office telephone call. He did record some of the office conversations with particular visitors. He would know in advance that he wanted it taped. He would think it was going to be official enough that it was worth making a note of what was said. Often the reason for that was to make sure of what he said so that other people could have heard what he, Burke, said about a particular subject as much as it was what the other person would be saying to him.

Q: Was this with or without the knowledge of the other people?

Admiral Weschler: I would say that it was about 70% without knowledge and 30% with. This was before the days of the beepers in the lines and that sort of thing. However, that Washington as I knew it, almost everyone, when they were talking about anything on the telephone, expected to be taped. There was a lot of concern about eavesdroppers from other services as well as from outside agencies that might want to be getting information, so I'd say that the atmosphere was not all that naive. There was an awful lot of sensitivity to other people getting information, and I don't think many people would have been surprised if they had learned that things had been recorded.

Q: How were his relationships with members of the press?

Admiral Weschler: He wasn't an easy man to get an interview with, simply because he felt he was that pushed, but he made it a point to be available a reasonable number of times. When I mentioned the deputy chiefs and the Vice Chief, Chinfo was always included in those conversations. Chinfo was one of the first to be sent for in almost any situation, and if Chinfo told Admiral Burke he ought to have the interview, he had it. It was that simple.

He wouldn't let himself get in for every daily situation that was coming up, but if Time or Newsweek or one of the big magazines or a newspaper alliance wanted to do an in-depth conversation, then he was available. As much as possible, he tried to be sure that he got the questions in advance. He wouldn't memorize the answers, but at least it gave him a chance to have his thoughts together as to what he was going to say. Frankly, I think he got along very well with the press, because he was very thoughtful and very frank in his discussions with them. He knew that he had an opportunity, and he had something to say, and so he tried not to be mealy-mouthed. He really tried to give them some data that he thought was worthwhile. So they usually ended up with a good article, which they liked.

Q: Did he enjoy that kind of situation?

Admiral Weschler: Yes, because I don't think there was an antipathy. I don't think it was at all like the Vietnamese situation, in which there was a "we" and "they" kind of thing between the military and the press. This was much more in the World War II environment, where the press was very much our allies. At the end of World War II, most reporters were bosom friends, and you felt closer to them sometimes than a lot of other personnel you might have bumped into. It was much more that kind of atmosphere in the '50s, and so I think that he was 90% in their camp, you know, and wanting to work with them. He was cautious enough because of the B-36 controversy and so on, that he wasn't a fool. But he didn't regard them, nonetheless, as laying for him.

Q: There was no "60 Minutes" in that era, either.

Admiral Weschler: There was a Drew Pearson, however.*

Q: Did Drew Pearson cause any problems?

Admiral Weschler: Drew Pearson got a few people, but he never got Admiral Burke, and I think Admiral Burke was determined that he wasn't going to. That comes back again to these slush funds and things like that. He said, "If any stupid little thing like that gets me in trouble, I really would feel that I had been let down." So all of us were very sensitive to that kind of thing.

Q: You described the admiral when he first came in bending over backwards to be kind to the people that he had been jumped over. Did he relax and grow comfortable in the role over time?

Admiral Weschler: Yes. By the end of the first year, even with Admiral Wright and Admiral Stump, he began to be the

---

*Andrew Pearson was a muckraking syndicated newspaper columnist, the predecessor and colleague of today's Jack Anderson.

CNO, because he was. He knew that he had information that they wanted, and he would call them regularly. They had secure phones, and he made a point of chatting with them. But you could tell over the year that he was getting more and more relaxed and that when the phone rang and it was one of the chiefs, it wasn't a "drop everything" kind of thing as it had been initially. I remember the first time Admiral Wright called and Admiral Burke said, "Tell him I'll call him back." That was sort of a milestone. You knew that he was the chief, though, no question about it, and these other admirals knew it. He had to recognize it from the demands on his time, and that's just the way they had to fit in.

So I'd say by the end of the year 1955 that it was pretty well clear, and there had been a lot of motion. After all, people saw the handwriting on the wall, and there were a lot of people who were retiring, and he did what he could to recognize the good ones, to allow them to continue to move up. Admiral Briscoe, for example, who was one of those who was passed over for CNO, ended up as CinCSouth, with four stars. So where those things were possible, things had been done. But yes, he relaxed, and I'd say by the end of a year, 18 months, he was very much in charge and everybody knew it and was relaxed with the situation.

Q: As it got toward the end of the two-year term, did he get any assurance he was going to go beyond that?

Admiral Weschler: I'm trying to remember when he knew he was going to carry on. He didn't know yet in August 1956, his first anniversary as CNO. I think it must have been about spring of the second year that he became aware that he was going to be asked to stay on, and I think it came up in connection with projects that he was thinking of. All of a sudden, he began to talk about things that he ought to do now in order to get them going. I think that he shared with us, with the staff, some time around that time that he was going to stay on for a second tour. As a result, his 180 days began all over again of getting some things accomplished, and the tempo picked up. The winding down was over and we were then back on a new crusade. By the time I left in December of '57, he was still going strong on that second tour.

Q: Did you detect any political leanings in Admiral Burke?

Admiral Weschler: None at all. I'm interpreting your question. He certainly tried to never allow the words "Republican" or "Democrat" to be in his mind or to be used in a conversation. As far as his having any aspirations to a position in the political world, that did not apply to him. I think he felt that being a naval officer was really better. As a matter of fact, he had a very interesting outlook, and I wish that we could to some extent make everyone aware of it. He said, "Tom, you ought to understand the role of the CNO and the Secretary of the Navy." He said, "The CNO is a nonpolitical office. I am a military representative, a naval officer. The Secretary is assigned by a political party to help the Navy achieve its purposes. To the extent that anything political is supposed to be done in the Navy, it ought to be done by the Secretary of the Navy. He can go over and act as the buffer between a political Congress and the apolitical Navy. If anybody's going to get sacrificed in the process, it's going to be the Secretary of the Navy." That's the way he looked at it. You may recall that Secretary Sullivan resigned when that aircraft carrier was canceled.*

Admiral Burke said, "That's just the way it should have been. That's what he's for, is to do that." It isn't up to the CNO to resign. He had presented the requirement and the requirement is still valid, but the fact that it wasn't fulfilled by the Secretary of Defense was a political problem, and therefore the Secretary of the Navy should be sacrificed.

---

*Secretary of the Navy John L. Sullivan resigned his office in 1949 after Secretary of Defense Louis Johnson arbitrarily canceled the aircraft carrier <u>United States</u> (CVA-58) after construction had started.

I say that because I think that John Lehman is the most political Secretary we've had in a long time.* He is doing more of that sort of thing, of being the political aggrandizer. My only objection on occasion with Lehman is that the Secretary is also trying to reach in and establish the requirements. I've already indicated that Admiral Burke had a great problem with Secretary Thomas about who was going to appoint the senior officers of the Navy to their new positions. I think Admiral Watkins is having that same problem with Secretary Lehman today. I think Secretary Lehman would like very much to name who's this and who's that, and Jim Watkins is trying to preserve the right to nominate individuals for the different jobs. So I see some crossing of that very delicate line between those two right now.

Q: Did Admiral Burke believe that naval officers should vote?

Admiral Weschler: Yes, he did. As a matter of fact, he did vote. I don't have any idea who he voted for; he never discussed it with me. We talked about that on occasion. He thought it was a very important thing to exercise your franchise, and just because he was representing a

---

*John F. Lehman, Jr., served as Secretary of the Navy from 1981 to 1987. Ironically, Admiral Burke's recommendation was helpful in Lehman being appointed to the job.

nonpolitical group didn't mean that he couldn't be a citizen first.

Q: The Sputnik was launched near the end of '57.* Did that have any impact in CNO's office?

Admiral Weschler: Yes I remember being at a party attended by Secretary Gates, Admiral Burke, and obviously lots of others; as an aide, I was present. The newspapers were all full of this Sputnik having been launched and that this was the end of an era, how we had been scooped, and so on. I can remember Secretary Gates coming over to Admiral Burke after, perhaps, he'd had the fifth conversation with somebody who was shaking his head about this terrible situation in which we were. Secretary Gates said to Admiral Burke, "You know, I just can't have anybody else come up and tell me all these sad stories about how awful it is that we don't have a Sputnik and don't have any program like this."

Admiral Burke said, "Yes, I know it's bad, but what do they want us to do? We can't invent one," or something like that. So it was a certainly much talked about event, and the military were looked to as having missed the boat rather than to an R&D program or NASA or some other

---

*On 4 October 1957, the Soviet Union launched Sputnik I, the first articial satellite. It caused great uproar in the United States, which had expected to be first in space.

community which might have a space mission.* So OSD did some very quick studies immediately thereafter to determine how much this might be a military shortfall or whether it really was some other agency of government that ought to be involved, and whether the Defense budget could stand such a program.** I think they decided that by and large it was not something that the services could do a tremendous amount in. They could contribute a little, and they certainly had satellite programs, but it wasn't basically their responsibility to go after it and do it.

Q: How much was Admiral Burke personally involved in Polaris, giving it momentum and so forth?

Admiral Weschler: I don't think there's any doubt but that he was the first sparkplug. As a matter of fact, Admiral Raborn had what he called the "CNO hunting license."*** Admiral Burke dictated a letter which, in effect, said, "Anything Admiral Raborn needs to do this job is hereby made available to him, and if anybody doesn't understand what's written on this piece of paper, I ask you to call Arleigh Burke." That was the essence of the letter. Admiral Raborn used to carry a copy in his pocket, and if

---
*R&D--research and development; NASA--National Aeronautics and Space Administration.
**OSD--Office of the Secretary of Defense.
***Rear Admiral William F. Raborn, Jr., USN, was the director of the Polaris project. His oral history on Polaris is in the Naval Institute collection.

anybody ever started giving him any difficulty, he said, "You haven't seen my hunting license." And he'd bring it out and show it to them. He saw Admiral Burke at least once a week, and Admiral Burke frequently would go over to Admiral Raborn's briefings.

In the first year or so that this project was going on, it was not discussed with us. I was unaware, as an aide, as to what had happened from that summer of '55 until the thing really got going about nine months or so later. During that interval, a Navy commander, a classmate of mine, had been appointed a special liaison for Project X. None of us knew what it was, but whenever Tom Walker arrived, Tom Walker would go right in and see the admiral and talk to him about what was going on and then go off.*

He was Admiral Raborn's informal liaison initially on the program when it was just getting started, shaking out liquid fuel versus solid fuel, how fast they could get a submarine together, deciding to cut the George Washington in two and insert the missile tube section, and things like that.** Once the program got going and approved by Congress, then they didn't have to have all that secrecy about it, and you began to read more about it in the press.

---
*Commander Thomas J. Walker III, USN.
**Originally slated to be the attack submarine Scorpion (SSN-589), the vessel was cut apart and had a 130-foot section inserted to house the missile tubes. She became the USS George Washington (SSBN-598).

Thomas R. Weschler #4 - 355

Q: Did Admiral Burke reserve for himself a lot of the decisions on Polaris or did he delegate?

Admiral Weschler: I don't think he reserved any decisions for himself. I think he felt that that was Admiral Raborn's job. Admiral Rickover, as you know, was a part of that program but not directly. Since the nuclear submarines were being provided, in effect, by Admiral Rickover, he had to be aware of what was going on and to sort of approve what it was doing to the submarine shape and size and whether it could still be adequately powered, whether there could be all the electricity that was needed. So Admiral Rickover was much involved, but the decisions came from Admiral Raborn. And there was tremendous reliance on industry. I don't know of any program that had more reliance on industry as teammates than did the Polaris. It had a steering group which was headed up by the presidents or senior scientists of maybe six or eight companies, and they were the ones who were really putting their very best into the show, and it was their recommendations that were pretty much coming forward in giving the steer.

Q: We've talked a great deal about Admiral Burke. I know you had a career after that. Is there anything else we should mention before we do move on?

Admiral Weschler: If there is, I'm not thinking of it at the moment. Why don't we just leave it at that and if I come across something else later on, I'm sure he influenced me in lots of ways, and I'll think of them as I go along. I'll say, "Well, here's a Burkeism," and I'll mention it. But I think we've covered the essence of it.

Let me just say, when I was leaving him, he asked, "What would you like to do?"

I told him that I wanted to go to sea; that was the big thing. I said that my only regret about having stayed with him in Washington was that I'd been there for two and a half years and that other classmates were going to sea, and that that's where I wanted to be. So he said, "Okay, go see your detailer and get yourself something worthwhile."

I was lucky enough to get orders to be exec of <u>Canberra</u>, so I left and reported immediately to the Mediterranean. I came back home with her, and then she operated in and out of Norfolk.

Q: Did you express a specific preference for where you'd like to go?

Admiral Weschler: I did to the extent that I wanted to get deployed, if possible. I don't remember saying anything about East versus West Coast, although I personally preferred the East Coast. I had had a lot of West Coast duty in World War II, and I tried to keep it as a facet of my professional life that I moved back and forth from one ocean to the other. I really wanted to know the world rather than one particular ocean area. So I have a hunch that other things being equal, I would have taken the Atlantic Ocean professionally. It was time to get a little Atlantic duty, and particularly the Mediterranean.

Q: Was there a value in going to a heavy cruiser as opposed to having another command?

Admiral Weschler: I thought there was. One of the advantages of being in Washington all that time and being an aide and having a lot of people waiting to see the admiral was that I could have conversations with them. I asked them, "If you were going to sea today, where would you go, and why?" I'm sure I must have asked that of about 50 people.

As I mentioned to you, Admiral Sides was the missile czar, and Admiral Sides became a great personal friend. He was leaving to be the first cruiser division commander of the guided missile cruisers. Before he left, he said, "I'd love to see you in the cruiser division, so when you're coming to sea, why don't you ask for <u>Boston</u> or <u>Canberra</u>?" Well, by the time I came to sea, he had practically finished his tour, but he had planted the seed, and here were these new guided missile cruisers. I was an ordnance PG, and I really thought they sounded pretty exciting. So I think it was the combination of the guided missiles and a cruiser as exec, which was a working position that I thought was worthwhile. Having had command of a destroyer, I thought I could learn a lot in the cruiser and then could still get command one more time either of a cruiser or a squadron. There would be one more shot at that.

Q: It wound up that you did relieve a classmate who'd gone to sea ahead of you, Jerry Norton.*

Admiral Weschler: That's right. Jerry Norton, who was an eye unsat, exactly as I was, and he had had a marvelous tour with Captain Mauro.** When I got there, Captain Frank Brumby was in command; he happened to be a classmate of my brother's and been an OpNav friend. He was one of those who had come in and out of the front office any number of times, so that I knew him professionally, although I had never met him socially.

---
*Commander Gerald S. Norton, USN.
**Captain Charles T. Mauro, USN.

Thomas R. Weschler #4 - 359

I really enjoyed that tour. I'm trying to think of any particular highlights. The biggest thing I think that we accomplished while I was on board is unusual. I don't think it's ever going to go up in lights, but we were the ship in which the unknown soldier from the Korean War was selected. That was a tremendously complicated procedure and was done with much fanfare. But, you know, as far as its having any application to anything else that I was going to do professionally, it couldn't fit into that picture. It was just one of those that had a lot of protocol. It all had to be done right, it all had to be done under TV cameras and all sorts of people wandering around, and it all went like clockwork. Canberra and Boston got rave notices for what was done, and so it was very good for all of us in fitness reports for what we accomplished that time.

Q: Where and when did it happen?

Admiral Weschler: I relieved in January of '58, came back, so this was probably about May of that year.* For this selecting of the unknown, they had three bodies that were unknowns that were taken from different sites in the U.S., and so that they would have no idea of which came from

---

*The ceremony took place off the Virginia Capes on 26 May 1958 and also involved the cruiser Boston (CAG-1) and the destroyer Blandy (DD-943).

where, they were transferred by destroyer to <u>Boston</u>. Then <u>Boston</u>, the cruiser, came alongside <u>Canberra</u>, and the bodies were transferred at sea to <u>Canberra</u> and put into our missile magazine. There the three bodies were laid out and teams of hospital men, skilled as morgue attendants, went in and put the bodies in formal caskets, and then they left. After they were out, a team went in and shifted the positions of the caskets, and then they came out. Then another detail went in, and with no guidance, picked whichever casket they wanted and brought that casket out on deck, and that became the unknown. The other two caskets were transferred to a destroyer for burial elsewhere, and the one that was on the fantail then was transferred to a destroyer which brought it up to Washington Navy Yard.

It sounds very complicated, but what they were doing was making sure that no single individual had any idea which body ended up in which casket, and that no one of the teams, no matter how much you interviewed them, could give you the final answer as to which one was where. It all had to be done fairly quickly because we had many next of kin of those who had died in the Korean War and many VIPs and other visitors on board.

Q: Who did the final picking of the body?

Admiral Weschler: There was a hospital corpsman first class, Medal of Honor and Purple Heart winner by the name of Charette.* He was the one who went into the space and selected one of the three caskets there, not knowing which was which. He put the wreath on top of one of the caskets, and then the team went in and brought that one out.

Q: Did you as the exec have to run people through rehearsals beforehand?

Admiral Weschler: Oh, yes. I bet you we rehearsed that procedure about five times before everything took place. Interestingly, I was allowed to levy for crowds from the ships in the harbor, and so we would send over and say we wanted 20 officers who would be the VIPs who were coming aboard, and each one of them would be Admiral Wright and Admiral Uptyump, whoever it might have been, who was coming. Others acted as the families who had lost people in the Korean War, who were there as representatives of the civilian public, and others who would be the crews of the various ships who would be participating in the ceremony, and they would all get in their places.

We did that because we wanted to have an idea of how tightly packed the ship was going to be, so that we weren't

---

*Hospital Corpsman First Class William R. Charette, USN, who was awarded the Medal of Honor for his heroism while serving with the Marine Corps in the Korean War in 1953.

Thomas R. Weschler #4 - 362

making maneuvers with the caskets that actually on the day we'd find were impractical because of the crowds. I think we were about as thorough in anticipating all the problems as one could be. Then it came off well when it was done. The cruiser superstructure, with the guided missiles on their launchers, was a beautiful backdrop, and we had wonderful weather. It really was quite a ceremony. I saw some films that were taken later and pictures of the fantail with the crowds. It was very impressive, very suitable, and, I think, made a very fitting occasion for this selection of an unknown soldier.

Q: Where did it take place geographically?

Admiral Weschler: It took place in the Norfolk area, and then ultimately the destroyer came up to Washington.

Q: You had been a small ship sailor pretty much up to then, except for the *Wasp*. What kind of adjustments did you have to make to this far larger crew?

Admiral Weschler: I had been the gunnery officer of a cruiser for two years, and I had been the gunnery officer on CruLant's staff in '49 to '50, so that had gotten me used to cruisers and battleships. I think the principal thing that I felt as exec and that later on convinced me not to seek to be commanding officer of a cruiser was that every head of department was about as competent as a normal ship's skipper. As exec I felt that I was calling on the talents of six or eight destroyer skippers. Unless I were awfully dumb, things were going to be done very well.

I know the captain had that feeling about myself, and about all these others, that the best thing he could do was get out of the way and let us function. I must say Captain Brumby was easy to work for, and after him, Captain Charlie Smith.* I thoroughly enjoyed it. They placed a lot of confidence in me, and I hope that's what I did with these heads of departments. But as a result, I didn't want to be commanding officer of a cruiser because I couldn't see that much challenge in it. I felt I would get a lot more challenge out of working as commander of a squadron, and I think I made the right choice. I think that's precisely the way it worked out.

Q: When you were in the Canberra, did you get the idea that the CO didn't have too much of a job?

Admiral Weschler: Yes, frankly, that's what I say, though it is a great responsibility. I'm sure that you can get execs who will flub it, and I'm sure you get heads of departments who, every now and then, have to be canned.

---
*Captain Charles H. Smith, USN.

But, by and large, if the skipper is well served in department heads and exec, there is not a great deal of challenge for him <u>internally</u>. There's a chance for the CO to look out external to the cruiser and to do much in connection with employing the cruiser well in battle or thinking about how he fits into the type command or the division. That's where he can put his effort. But in a lot of peacetime requirements and single-ship operations, there is only so much you can do. Pretty soon the schedule is locked in for a year, and then you just have to sit back and go along for the ride.

Q: Can you talk some about the operations while you were on board?

Admiral Weschler: I think the principal thing that came up in connection with <u>Canberra</u>'s time was a gradual appreciation of how warfare was changing. You'd say that that ought to be obvious right away--that it's a guided missile cruiser--but that's only the beginning.* Because it was a guided missile cruiser, we were looking at the whole business of antiair warfare. Two people whom I think influenced the role of missilery in antiair warfare most were Admiral Lawson P. Ramage, Red Ramage, and Admiral Ricketts, both of whom were cruiser division commanders

---

*The <u>Canberra</u> was armed with Terrier missiles.

during the time that I was in Canberra.* Admiral Ricketts rode us for quite a spell on a deployment, and Admiral Ramage came aboard for one exercise, which was a very significant Second Fleet exercise and was most imaginative.

The combat information center had to be redone in order to get the information flow that was appropriate for guided missiles. And we learned how complex it was! You had to have the air search radar find the target initially, and then have the basic radar of the missile system guided onto it by the air search radar. Then you had to get the radar within the missile itself riding the beam that took it to the target. Marrying these three different systems was very complex, and you had to have special equipment in order to do it. The comprehension of the difficulty was slow to reach the fleet and slow to get around even within the ship.

The other aspect that goes with it is that in World War II you relied pretty much on your chiefs to know how the equipment worked. But now that we were moving into missilery, there were few chiefs who knew all this, and most of the missile men who served knew only one small piece of the system. So the officers were thrown into a

---

*Rear Admiral Lawson P. Ramage, USN, who became a vice admiral and whose oral history is in the Naval Institute collection; Rear Admiral Claude V. Ricketts, USN, who eventually became a four-star admiral.

role of having to know the technical side of it enough that they could be imaginative in developing tactics for usage.

I cite Admirals Ramage and Ricketts again, because both of them, as individuals, went to the stacks of these different pieces of equipment and would manipulate every knob themselves until they really had the skill and feel of that particular function, and then would go to the next one. They, as flag officers, were sometimes the ones who thought of the new patterns of how to employ the system, over and above what the individuals within the ship had been able to come up with. I found them sort of revolutionary in their approach and their comprehension, and it really put everybody on his toes! The initiative served to shake up a lot of people and get them thinking, "Gee whiz, that admiral has been aboard six weeks and he already knows more about this system than I do, and I'm finishing up a year or a year and a half on here. I'd better get with it." So it was that kind of fire that they were setting.

Q: Can you give an example, say, of Admiral Ramage's imagination in this? Was it new tactics?

Admiral Weschler: It's hard to pick out some particular thing at this moment, but it was the way that he tied concepts together. It was the teamwork that he engendered.

And I don't mean teamwork in terms of people in CIC; I mean teamwork within the fleet. He was devising patterns that we now take for granted of how to fit the combat air patrol, the guided missiles, and the guns into a firing pattern when an aircraft was closing.

I'm not positive of it, but I think it may have been on Admiral Ramage's watch that we first heard the term "salvo the CAP," referring to the combat air patrol that was chasing a target, trying to shoot it down. When the target moved within guided missile range, then the order was "salvo the CAP," which meant break off the CAP and get them out of there, because now you were going to give missiles free, and the missiles would be allowed to fire to shoot down the target. If Admiral Ramage didn't do it first, it was his concept, at least, of establishing these areas that one system had it here, then another weapon system had it there, and then finally the guns took over. That kind of coordination was slow in coming and it was formalized under people like Admirals Ricketts and Ramage to make the whole fleet work together and extend our AA competence over a tremendous field.

Q: Was there any body of doctrine for use of those ships when you arrived?

Admiral Weschler: Practically none. We were trying to

develop that body of doctrine.

One other aspect that I want to comment on was the shortage of missiles. We didn't have that many missiles to fire, and I think the feelings that I had then are probably still very much those of the fleet today, that when you have a missile allowance of maybe two or three a year, it's hard to say that you're competent and that you have an assurance that you can handle the missile battery excellently. If you fire three and you get one hit and miss two, you feel awful. If you fire and hit with two and miss one, you think that you're pretty good. I don't think either number amounts to a row of beans. You didn't really know what you could do.

Q: Those two ships, the Boston and Canberra, were seen as revolutionary at the time, as they were, but in retrospect, weren't they pretty rudimentary in terms of AAW systems?

Admiral Weschler: Yes, because of all of this other equipment it took to support their capability. The ability to hand off from the air-search radar to the missile system radar was just in the beginning stages--much too complicated and much too slow. I think the fastest we were ever able to make some of these transfers was perhaps one to one and a half minutes for transfers today that we want to do in five to ten seconds. The aircraft were not that much slower in those days, so you couldn't justify four or five times the time interval. They were just the beginning of the new techniques, and people had to grasp the overall look at things that people such as Ricketts and Ramage were bringing in order to get the equipment to have the response that it was going to take to do the whole job. We had a missile at sea; that was the biggest thing.

Q: Was there anything akin to NTDS then, or were you still pretty much adapting the old manual method?*

Admiral Weschler: I don't know of anything that we had that was more than high-speed teletype. That's the type of information we were passing around, sort of like the Link-14 to give ourselves the guidance on what was going on.** The cruiser was getting the word, and the carriers got the word, but I don't think the destroyers were really even into the teletypes that much in order to respond.

I just thought of an aside that might be of interest. The dummy guided missiles aboard <u>Canberra</u> were painted a blue and gold. They were used for missile-handling drills and for display on the launchers. They weren't painted a dark Navy blue and a bright gold, as you might have

---
*NTDS--Navy tactical data system, a computerized, automated system for tracking and responding to radar contacts.
**Link 14 is a data link for passing NTDS information between ships.

expected. They really ended up being not quite powder blue, but on that side of blue, and the gold was really more of a yellow. Canberra made a midshipmen's cruise in the summer of '58, and we were in Goteborg, Sweden. After we came up the channel and anchored, we ran these missiles up on the launchers. Even out there in the harbor, we could hear the cheers from the shore as these blue and yellow missiles went up on the ramp. Those were the Swedish national colors, and the Swedes assumed we had painted the missiles to suit Sweden, so we got the greatest round of applause you've ever heard. We left those missiles up the whole time we were there. It was the greatest thing we could ever have done.

Q: Do you have any recollection of Sixth Fleet operations from the period just after you came to the Canberra?

Admiral Weschler: No. As a matter of fact, when I got to Canberra, she was in Majorca. Admiral Charlie Melson was the cruiser division commander at the time, and they had just about completed their tour.* I had stayed a little longer with Admiral Burke than I had expected to initially, so that it was January of '58 before I could get there, and it was just about time to come home. So we had Majorca and

---

*Rear Admiral Charles L. Melson, USN, Commander Cruiser Division Four. Melson eventually retired as a vice admiral; his oral history is in the Naval Institute collection.

then we went off and did something; I think it was some sort of an AA gunnery shoot, and that was really about it, and then we started for home.

Of the activities for Canberra in addition to the AA exercises that I've talked about with Second Fleet, the biggest event was the midshipmen's cruise, which was a fine experience that involved Captain Charlie Smith. I'm trying to remember any significant events from that cruise other than the wonderful welcome in Sweden.

Captain Smith, somewhere along the line, had had a chance to bump into Prince Juan Carlos of Spain. Canberra came into Vigo, Spain, which was sort of an unusual port, not one that we visited often. There is a strong Celtic influence in the people, and it is a completely different Spain from Madrid or Barcelona. Canberra was alongside, and directly astern of us was the beautiful Spanish schooner, the Juan Sebastian de Elcano. The Prince was aboard the Juan Sebastian, and so Captain Smith had the Prince aboard for dinner. Later the Prince had Captain Smith aboard the Elcano. That's of great interest to me, because I've seen Elcano a lot since then as a tall ship, and I know that she still is very much in the Spanish King's eye. Whenever Elcano does any significant operation and returns, the King will usually have her perform a special review for him. Any sight of Juan Sebastian de

Thomas R. Weschler #4 - 372

Elcano always reminds me of Vigo, Spain, and that time when we were together.

Q: The Prince must have been pretty young at that point, wasn't he?

Admiral Weschler: He was 20 or 21.* He wasn't any more than that. He might have been a midshipman. I'm sure he wasn't an officer yet.

Q: Speaking of midshipmen, what kind of training program did you put on for them in the Canberra?

Admiral Weschler: Well, as you know, pretty much what you do with midshipmen is dictated by the Naval Academy. Their whole procedure is laid out. But the advantage of having Canberra assigned was that we were something brand-new and we had a chance to stimulate their imagination. So, regardless of anything else that the midshipmen did, they were all walked through the missile battery and given a demonstration. The fact that we were able to carry nuclear warheads was not something that was discussed, but that became apparent as they saw the layout. Frankly, in those days, we didn't have any nuclear warheads aboard. We were simply capable of carrying them.

―――――――――
*Prince Juan Carlos was born 5 January 1938.

I think the thing that was remarkable that had to be developed for Canberra and Boston was the ability to handle the damage of a serious missile fire. They had never had so much inflammable explosive assembled in a single large space as we had in that missile magazine. They were used to sprinkling systems, but a sprinkling system really wouldn't do a lot if there were a major fire. So the big question was, how to get a tremendous amount of water into this space in a hurry in order to flood out the fire, and at the same time not sink the ship, because that missile magazine was a huge area.

There had been a lot of engineering studies to justify the system installed, but BuShips decided it wasn't sufficient. Then they did more studies that ended in new installations for the later guided missile cruisers. BuShips devised a means by which a sprinkling system could be supplemented by opening holes as big as three feet across to allow mountains of water to come pouring in, so that they felt they could flood a missile magazine in seconds. It was a fantastic thing to contemplate, but much different from what we had when we started. I think it was the appreciation that BuShips got from seeing the spaces and studying the problem and our asking questions about, "What do we do if?" that made them aware of the fact that more needed to be done.

The midshipmen certainly became aware of what we had

and could recognize that it was a conversion, but I think we also could relate to those who said, "Okay, but it doesn't look very sophisticated." I don't think we were on that first go-round. We had a lot of capability, but it was all in one spot, and you could tell you'd taken a turret out and put this in in its stead.

Q: Was the barbette still left in?*

Admiral Weschler: No. All that had gone, and we had taken over the space that had been available for the catapults and the aircraft stowage, so that you really had a lot of the fantail.

Q: There was a big deck house back there too.

Admiral Weschler: That's right. That part of the deck house remained, and the missile launcher was on top of it. Then you had an area within the deck house where you put on the wings and fins. As the missile came up, it stopped and was winged and finned and then went on up to the launcher and was ready to go.

Q: That was done manually, the wings and the fins?

---

*A barbette is an armored cylinder that extends down into the ship, below the turret itself.

Thomas R. Weschler #4 - 375

Admiral Weschler: Yes. They had to be there and were put in place, and it could be done very quickly. You had to have people standing there to put them on, and then the missile went on up. When you brought them back down, the same thing; wings and fins had to come off, too, to strike a missile below. Then there was something that in later years came to be called the "Coke machine." It was the series of open canisters in which you could strike down your test missile and then cycle over to a live missile and bring it up.

We had different kinds of missiles, the missiles that were used with the conventional warhead and those that would have been capable of taking a nuclear warhead if needed. These things were very interesting to the midshipmen, and, I think, gave them a feel of the wave of the future. They also went up and saw the missile control equipment and radars. Aside from stimulating them with this, that was really all the "new Navy," we were able to work into their time on board.

Q: Were there any special security precautions for this missile magazine?

Admiral Weschler: Oh, yes, because it was such a danger. It was very similar to the way that we handle a nuclear space today. You had to have tight security, you had to have a missile battery badge in order to get into the space. There was a log-in, log-out procedure. As you can imagine, overseas it was an area that almost all our VIP visitors wanted to see. We wouldn't do it for a conventional civilian group, but if there was somebody from the Swedish Government, a senior or the ambassador or someone like that, he was almost always brought back. You'd get the word, "Line up the missile team." Then you knew they were going to come in, and they'd get the five-minute spiel on what went on in the winging and finning area, and the general layout: "See, here they are down here." Then they'd go out, and you'd run the missiles up and train them around, and they'd say, "Thank you very much." We were ready to do that all day and all night at a drop of a hat!

Q: Did you feel, though, that this setup was no longer classified information, that it had pretty well been shown to enough people that it was compromised?

Admiral Weschler: I think we recognized from the beginning that the big thing about it was the internals of how the missile worked, the beam-riding aspects, the radar and so on. That, of course, we didn't discuss any more than the most general statement, "It's a beam-rider," or something like that. So we really weren't worried an awful lot about doing these other things. It was physical security against others that was really the danger for this kind of an installation. That magazine was so sensitive that any sabotage in there could have been gross and could have wiped out the ship. That's all there was to it.

Q: You'd been a gunnery officer. How good was the gunnery in the Canberra?

Admiral Weschler: I thought it was pretty good. As a matter of fact, I enjoyed the fact that we still had turrets. The fact that we could fire the missiles and at the same time still have turrets and a good AA battery was sort of comforting. We were not all switched over, and it made us feel very ambidextrous, that there was hardly any phase of warfare we couldn't contribute to. And I think that we had good people. You know, it was a good cruiser, and although it wasn't one of the new rapid-fire ones, which everybody wanted, it still could put out the bullets.

Q: As it turned out, there was no need for a rapid-fire cruiser.

Admiral Weschler: No, we didn't use any of them very much in their basic role. We weren't as much of a flagship as a lot of other people would have liked. You know, the Salem, Newport News, everybody was getting outfitted with more and more communications gear. Canberra didn't get a lot of that. It was okay for a cruiser division commander, but that was another thing that ComSixthFlt noted, that it just didn't have the number of circuits and the flexibility that they needed to establish the AA nets and to do everything in the fleet that would have been desirable.

Q: As an exec, you were probably just as grateful you weren't a fleet flagship.

Admiral Weschler: Yes. I think you're absolutely right. I think this is where, by not being one, I think that I perhaps have the views that I have on cruisers. Had we been a fleet flagship, I'm sure that the CO would have had a thousand things to do there, because, as you know, he is, in effect, another chief of staff, and he has some of the most demanding ship riders to accommodate. He's busy all the time putting out the fires of friction between himself and the staff and trying to make sure that the ship is run well to suit the admiral. In that case he becomes sort of a super exec, and the exec is running the internals. I never got in that situation, and I'm just as glad.

Q: Do you have any recollections about the Marine

detachment in Canberra?

Admiral Weschler: I do, because the Marine detachment was such a key part of that unknown soldier arrangement. Captain Paul Helsher was the senior Marine by the time we had that transfer.* He just couldn't have been better. He was ex-enlisted and had a wonderful feel for drill and for precision and control. He put together the details of men for the unknown soldier ceremony, and he ran a very good Marine detachment. He was a great one for having them out on deck, running through all of the physical fitness training, doing various drills with small arms, with manual at arms, and making sure that they were crisp. Through him, I got a good feel for the detachment and thought it was a good unit.

Q: Was there an emphasis on spit and polish despite not being a fleet flagship?

Admiral Weschler: Yes. I think that any cruiser prides itself on that. You want to have a quarterdeck that really sets the pace. Captain Brumby, who was my first skipper, was the son of four-star Admiral Brumby.**

---
*Captain Paul M. Helsher, USMC.
**Frank Hardeman Brumby was in the Naval Academy class of 1894. His top assignment was as a vice admiral, Commander Scouting Force in the early 1930s. He retired in 1938 and was subsequently advanced to the rank of four-star admiral on the retired list in 1942.

Thomas R. Weschler #4 - 380

Q: For whom a destroyer escort was named.*

Admiral Weschler: Yes. There wasn't any doubt in his mind that he wanted a ship that his father would have been proud of, and he ran it that way. Captain Charlie Smith was one who very much aspired to be a flag officer, and so he wanted a ship that reflected the pride that he had in the ship, and he wanted it to be one that people would say, "Who's the skipper of that?"

And he'd say, "That's my ship." So I think I had two good skippers and they insisted on having the ship look well, and I think it did.

Q: Was there still a good bit of formality in the ship in honors and courtesies and wardroom decorum and so forth?

Admiral Weschler: I'm trying to think where I might have been to establish a feeling for such a judgment. I don't think there's any question but what the answer would be yes. Not as much as in the '49-'50 era when I had been the gunnery officer of CruLant. I remember then the battleships and cruisers as being very strict in what was done. This was now '58-'59. I think that there had been some softening of that, and part of it is because each of

---

*USS Brumby (DE/FF-1044)

us, as we came along, was not likely to have been shipmates with cruisers and battleships all our professional careers. There was a lot more of the destroyer Navy and the amphibious Navy flowing in, and I think that softened the edges of some of this. So I think there was an easing of it, but still a very noticeable difference between going aboard Canberra and going aboard a destroyer. I think you would have felt it right away.

Q: Did you have a bugler, for instance?

Admiral Weschler: Yes, we had a Marine bugler, and, of course, he was busy all the time. I remember that my children came aboard, and they enjoyed being there because they liked to hear the bells rung and the bugle calls, and that sort of thing. They liked the whole thing, the beautifully stoned decks and the fancy work that the sailors had made--the macrame all around. Those were the things that caught your eye, and people thought this was really pretty great. When we were on that midshipmen's cruise, we really wanted to put our best foot forward. After all, we were with the British and Swedish and Dutch and Spanish navies, and whenever you're with other navies, you want to make sure your own looks pretty good. We didn't let down at all in that.

Q: I had the feeling when I was in the New Jersey that people wanted to make the ship look good as a matter of pride, as if they owed that to the ship, not that they were being forced to. Was it that way with you?

Admiral Weschler: Yes. I would say that that was part of it, and that helped again to make it quite easy to run the ship. And people weren't as crowded. When I think of the living spaces in a destroyer where it's much more like in a very small house with a lot of kids, one person moves one thing, and the whole room looks topsy-turvy. You get a cruiser with people spread out through large living spaces, and even if they've been down there living in the space, all of a sudden it doesn't look that bad. There's room enough to absorb people without being out of order.

Q: How well did she ride?

Admiral Weschler: That class of cruiser, and Canberra was no exception, had what I called a pendulous bow. If you got down there forward of turret one in any sort of a seaway, the bow had a funny way of rocking that gave you the impression it was going to come right off. And you recall that the Pittsburgh lost its bow in the typhoon in 1945.* Well, it wouldn't have surprised me if Canberra

---
*The heavy cruiser Pittsburgh (CA-72), a Baltimore-class sister of the Canberra, lost her bow during a typhoon on 4 June 1945. It was subsequently replaced, and the ship returned to service.

had dropped its bow a couple of times when we were crossing the Atlantic. I went down there with the chief engineer two or three times to look at that thing, because I was sure that those stanchions were working and that it was going to come loose. But they had done a special shipalt after the Pittsburgh lost its bow, and they had done at least one more stiffening since then.* So we decided it wasn't going to come off, but it sure was something to see. You didn't want to be up there because you just couldn't have any feeling of security.

Q: It sounds almost eerie, the way you describe it.

Admiral Weschler: Yes, that's why I called it the pendulous bow. That's just the way it felt, as though at any moment it was just going to swing right over and come off.

Q: Did this same pride that we talked about in the crew manifest itself in the disciplinary action? Was that fairly easy for you?

Admiral Weschler: Yes. As I recall it, the role of the exec in this time frame was beginning to be under the new

---

*Shipalt--ship alteration.

law, so that the exec could have a preliminary mast and a screening mast, but you really couldn't take final action on many things, nor did the captain want you to. So that the captain really had to go through the final routines. But because of the fact that they knew everything was going all the way to the captain, there was a lot of emphasis, I think, by the chief petty officers, on trying to get things solved at their level. By now we had come through the rapid outs at the end of the Korean War, and we were now back to a point where we were getting long-term personnel in the Navy. So the restlessness that I felt in that era, '53-'55, was pretty well gone. We now were dealing with more permanent ship's company and people who wanted to be there.

I think Admiral Burke had had an impact on what was going on in the fleet. I think there was the feeling that somebody cared and that deployments were beginning to get under control, and there was a little more regular life to what was going on at sea. You deployed and then you came home and operated out of your home port for more reasonable periods. It was not a time of stress in the personnel side of the Navy, and I found it to be a reasonably happy situation with a lot of continuity in the personnel and those who were available.

Q: Was the ship a popular tourist attraction in the United States? Did civilians come to see her?

Admiral Weschler: Not all that much. We came into Norfolk; that was home port. That naval base was so huge that if people came in, they drove around the piers, and that was about it. We took our turn at being the ship for public visiting, but I don't recall, even though we were a guided missile cruiser, that that many came along. If we were in a port, a special port like New York, which we got to at least once or twice, then we would be overwhelmed, and then you put on the missile display for everybody under the sun, and that was wonderful. But aside from such visits, I don't think we saw all that many.

Q: As far as people within the Navy, had some of the curiosity value worn off by the time you got there?

Admiral Weschler: Yes, definitely, because there were other ships being contemplated then, and I think they just thought these were the forerunners and there were going to be an awful lot more coming along, and that when they built them from scratch, that was going to be the real McCoy.

Q: Anything else on _Canberra_?

Thomas R. Weschler #4 - 386

Admiral Weschler: I have one name to drop that I think might be of interest, just going back to Admiral Burke and coming up to <u>Canberra</u>. Admiral Burke was eagerly sought by a lot of the reserve groups to come speak to them. One of the people who came in to see Admiral Burke often when he first came in as CNO was Bernard Baruch, Jr., who was a stockbroker and investment counselor. He had picked up a lot of his father's background, not all his father's competence, but nonetheless was capable and well thought of in business.*

However, he was a bit of a problem to handle, in that he would come in with poorly thought-out ideas. Nonetheless, Admiral Burke tried to be receptive to him and did see him on a couple of occasions, and went up to New York and spoke to the intelligence company of Naval Reserve that Bernard Baruch, Jr., was a member of. But later, he was one that the admiral asked me to make sure was taken care of, without bothering the admiral directly.

One of the things that Baruch was working on, which later became worthwhile, was trying to get the merchant ships of the United States into some sort of an intelligence reporting network. It was never formalized, but when the merchant marine officers would come through various schools that the Navy had, they were asked that if

---

*Bernard Baruch, Sr. (1870-1965) was a long-time businessman and statesman, highly respected as a presidential adviser.

ever they saw unusual things out on the high seas, not to hesitate to send messages back to the naval districts or to Washington, so that they would be acting as eyes and ears around the world and giving us an informal network. And I think Baruch was useful in getting those kinds of ideas established.

When we were in New York in '59 with Canberra, Bernard Baruch, Jr., learned that the ship was in and that I was aboard as exec. He was kind enough to say, "Won't you join me at my place in Oyster Bay?" He sent this huge limousine in to get Captain Smith and myself, and we were whisked out to his beautiful home on Oyster Bay. He had a big swimming pool, large old home, wonderful setting. We thoroughly enjoyed it. While Captain Smith and I were there having this wonderful time, a visitor was announced, and, lo and behold, it was Commander Sheldon Kinney and his wife Lee dropping by.* They had known the Baruchs from some previous experience in the Long Island area, and I thought that was interesting. That's the first time I had bumped into Sheldon Kinney since the Naval Academy, and I thought, well, you can't meet somebody under nicer auspices than to be guests of the Baruchs on Long Island at their Oyster Bay home. That's just an aside, but at least it gets names

---

*Commander Sheldon H. Kinney, USN, was essentially a contemporary of Weschler's, having graduated from the Naval Academy in the class of 1941. Kinney eventually retired as a rear admiral.

connected across the years, an incident that I've often reminded Sheldon Kinney of when I see him.

Q: He worked in that area, at Fort Schuyler, for a while after he retired.*

Admiral Weschler: That's right. And I'm sure that some of those same friendships were in the background of his going to Fort Schuyler and leading him into the job that he has at present, with the World Marine University that he's working on.

Q: You went from there to a BuOrd tour in Pittsfield, Mass. How did that come about?

Admiral Weschler: That, I think, was a very interesting change of duty. One night when the ship was away, the phone rang at our home in Norfolk. <u>Canberra</u> was down at Guantanamo at the time. This friend, Charlie Norris, told Trina that he had just heard that I was going to Pittsfield, Massachusetts, to be the BuOrd rep.** Trina said, "Oh, Charlie, I just can't believe you. Call me tomorrow morning if you think that that's true." So she hung up.
_____
*Following his retirement from active naval service, Admiral Kinney served as superintendent of the State University of New York Maritime College.
**Captain Charles R. Norris, Jr., USN.

Inside of 15 minutes, Charlie was back on the phone, and he said, "Trina, I know you think I've been drinking. I'm telling you the truth. Your husband is going as BuOrd rep to Pittsfield."

Trina said, "That can't possibly be. Tom hasn't done anything that bad." That was her reaction.

About that time Observation Island showed up down in Guantanamo. That ship was working with the Polaris missile project, although I didn't know it at the time. I simply knew that Observation Island was a converted ship and that they were practically using first class petty officers as deck hands because she had a complicated set of equipments on board. They didn't have room for many people, and so they were pressing the petty officers into service. An officer out of '34, Bud Slack, was the skipper, an ordnance PG and someone I knew slightly.*

I bumped into him over at the club at Guantanamo, and asked him in general what was going on. He said, "The Polaris missile program is moving along fast. It's moving into various test areas. We're beginning to get equipment, and some of the people involved are at GE at Pittsfield and at Lockheed," and so on. So at least I now had a few ideas about areas and places.

When I came back to Norfolk, which was, let's say, a

---

*Captain Leslie M. Slack, USN, was the first commanding officer when the test ship Observation Island (EAG-154) was commissioned on 5 December 1958.

week or so after my wife had had this phone call, she told me, almost in tears what she had heard, and said, "Now, you get on the phone and find out."

So I called Ben Pickett, who had been a classmate of mine at MIT and another ordnance PG, and he was the detailer for BuOrd.* He said, "Absolutely right, Tom. You're going up there. Your title is BOTLO NIROP Pittsfield."

I said, "You've got to tell me what those initials mean."

He said, "It stands for BuOrd Technical Liaison Officer, Naval Industrial Reserve Ordnance Plant, Pittsfield," and it means that you are the special Polaris representative at Pittsfield, where they are building the guidance and fire control systems for Polaris."

I said, "Well, is it the same as an inspector of naval material?"

He said, "No, you're working directly for SP, for the Special Projects Office. This is a good job. I'm really not hurting you at all. You really ought to feel glad that you're getting it. You're going to be relieving Archie Soucek out of '37, and I think it's the way to fame and fortune."**

I said, "Ben, I've got to take your word for it.

---

*Captain Ben B. Pickett, USN.
**Captain Archie H. Soucek, USN, who retired 1 July 1959.

Okay. Sounds all right to me because I'm shipmates with the Polaris idea. I'd really like to get in on it."

So that was how it came about. Because of my background and this detailer who thought that he was doing me a favor, I joined the Polaris program, and he was absolutely right. I stayed in Pittsfield about a year, and during the year that I was there, I was selected for captain. With that year's experience, I had an opportunity to come back to Washington to head up the Polaris fire control and guidance section. I regard that Pittsfield tour as being one of the best and most exciting I ever had. It introduced me to industry, was my first real contact with civil service, and was my first experience with all of the technical side of the Navy from the standpoint of conceiving and building equipments.

It was a major learning experience, and also, I think, a heartening one, because I found that we had some of the most capable, dedicated people in civil service that one could want. I don't know how we had all those people at the right place at the right time, how we recruited them and how we held onto them, but that Polaris program was a tribute to a lot of people, and the Navy civil service were a key part of it.

Q: Why did they pick you?

Admiral Weschler: I was an ordnance PG. The guidance and fire control was put together by Dr. Draper, who had been one of my profs at MIT. MIT was one of the contractors in the group that I was going to administer, and the other teams that were involved were GE Pittsfield and Sperry Gyroscope in Long Island. So with the MIT connection and the specific educational background, this seemed like the right kind of thing. The rest of it was availability. The tours in cruisers were nominally 18 months at that time, and I'd been aboard just about 18 months, so I was due to roll during the summer. They needed somebody because Archie Soucek was about to retire. Thus I was available on time and had the right tickets for this particular billet. Then, having been there for a year, the officer in Washington was due to move, and he was looking for a relief. I ended up relieving Frank Herold, who was an electronics PG, EDO.*

This was another thing that impressed me about the whole Polaris program: it was a conglomerate of all types of naval officer talent. It didn't matter where you came from; it mattered what experience or professionalism you were able to bring to the job. So we had submariners, surface sailors, aviators, EDs, all working on the project, all mixed up and interchanged and moved around and relieving each other. It was a tribute to Admiral Raborn,

---
*Captain Frank B. Herold, USN.

Thomas R. Weschler #4 - 393

who said, "I've got a job to do. I want the talent. Now get it for me."

Q: What was the basis for your initial hesitation in going to Pittsfield?

Admiral Weschler: I never really had that hesitation, except what my wife had engendered. She felt, based on general hearsay, that one of the ends of the line was to become an inspector of ordnance or materiel in some out-of-the-way place. She suspected that it was a place to be left to die, and then you'd retire from there. Pittsfield is enough off the beaten path that if I tell people today that I lived in Lenox, Massachusetts, and worked in Pittsfield, they say, "Oh, were you going to college?" They can't imagine anything in that area that would call for the presence of a commander or a captain. I think Trina was just putting it in the conventional framework and didn't know the special nature of the job. We didn't know SP well enough at the time to realize that they were putting top talent wherever anything was going on. There was an inspector of naval material at Pittsfield, a commander's billet. It was not of the same character as the BuOrd technical liaison officer.

Q: You said you had a lot to learn in that job. How could

you be effective, then, staying only a year?

Admiral Weschler: Well, you could be effective because everybody was learning. It was a new program. Everything that was being done was being done to a new sheet of music. There were a lot of details to supervise, a lot of general programs to administer. The dovetailing, which was the level I was working on, was to make sure that what was going on at MIT was being recognized by GE or that Sperry was doing its part, because these pieces of equipment had to fit together. It might well be that there were manufacturers trying to meet tolerances that had been set, let's say, by MIT. They might be having a terrible time meeting a particular tolerance. You could get back to Dr. Draper's group and say, "This is what we're finding. Is it possible to relax it?"

If the answer was no, we'd say, "Have you been able to meet it in the laboratory?" Usually the answer would be yes. "I need one of your experts from the laboratory, then, to get down to Kearfott and find out precisely what they're doing because they're now on their sixth item and there isn't a one of them that comes near meeting the specs. Help them out." It was that kind of coordination of being sensitive to problems as they were arising and having the talent or the dollars or the ability to call on Washington to get other talent to put out the fires as quickly as they came up. You could do that without an awful lot of experience, but thank heavens for that year in the field by the time I went to Washington. Now I had a chance to recognize what the whole national production picture was, and to be able to play the role nationally that I learned to play in a region.

Q: What was your piece of the action, then, when you were at Pittsfield? What part was it of the whole?

Admiral Weschler: The missile guidance and the fire control system--the guidance package which flew with the missile, and the fire control system, which stayed in the submarine and controlled the spin-up, arming, initial setting, and actual firing of the missile. The teamwork required across a major set of industry was phenomenal. Everything from the beginning was second-sourced, so if any one company fell on its face, you always had another one ready to go.

In things like the guidance gyroscopes, which were the whole key to accuracy, we had three manufacturers from the beginning; we had Honeywell, AC Spark Plug, and Kearfott. Those gyros were so demanding that there were times when we would have perhaps 60 of them in process and maybe two were meeting the specifications! Yet we had to get them. We were turning out a reasonable number, because we knew when every one of them had to start going into its guidance system to meet the final delivery timetable. That was the kind of thing we were working on, and gyros probably absorbed six months out of that year's time, because they were the biggest bottleneck all the way through.

One other thing that I think is important to highlight here is the teamwork between the Air Force and the Navy. The Navy was working on the Polaris project. Meanwhile, the Air Force was working on the Minuteman. Everything that we were doing at Lockheed, the system contractor, and around our contractors, the Air Force was doing around its Ballistic Missile Systems Division, which was headquartered in Los Angeles. We used to stop by Los Angeles to visit their guidance and fire control division and see what they were doing, what luck they were having. If we were having any problems, we'd tell them where we were stood.

Dr. Draper was the adviser to both groups. We were using the Dr. Draper principles all through both inertial guidance systems. We had agreed with them that we would have three manufacturers of gyros different from the three they had, and when we began to procure transistors, we used different sources. In that way we could back up each other's program. We made some of the most fantastic changes in the course of the life of these early missile programs. The whole electronic industry was growing up. We moved from straight circuitry, to potted modules, to circuit boards, to the beginning of the microcircuits as we know them today, and that all happened in perhaps three years.

We would show the Air Force what we were doing as our approach to it, and they would tell us what they were doing. In one case, where the Air Force had a very rigid specification on a transistor, we were able to take the first rejects of their test and use them in our program. We did a lot of backup and a lot of working together, which at the time, critics of the Defense Department were not willing to believe. These critics thought of us as two contesting missile programs. The teamwork was really the way that it was going! Brigadier General Duffey, who was the head of fire control and guidance at that time for the Air Force, is now retired and serving as the head of the Draper Lab at MIT. He has been doing a lot of work with NASA on the space projects.

Q: Did you have much contact with Dr. Draper personally on this?

Admiral Weschler: He was a member of the steering committee for the Polaris project. I used to see him probably once a month or so up there at the laboratory, and I was in his lab at least once a week. After we moved to Washington, I saw him less often.

Q: Would it be fair to say he made a substantial contribution to that?

Admiral Weschler: I don't think there's any question. I think Dr. Draper's ideas, as incorporated in the guidance systems, were the real heart of our success in the whole field. He was brilliant. Without him we wouldn't have gotten to the moon, and without him I don't think we'd have the progress that we've made in satellites today.

Q: Did you get out in the Observation Island for tests?

Admiral Weschler: Never in the Observation Island. By the time that I got down to Washington and would have really been doing some of that, they were past the Observation Island era. We used her a lot for the initial launching module. They had her when they were checking out the various kinds of rolls and pitches and motions that equipment could handle, going through simulation, being sure all that was taken care of. By the time I got there, we were doing the firings from submarines, so the firings that I watched were aboard the George Washington and the Robert E. Lee, the first couple of submarines coming along, and we would do the test firings from those.

Q: Where did you get your requirements as far as accuracy? Was that from OpNav?

Admiral Weschler: I would say that it was a combination. I think that the MIT lab specified what they thought they could meet, and then they took what they thought we could do and cranked it back through to see what that kind of a warhead would be needed to get results and what warheads could do. We had to know whether there was a match between what was possible and what then was needed. If it didn't quite fit, then there might have to be a refinement, go back and say, "MIT, we hear you, but we need X." So it would be a talk back and forth between what was desired and what they thought was feasible and then still be able to get it done within the time frame. But I'm happy to say that from the beginning, they actually were achieving the accuracy that they wanted, and then there began to be a little more accuracy than we had initially called out. So that was very healthy.

Q: How much pressure was there from that time schedule?

Admiral Weschler: Relentless. As you may recall, the Polaris program created a whole bunch of things that never existed before. It was the first time that anyone took what was essentially major R&D and laid it out as a production schedule. As somebody said, "They took ten miracles in a row, gave them a timetable, and achieved it." That's just about the way it was. The gentleman whom I would give credit to after Admiral Raborn, who was the whip for this whole thing, was Levering Smith, now Vice Admiral "Sir" Levering Smith.*

Levering Smith was a chemical PG, and he became the technical director of the project, primarily because solid fuel was the big thing that the Navy was contributing to this missile design. MIT was conceiving the guidance system. The AEC was pretty well putting together the warhead and the bomb that it was going to carry.** Then the other big thing was putting together the rocket motors of solid fuel. That was really the biggest challenge that had ever come up, and that's where Levering Smith fit in.

Then there were the mechanics of getting the missile launched from underwater, getting it up into the air, and igniting, and making it go through all the stages properly. That's where Lockheed came in with all sorts of subcontractors. The Navy threw the challenge to Lockheed as the prime contractor to do all of this development and coordination work, rather than the Navy trying to fit all the pieces together for itself. That was a revolution, and that's why the steering committee was so important. It

---

*Captain Levering Smith, USN.
**AEC--Atomic Energy Commission.

consisted of the presidents or chief executives or senior scientists of all of these companies sitting there with Levering Smith, listening to what the problems were and making sure it would go, and then once a week having a report to Admiral Raborn as to where they were versus where they were supposed to be.

That's when things like PERT charts were invented.* The first time they were ever developed was on the SP program by Gordon Pehrson, who came to us from Chicago in some management position out there.** He's another one of those that Admiral Raborn found and gave his head. The first thing you know, he created this whole business of "how goes it" and where we were supposed to be, and the planning charts, so that you had something to report against. It was his job to have these indicators coming in so that while the technical groups would be saying, "This is what we're doing and where we are." This other group was saying, "This is where you're supposed to be."

When you met on Monday morning for this weekly report, you were always presenting where you thought you were versus what this other team, your buddies, were saying you should be. Admiral Raborn might say, "What's going on here? I don't like that. You're in trouble. Explain to

---

*Program Evaluation Review Technique, a system of laying out milestones to be achieved and a projected timetable for their achievement, then measuring progress toward the goal.
**Gordon B. Pehrson's oral history on Polaris is in the Naval Institute collection.

me how you're going to get out of it." Then he established these different color-coded levels of problem: "In trouble, but I can solve it," "In trouble, but the technical director can solve it," or, "In trouble. Admiral, you've got a problem." Those were the three kinds. He told us, "If I ever hear, 'Admiral, you've got a problem,' and I haven't had a warning about it, you're in trouble." So each weekly review was an important session, and everybody knew that's just the way it was. There were people going around whose job was not to spy, but in effect to know everything that was going on and whether or not it was meeting the schedule. They were giving their own best analysis, which might be completely different from what you, as the technical director's representatives, would be saying about the problem and its seriousness. But those things got debated with the boss and not with anybody else.

Q: Did the fact that it was such a new thing create problems in establishing these milestones, because maybe you didn't know what you needed to achieve?

Admiral Weschler: I'm sure that's true, but, as I say, we put milestones on for everything anyhow. The idea was that you knew that just backing it down from where you had to be at the end to today--if you'd come at it from the finish point, you would establish a deadline. Then you could come up this way from where you were and you might very well find that you had six months or six minutes, but you knew you could establish a time frame from one end or the other.

As long as you didn't have too many of these imponderables, you could box yourself in enough to know whether you felt you could make it or not. That's the kind of thing, then, that would lead you into saying, "Boss, we've got a problem." And then you'd get new talents. That's when you might very well bring in a couple of more experts whose job was simply to address themselves to this issue, help you to delimit it, and see whether or not there might be another approach that could do it. That's why I say it was R&D but being done on a production schedule right from the beginning.

Q: Were there any special requirements for the guidance system because it was a solid-fuel missile?

Admiral Weschler: There weren't any that were different from what it would have been on a liquid fuel, I don't think, but the principal thing that the guidance system had to do was determine when cutoff would take place, and when it would cut on again if you needed one more spurt to put it into the right trajectory. So it controlled the signals that had to be given to the motor. It was much more of a problem for the fuel manufacturers to devise a means of turning on the motor and turning it off so that if you wanted a tenth of a second acceleration, you could get it. It was much more of a problem from their end, and trying to get nozzles that could stand the intense blast pressures.

By now, we're used to working with these very high heats and pressures, but in those days, all of this metallurgy was brand-new. There was hardly anything that was being done that wasn't right at the threshold of science. They must have spent weeks trying to get one kind of metal which would allow those rocket nozzles on the second stage to remain intact throughout the flight dependably. It was a revelation to me. It was U.S. R&D and manufacturing know-how, in one of the most exciting environments that I can imagine. I believe every person who was in it was really working for Uncle Sam and not just his company. A lot of the people who were there as young civilians really got painted golden and went right up through their companies. The head of Lockheed missile and space division today, Bob Fuhrman, was one of the junior engineers working on the Polaris program when it got started.* That kind of thing repeated over and over. They learned how to work in this environment, and probably few programs could have given them the insight that they gained in Polaris.

---

*Robert A. Fuhrman.

Q: Did you have any benefit in that tour from the fact that you had been in a guided missile ship just prior?

Admiral Weschler: I'm sure it was some. I'm trying to think where. I think it was probably at GE Pittsfield more than it was when I got to Washington. The part that I'm coming back to there was that all the equipment that was developed at GE had to be very thoroughly tested before it could be moved out of the plant to the ship. Having worked with Canberra and known what elaborate test procedures we used for checking out the missilery on a repetitive basis and checking out all the fire control gear that we used there, I was familiar with the procedures and the pamphlets and the way that it was done. So when we came to devising acceptance tests for Polaris equipment at GE, I had a good feel for what they ought to be like, and I could make some contributions or at least have a feel for what we were coming up with.

One other thing that was helpful was the fact that anybody who's been aboard ship and goes into an overhaul knows what the conditions are in a ship that's building. We made sure that the equipments that were being devised at Pittsfield were going to be ready to go aboard ship exactly as they were delivered, that they didn't have to have various pieces assembled by people unused to the critical nature or purpose of the equipment.

We had a bad experience with part of the gear that went aboard George Washington, but we learned very quickly. George Washington was about two-thirds finished and they started putting the fire control equipment on board, intact, as we had delivered it. The ship itself wasn't sealed off, and so all of the normal welding was going on and all of that dirt of the yard was coming in. In about four weeks, we examined that fire control equipment, and it was terrible. Every bit of that gear had to be taken out of the ship, brought back to the factory in a special truck, cleaned, and then returned. From then on, none of the fire control gear was put into a submarine until the ship was ready and the air-conditioning was in operation so that it was, in effect, a protected environment. When that was done, then the equipment was taken down and put in place so that it operated in a clean environment that it was going to be seeing for the rest of its life and was spared the usual overhaul abuse.

Q: What would you say was the biggest problem you had while at Pittsfield?

Admiral Weschler: I'd say the biggest problem in that job at Pittsfield was the gyroscopes that were coming from three manufacturers who were trying to build them to spec. Those were in the days before we knew what clean rooms really were. Now if you tell me that you need a space which is clean to the nearest micron, probably a third of the plants in the U.S. have places where that's being done. At that time it was unheard of. This was the first time that we really began to get into the business of people having to wear all of the fancy uniforms, as though they were going into an operating room, absolutely clean environment with multiple filters and all that. We were establishing manufacturing requirements and tolerances that the industry had never faced before. Gyroscopes, which were so picky in their dimensions and tolerances, were right on the ragged edge of what could be done.

Another thing that was brand-new was that the guidance system was demanding in terms of weight. After all, we're now dealing with what is being carried by this missile up into space. Everything there is to make it go boom, with the exception of the guidance system. If your guidance system is too heavy, it affects the weight of the warhead. The warhead and guidance system combined have to meet weight, or else the range falls off. Well, we were working against a target of, let's say, 1,500 miles, and every ounce we could get out of the guidance system was probably worth another few miles.

Finally, having made every adjustment we could possibly make, cranking down the weights of the gyros and all the rest of it, the systems review team decided the only thing to do was to start making these guidance systems of beryllium. Well, beryllium was a brand-new metal. It looks somewhat like aluminum, but it's as strong as steel, and about the same weight as magnesium. It is deadly poison when you machine it in terms of particles that get into the air. So in order to install a beryllium facility, we had to get a space that not only was absolutely clean, but now the workers had to wear masks so that they were protected against the particles, and you had to have a high-speed air changer so that there couldn't be any concentration of particles build up, and they had to learn to machine beryllium. We had never worked with it before, so this was a whole new kind of metallurgy that had to be learned.

The plant had to be built as a production plant at GE when no one had even worked on this metal before. What kind of bits and lathes and drills and all such technical questions had to be learned from scratch and turned out as an operating plant. Everything had to be special ordered and made for this application. It was a challenging assignment. The guidance systems ended up being made of beryllium and worked wonderfully, and everything was fine. We probably added 200 miles to the range of the missile from making that kind of a change. It was worth it, because it gave the submarine that much more flexibility in its operations at sea. So there were lots of challenges, and it's hard to pick out the one, but I still think the gyros were our biggest problem.

Q: At what level would that kind of decision have been made to go with beryllium?

Admiral Weschler: It probably would have been made at the steering group. They would have made the recommendation, and the technical director would have approved it and told Admiral Raborn, "This is what we're doing. Stand by for some big bucks." Admiral Raborn had been given one pot of money. It's the only time the Navy has operated this way and the only time the Congress has really appropriated this way. They appropriated money to the SP program, and it was used as necessary: R&D, production, testing, training. The only exception was that the ship construction funds still came out of the SCN budget. The SP money was not assigned to all the different line items that we're used to, so it could be sort of apportioned within the SP to budget as needed. There were only the broadest kinds of controls by Congress on it. The virtue was that we could do these kinds of things, like suddenly go into beryllium manufacturing without having to go back and get a new procurement line from the Congress. The timetable would not have permitted such controls.

Q: What kind of a working-hour demand did this job place on you?

Admiral Weschler: As far as Pittsfield was concerned, 8:00 to about 6:00, I would say, were the normal hours up there, but I spent an awful lot of time on the road. I was probably out of the office two days a week, running around this circuit which ran from Minneapolis down to New Jersey, Long Island, and Boston, with an occasional trip to Washington. When I was in Washington running the job, it was largely the same, 8:00 to about 6:00 and, again, a lot of time on the road, probably bunched more so that we might be half a week away, and then back for a week and a half, and then another half week away.

Q: Was it the Navy's responsibility to check on the personnel reliability of the employees in these companies, or did the company have to do that?

Admiral Weschler: For security checks, this was essentially the task of the Navy, working with other federal agencies. It was up to the company to ensure that its plant and personnel were administered exactly as the Navy's security requirements directed.

We had a section of SP whose job was to go around and verify that all of these programs were being effectively administered. In addition, even though we were there as the special technical people, there was a resident inspector at GE Pittsfield who did the normal functions of government procurement, and so they were being audited and inspected and so on by the regular team.

Let me make one other comment in connection with industrial security and confidentiality that I think was unusual. You're seeing more of it today, but at the time I think it was absolutely unique. I mentioned that we were second-sourcing a lot, that we always made sure there was no single manufacturer, so that if one fell on his face, then somebody else was ready to go. That also prevented us from ever being hamstrung. Nobody could hold us up, saying, "I'm sorry, I'm not interested in the contract unless these items sell for twice as much." That could never happen because you always had somebody else to go to.

Well, companies were devising very special methods of doing these things, like building these gyros. After a time, we would say, "You, whoever you are, go over to that other company, and I don't care if you have to take the lathe operator with you, or the mechanic on the line, I want you to go there and train that person to do it the way you're doing it so that their production line starts matching yours in capability."

Now, that was working at a level of detail and technical transfer that had never before been allowed within American industry. When we brought Hughes into the guidance capsule business, building electronics, we gave a contract to Raytheon, which said, "You will ensure that Hughes is able to build guidance packages as well as you are by the end of this contract."

We gave Hughes all of the specs. We said, "You have the specs and now we're giving you the transfer of data from Raytheon, and at the end of it, you ought to be able to build them so that they meet the specs as well as those from Raytheon." That's the kind of thing we were doing. That was unusual, and it took some selling to get management people to accept it, but after a while they did. They knew we were serious and that we'd done it with others, and they came around. It didn't stop them from being competitive in connection with dollar costs, because now their own labor and materials and total productivity all came into account, but it certainly made sure that we had a broad technical base.

Q: Was there a second source for the types of equipment you were getting from GE?

Admiral Weschler: No, there was not. The reason for it was that it didn't fly and it was not as near the state of the art. Everything that flew was second-sourced. The equipment within the submarine itself often, as with GE, we had single procurement, but it was procurement in an area in which we already knew there were others who could do this kind of thing. It was the GE guidance packages and electronics they were putting together for the missile that was in that second-sourcing requirement.

Q: Were you developing a training package for the sailors who would have to run the gear?

Admiral Weschler: That's right. In addition, we ran training programs right at the factory from the beginning. The initial skippers and execs and leading petty officers of the first ships came through GE and MIT and Sperry and so on, and saw the equipments and were trained with them. They helped on the factory acceptance tests. That was perhaps the only way they could see a piece of gear in operation and be convinced of what our support policy was. Let me explain that.

A typical piece of gear aboard ship, a technician who operates it wants to be able to say to himself, "If it goes down, I can fix it." The more intelligent he is and the more he's been trained, the more that's the way he thinks about it. What we wanted to convince these people was that the last thing you wanted to do was try and fix something in the guidance system. Before the guidance system was delivered, it was put on a centrifuge and spun at high speed, and while it was spinning, it also rotated, so that everything in it was being stressed at speeds comparable to the speed-up of the missile as it went into flight. So if it had any cold solder joints or anything that was loose, it was likely to come apart.

After it had been shaken, rattled, and rolled--and it was really quite a program that it went through--we didn't want anyone taking that guidance package and deciding that what it needed was a drop of solder on joint X. If he does work that isn't thoroughly tested, then when the missile is fired, the highest probability is that any failure will be in the fix that he just put in. We tried to convince them of that, and we gradually did.

I went aboard a submarine and talked about this. I can remember one guided missile man, a chief petty officer, saying to me, in effect, "Captain, I hear what you're saying. As long as the guidance systems stay up all the time like they're supposed to, if they meet your reliability criteria, I won't have any trouble accepting your maintenance criteria. But if the systems don't meet reliability, I'm going to maintain them." That was sort of the challenge that was in the air. Well, I'm happy to say that after <u>George Washington</u> went on its initial patrol with 16 guidance systems in their missiles and three spare guidance systems, they came back with all 16 missiles up and with two guidance systems unused of the three we had

Thomas R. Weschler #4 - 415

given them as backups. Ultimately, we cut the three spares down to two, and we never had any problem with reliability. But if we hadn't met it, those technicians would have been in there doing a lot of things that we didn't want! It was very interesting the way that it worked out. That reliability had been a prime goal.

Q: Did you put any kind of sailor-proof mechanism to keep them from doing that?

Admiral Weschler: No. There wasn't any way, really, to do it, because they could get into them. We gave them spare boards that plugged in, space guidance computers and space guidance systems, so there were a lot of things they could do, packages to change, but we didn't want them going beyond the specific board or package supplied. All that we could do was get the captain and all the technicians down the line convinced that the design and test systems were sound, and that because of these centrifuge problems and the like, it just didn't make sense to fiddle with them. Since they always had enough systems, and since the systems met their reliability requirements, they were willing to accept the guidelines.

Q: I've heard Admiral Raborn described as a great motivator on this program. Did you have to be a motivator at your level at GE?

Admiral Weschler: Yes. I was a motivator in part, but I think the greatest motivator I had was a wonderful fire control and guidance division civil servant by the name of Dave Gold. I think Dave Gold was probably one of the most brilliant men I've ever bumped into, and he was probably a GS-16 when I first met him. I think he was a GS-18 by the time he retired. He was absolutely superb. He had studied at MIT and knew what he was talking about. He was a match for almost any one of the conceptual engineers who worked on the project. He could smell double-talk almost before it started, and he was intolerant of anything but the finest performance.

As we were saying earlier about captain and exec, that one of them usually has to be the SOB, Dave was my SOB, and all I had to do was go around and pick up the pieces and try and keep people working. Sometimes I'd find everyone practically laid out with the reaming that they'd just had. Then I'd have to inspire them again and say, "I know you can do it. Dave's absolutely right, and you know it in your heart, but ..." and then get them all back up and motivated. So I had that kind of motivation rather than holding their feet to the fire, which was sort of done for me.

Q: Since the checkbook was open, was there any way that money could be used as a motivator?

Admiral Weschler: No. I don't recall anything where there were premiums. There were no premiums on early delivery. I'm sure there were penalties, but the penalties on the early contracts were probably minimal, because everybody, again, knew it was such a series of miracles. But as we got into production, then there were penalties. And because the contract was so very closely administered through the regular audits and through this special group that we had, I think probably it ended up being a fairly economical system overall, despite what we were doing. You just can't have everything operating in the full light of day and in the glare of publicity and not have it stay pretty pure. That was what we found for the early years. Afterwards, when we got into production, then we used all the usual kinds of incentives to make it come off. But I think every company was on its mettle not to be the one who failed. For instance, if in that whole chain suddenly Hughes had been the only one that hadn't produced and you were saying, "I don't have a program because of ..." that would have been the worst thing that could have happened, I think, in their professional view.

Q: And they had the goad that there was a Raytheon, for

example, who was ready.

Admiral Weschler: That's right, who probably wasn't having the same trouble, because they didn't have to share every word the second they said it. They could say, "Oh, now I've got it," and they knew full well that they were going to get all the brownie points out of that and be able to sit at the steering group and say what they had achieved. The other contractor would be squirming, trying to figure out what's wrong with his engineers. So there was a lot of good peer pressure on everybody, and I think that was productive.

In retrospect, Paul, I think one of the things that impressed me about the Polaris program was the value of the total across-the-board look that the Special Projects people took for the Polaris introduction to the fleet. In other words, instead of designing a missile, which it might have done, or designing the missile and the submarine, which it might have done, Special Projects also took in every aspect of the program. That included procurement, testing, training of personnel, working up the manning of the submarines, developing the total logistic support plan, the concept of the tender which could be used overseas to support the submarine, the length of the patrols, the number of spare parts that had to be maintained in the system, everything right up to overhaul and maintenance and cyclical testing of the missile to ensure its reliability.

Every aspect of it from beginning to end was included in the initial planning. As a result, I think it was one of the most economical packages we ever bought, because everything that was bought fitted into the same matrix, and we didn't have the usual guesses and fumbles that went with it. Spare parts were being procured at the same time that the production line was still running, so that they weren't an afterthought or a special procurement that cost a lot of money. That, to me, was a very significant thing.

Let me just make a point about how this experience benefited me in later years. I was so grateful to the Polaris program when I came to be the CNO's manager and to coordinate with the Naval Material Command on the design and procurement of the Spruance-class destroyer and the Virginia-class cruiser. As much as possible, I went back to the SP concept and tried to procure the destroyer and the cruiser along the same lines. I have to say I was ably abetted in that, because Admiral Galantin, who was the second director of SP, was the Chief of Naval Material.* He knew exactly where I was coming from and was encouraging me to follow that same pattern.

Q: What do you recall specifically about the Washington

---

*Admiral Ignatius J. Galantin, USN, served as Chief of Naval Material from 1965 to 1970. Previously, he was Special Projects Officer from 1962 to 1965.

phase of your Polaris experience?

Admiral Weschler: The office I had in Washington was really the progenitor of the office I had in Pittsfield. It, again, was the design and development of fire control and guidance systems for the Polaris missile. It included not only the first generation, which was already under procurement by the time I got to Washington, but also the second generation in which we were updating the fire control equipment, moving from an early generation computer to one of the new, modern, fast, highly capable computers that made us prepped for the challenges of the next decade.

We discussed accuracy of the guidance system a little bit once before; whatever accuracy you have, you always want to improve it. As we were building the gyros and as Dr. Draper was working his formulae, he kept finding ways in which he could refine and improve the accuracy. So the second-generation guidance system was significantly more accurate than the first. The first was moving into a production phase and at the same time the research and development for the second generation. It kept the teams in place and kept challenges to industry. New players did come aboard as somebody else either dropped out from choice or simply wasn't competitive as we moved into the next phases.

Q: I've heard the thought that it's harder to maintain a top-flight organization than to create one because you don't still have that pioneering spirit and motivation. Did you get that far in the Polaris program, to the maintaining phase?

Admiral Weschler: I was leaving Polaris just about the time that maintenance was coming along. There were a certain number of us, of which I was one, who felt that SP, as the very special entity that it was, couldn't justify itself as a long-term part of the Navy. Sort of like the "sunset laws" that they're talking about with various congressional laws, I felt that agencies which can be created ought to also have their demise considered. I thought to do away with SP and then go to a simpler maintenance group would have been very effective. However, I wasn't enough akin to the strategic world to recognize the Poseidons and the Tridents and the kinds of things that would be coming along later.* As a result, there were continually new challenges and new hardware.

I think SP has really served very well. I have a feeling that they did have some growing pains as they moved along, that there were attractions to other programs that were a little bit more exciting when SP got into a sort of steady state. As some of our top-notch people approached

---
*Poseidon and Trident are successors to the Polaris as submarine-launched ballistic missiles.

retirement, I think they would have had a hard time recruiting exactly the same level. However, that's speculation. I know that SP continued, and then gradually I began to see why, and I don't have any fault to find with the fact that ultimately it did continue.

Q: Do you think that one of the reasons it was able to continue to be successful was that it was sort of an ecumenical thing, that there were surface officers, aviators, and submariners all involved in it?

Admiral Weschler: Possibly. I really think that it was enough of an organization with a purpose, that as long as that fundamental purpose continued to be served, the organization had a place. The ones who had to be convinced of its value, I think, were the Congress and the Secretary of Defense. And I think that those two agencies really believed in it all the way through. Of all the programs that we have in the strategic nuclear world, it's the one that grabs the imagination most. For the United States, which doesn't really believe in first use, there's nothing like this program for deterrence. As long as that stays true, I don't think you're going to have any trouble with those who might otherwise try to put the heat on to get it out of existence.

Thomas R. Weschler #4 - 423

Q: I've talked to Commander Paul Backus, and he said that one disappointment Admiral Burke had was that the system didn't go into the Long Beach or other surface ships. He was boss of the whole Navy, and it would have been well for the surface Navy to have had a piece of it.*

Admiral Weschler: As you know, he fixed it up for both Long Beach and Albany. Those are the two. Within the NATO nations, Italy actually had designed the Garibaldi so that it could take a Polaris missile.** We never released the plans to them, but they had in effect a missile section where such missiles could have been put. But I think that Admiral Burke agreed, when it came to the battle of the dollars, that he just couldn't justify actually outfitting the Albany with the spots that had been held for it.

Q: What is your assessment of Commander Backus's contribution and role in the whole program?

Admiral Weschler: I should qualify my comment by saying that by the time I got to Washington, Paul had already made

---

*Commander Paul H. Backus, USN, was heavily involved in the Polaris program from the OpNav viewpoint. His oral history is in the Naval Institute collection.
**The Italian light cruiser Giuseppe Garibaldi was built in the 1930s and then extensively modernized between 1957 and 1962. Her after 6-inch turrets were replaced, one by a twin Terrier missile launcher and the other by four Polaris missile tubes. She test-fired Polaris but did not carry it on an operational patrol.

his contribution and moved along. I saw him, but he was already ancillary to the action when I got there in Washington. I gathered from conversations with him and with others that he had been an excellent gadfly, an imaginative person, and one who knew what we were trying to achieve and who wasn't accepting easy ways to get it accomplished. He wanted to make sure that we stuck to the objective and that we didn't compromise end results very quickly for expediency. I think that was good for a program like this, which was trying to blaze new horizons, that you had somebody in there who demanded success, who kept your feet to the fire and didn't let you pull off at the first opportunity.

Q: How closely did you work with Levering Smith when you were in Special Projects?

Admiral Weschler: Very closely. When I first got there, Levering was what we would call SP-20, which was the head of the technical section, and I was SP-23, which was the head of fire control and guidance section. So he was my immediate superior in that chain. While I was there, he moved up to become the number two in the project, the deputy director under Admiral Raborn, so I knew him in both roles.

As I indicated in some comments in the previous

interview, I just thought Levering Smith was one of the greatest scientists in uniform that I've ever met; he had a very sharp mind. I regard him as practically unflappable, that he was able to work with any of these scientists or industrialists and know what he was after and not be sidetracked or disarmed or put off by anything that was said. He kept driving ahead for what he knew was right, and he wouldn't take any compromise on something that he thought was fundamental to the project. He was a perfectly wonderful guy for this kind of thing in which we were trying to accomplish the chain of miracles.

Q: How much administrative work was required in his position?

Admiral Weschler: Not all that much. I would say it's because of the way SP was organized; there was a 10 shop, which was essentially all of the paperwork. He had to worry an awful lot about budget, the financial side of the house. He had someone to manage the budget for him, but every one of the financial decisions was an educated guess, and Levering was involved with those things right down to the gnat's eyebrow. The technical director had a certain discretionary budget which he could take care of, because if any one of our sections began to run over, he was the one who had to bail you out, and he had certain limits.

And, of course, the front office had other limits in the budget lines, where if you really had a tough one, you could go up there and get some help.

I think I mentioned to you the other day the way the program ran, that people would say, "I'm in trouble, I can fix it," "I'm in trouble, my boss can fix it," or, "We're in trouble. Admiral, we need you." Well, each one of those layers had to have some budget backup to make it possible, because you know as well as I do that it takes extra effort. You have to have the budget to do it. Levering was the one who created those pockets that were of the right size. That took some real crystal balling to make it all come out right.

Q: Was he one of the people who would say what individuals would be brought into the program? Who had that job?

Admiral Weschler: There was a separate section on manning, but I would say that the front office, which was Admiral Raborn and his deputy, did the bulk of the recruiting, but for anything that was in the technical arena, Levering would be in all the way. As he moved up the line and was coming over to the deputy position, I'm sure his voice was more and more heard, whether we were aware of it or not. I have a hunch he talked with Admiral Raborn on all those decisions.

Q: I'm curious in this area whether anybody ever had to be fired, or whether the people picked were so good that that was never necessary.

Admiral Weschler: There were, I'm sure, a couple of easings along. I'm aware of a couple that I thought weren't necessarily the best in the program, and they didn't stay there for an overly long tour. I think there was that degree of change of personnel, but as you've already indicated, since everyone who came was good, it doesn't mean that he was a foul ball. It just meant that in this rarefied atmosphere, he wasn't functioning as well as you had hoped for, and so you didn't damn him. You simply said, "He really is closer to average than I thought," and moved him along to be with his average counterparts elsewhere.

Q: Was there any concern about people getting compartmented into this Special Projects so they would no longer be well-rounded naval officers?

Admiral Weschler: Well, yes. I think you put your finger on a very excellent point. We had already seen this happen with nuclear weapons in the '47 to, say, '53 era. Some of those who had moved into nuclear weapons had gotten so specialized working with Admiral Hayward and working in some of those jobs that it had really taken conscious effort on the part of the CNO to get them out of this special program and plug them back into being line officers.* They had to have certain concessions to allow them to become exec and commanding officer of ships or squadrons in order to go on and have successful careers. I think SP was aware of this. I think Admiral Raborn, who was himself a line officer, always felt that this was the case, and after a couple of years in the program, if you went to him and said, "I think I've been here long enough," his principal comment would be, "Who's your good relief? And then I can hear you talking to me." So as long as you'd come up with some good relief, usually you could get moved along. They would cooperate in this by looking around for others they could bring aboard.

Q: I would think it would not be as hard to sell a potential relief on that as it would have been in some jobs.

Admiral Weschler: You're absolutely right, and as I commented also, many of the people in SP were engineering duty officers only of various persuasions, and they were a nice cadre through the organization. If they stayed four

---
*Rear Admiral John T. Hayward, USN.

or five years, this was one of the best places they could possibly be, and they were moving up in responsibility through the organization. Bob Wertheim comes to mind as a case in point. I first met him when he was a lieutenant commander in the program, and he was in and out of the program at least three times, ending up as Rear Admiral Wertheim.* I think he relieved Levering Smith in the program and ultimately was the head of the project. So you can see that it never seemed to hurt him and he, being an ED, could move along very freely.

Q: That's right. As an EDO, he no longer had that requirement to rotate between sea duty and shore duty.

Admiral Weschler: To keep going up. But he did leave the program, broaden himself in his own technical field, and then come back to it.

Q: Do you have any specific memories of working with Wertheim?

Admiral Weschler: No, I don't. I knew him, but other than the fact that we got to know and like each other socially and that I saw a lot of him, admired him tremendously, knew that he was savvy and wasn't at all surprised to see him

―――――――
*Rear Admiral Robert H. Wertheim, USN (Ret.), whose oral history is in the Naval Institute collection.

move along as he did, I don't have anything specific that comes to mind in connection with him.

Q: Any more on Admiral Raborn? Did you get a closer view of him when you were in Washington?

Admiral Weschler: Oh, yes. I hadn't really known Admiral Raborn all that well before I went to the project. When I was here at the Naval War College as a member of the faculty in '51 to '53, Admiral Raborn was then Captain Raborn and a student. When he left here, he had command of a carrier that had that fire here.* His ship was home-ported in Quonset, and there was an explosion of one of the catapults, and there were many serious injuries in connection with that and people rushed into Newport Hospital. I saw him around that time, and I know my wife, as a Gray Lady, a Red Cross assistant, was over at the hospital and saw Captain and Mrs. Raborn. So we knew that much about him.

I formed all my real professional appraisal of Admiral Raborn when he was there in Washington as SP. The thing I admired about him was, as I've indicated, that not being a technical expert himself, he still knew how to direct and

---

*On the morning of 26 May 1954, the USS Bennington (CVS-20) was steaming off Narragansett Bay when the port catapult accumulator burst, releasing hydraulic fluid throughout adjacent spaces. The resulting fire killed 103 officers and men and injured 201.

get the best out of people in that field, as well as the industrialists, who were usually the senior executives of their companies. He worked with them and had them energetic and enthusiastic for the program as though they were JOs working for the skipper of a hard-driving squadron. He was superb. He really had the leadership knack, and he knew that he had CNO and SecNav behind him, and he was very effective in the Congress in putting his points across. So he was really the right man in the right place. I wasn't at all surprised that he went on to research and development and so on.

I might just comment as a personal expression, that he didn't do all that well when he went over to CIA.* I think that was a completely different kind of challenge. He was then working with the straight bureaucracy that had a more routine job to do, and I don't think he had been shipmates with that kind of challenge. I think he simply was a name that the Congress recognized and was willing to accept, and that the President felt was a good man and had done a good job. When he was plugged in, it wasn't his cup of tea, and it didn't work out that well.

Q: How well did he and Captain Smith complement each other working as a team?

---

*As a retired vice admiral, Raborn served as director of the Central Intelligence Agency in 1965-66.

Admiral Weschler: Like a glove on a hand--it was that kind of thing, completely different personalities but both redheads. They got along very well together, and there could be sparks on occasion, but they were probably kept within the office most of the time. We just saw them as two people, what one didn't do, the other did, and they were Mutt and Jeff.

Q: In the midst of all this success, did you have any disappointments at all in the program?

Admiral Weschler: Well, I'm sure there were a couple of tests of missiles that had us disappointed. The guidance system was so crucial to accuracy and to performance, that in some of those early flight tests, any time that the guidance system didn't work 100%--as soon as any missile had a casualty, the first thing you wanted to find out was, whose section was it that had failed, and if it wasn't yours, you were grateful. But if it was yours, you knew that you were going to be at general quarters for the next week or two until you could isolate exactly what the fault was, and then come up with a fix. Or if it was a fluke, identify it as such and then go in and say, "It shouldn't have happened that time. It'll never happen again. We've checked over everything; everything's right. We're ready to go." That's hard to do. There were a couple of those. But aside from those, what I would call programmatic problems, I don't recall any real disappointment in it.

Q: You talked about the ten miracles that were needed. It seems to me this would be a good psychological edge for the leader to go to you and say, "The guidance thing is the critical thing. That's where we really need it." And then say the same thing about other areas to nine other people.

Admiral Weschler: Yes. Well, he probably did, and you all felt that way, that anybody could do this and anybody could do that, but who could do this? So we all thought we were pretty special, which is what he wanted to engender as a feeling, and we felt the same about our companies and what they were doing.

Q: It's good leadership.

Admiral Weschler: Yes, it really is.

Q: How did you go about recruiting your relief, then?

Admiral Weschler: Well, he just appeared in the system, which was really very nice. I thought it was interesting that the gent I relieved had been an ED, electrical engineer. I was a straight line officer, ordnance PG, and my relief was an aviation engineering duty officer. He became available in the system, had excellent credentials, very well known around the Washington arena, and particularly in the SP headquarters. Everybody seemed to know and like what he had been doing elsewhere. So he came over and in the minimum time frame was aboard and took the office, and I went off to the National War College.

Index

to

The Reminiscences of

Vice Admiral Thomas R. Weschler
U.S. Navy (Retired)

Volume I

Air Force, U.S.
In the early 1950s a team from the Naval War College spoke about carrier warfare to the students of the Air War College, 209-210; cooperation with the Navy on missile programs in the late 1960s, 396-397

Air War College, Maxwell Air Force Base
In the early 1950s a team from the Naval War College spoke about carrier warfare to the students of the Air War College, 209-210

Albacore, USS (AGSS-569)
Whale-shaped submarine that was ridden in the 1950s by U.S. CNO Arleigh Burke and Britain's Lord Louis Mountbatten, 310

Albany, USS (CA-123)
Cruiser slated to become flagship for the Atlantic Fleet Cruiser Force received a tour de force inspection by Rear Admiral James L. Holloway in 1950, 189-190

Albany, USS (CG-10)
Cruiser that was fitted in the early 1960s to accommodate Polaris missiles but received none on board, 318, 423

Ammunition
Efforts in the late 1940s and early 1950s by the Atlantic Fleet Cruiser Force to use up ammunition left over from World War II, 180-181

Amphibious Warfare
Role of naval shore bombardment in support of amphibious operations in the early 1950s, 195-198; voluminous operation orders in World War II, 204; amphibious raids in the Vietnam War, 204-205; role of logistics, 206-207

Antiair Warfare
On board the aircraft carrier Wasp (CV-7) in 1942, it was sometimes difficult to get radar information on planes that had been detected, 83-85; training in 1943 for the gun crews of the destroyer Sigsbee (DD-502), 106; replacement of fire control radars in the Sigsbee's gun directors, 107-107; use of cruiser guns against air targets in the late 1940s, 186-187; limited capability of the destroyer Clarence K. Bronson (DD-668) in 1953, 236; the Typhon air defense system was canceled in the 1960s because it got too big for the ships intended for it, 315-316; role of the cruiser Canberra (CAG-2) in the development of doctrine and tactics for the use of guided missiles in the late 1950s, 364-368; slowness of radar operations in the first guided-missile cruisers, 368-369

Antisubmarine Warfare
    Training for Atlantic Fleet ships around Guantanamo Bay, Cuba, in 1954, 239-242

Arkansas, USS (BB-33)
    Summer training cruise to Europe for Naval Academy midshipmen in 1936, 21-22

Armstrong, Vice Admiral Parker B., USN (Ret.) (USNA, 1942)
    Served as chief engineer of the heavy cruiser Macon (CA-132) in the late 1940s, 155-156

Army, U.S.
    Vietnam War Army officers, including General Harold K. Johnson, Army Chief of Staff in the mid-1960s, who were prisoners of the Japanese in World War II, 122-124

Athens, Greece
    Liberty for the crews of ships in Destroyer Division 302 when they were in Athens in December 1953, 232-234

Backus, Commander Paul H., USN (USNA, 1941)
    Imaginative officer who made a number of contributions to the Polaris missile program in the late 1950s, 423-424

Bahrain
    As the base for Commander U.S. Middle East Force, received a visit from the transiting ships of Destroyer Division 302 in late 1953, 227-229; liberty for enlisted men was sparse, 233

Banvard, Theodore J. (USNA, 1939)
    Went into merchant marine service upon graduation from the Naval Academy in 1939 because of vision problems, 33-34

Baruch, Bernard, Jr.
    Visited in the late 1950s by officers from the cruiser Canberra (CAG-2), 386-388

Bates, Rear Admiral Richard W., USN (Ret.) (USNA, 1915)
    Following World War II he conducted detailed analyses of various battles for the Naval War College, 207-208

Batista, Fulgencio
    Cuban President who evacuated with his family when Cuba fell to Fidel Castro in 1959, 319-320

Beach, Captain Edward L., USN (USNA, 1888)
    Naval officer whose popular writings led boys to aspire to the Naval Academy in the early years of the century, 12

Beakley, Rear Admiral Wallace M., USN (USNA, 1924)
As air group commander in the aircraft carrier <u>Wasp</u> (CV-7) in 1942, he jealously guarded the information available from radar, 82-85; on the staff of the Naval War College in the early 1950s, 84, 203, 210; as Commander Middle East Force in the mid-1950s, 228

<u>Bearn</u>
French aircraft carrier that the U.S. carrier <u>Wasp</u> (CV-7) kept bottled up in Martinique when the United States entered war in 1941, 47

Belgian Congo
As Belgium's Chief of Naval Staff in the mid-1950s, Commodore L. J. J. Robins arranged for CNO Arleigh Burke to tour the Belgian Congo, 281-282

Belgian Navy
As Chief of Naval Staff in the mid-1950s, Commodore L. J. J. Robins arranged for CNO Arleigh Burke to tour the Belgian Congo, 281-282

Bell, Commander C. Edwin, USN (USNA, 1939)
Had a difficult time working as aide to Admiral Don Felt, the demanding VCNO in the late 1950s, 327

<u>Bennington</u>, USS (CVS-20)
Experienced a serious fire while in Narragansett Bay in May 1954, 430

Bergen, Captain Franklin Steward, USN
Naval officer who began his career as a talented enlisted man on board the aircraft carrier <u>Wasp</u> (CV-7) at the beginning of World War II, 56-58

Bermuda
Base of operations for the aircraft carrier <u>Wasp</u> (CV-7) during neutrality patrols in 1941, 43, 45, 47

Betts, Lieutenant Sherman W., USN (USNA, 1931)
Served as aerographer of the aircraft carrier <u>Wasp</u> (CV-7) early in World War II, 64

Bill, Commander David S., Jr., USN (USNA, 1939)
Pulled a prank on Douglas Fairbanks, Jr., while serving in the aircraft carrier <u>Wasp</u> (CV-7) in 1942, 73-74; as chief of staff for the U.S. Middle East Force in the mid-1950s, 228

Blandy, Admiral William H. P., USN (USNA, 1913)
    Was relieved as Commander in Chief Atlantic Fleet in February 1950, just as the battleship <u>Missouri</u> (BB-63) was refloated after being aground, 170-172

Boston, USS (CAG-1)
    Guided missile heavy cruiser that participated in a May 1958 ceremony to select the unknown soldier of the Korean War, 359-360

Brown, Vice Admiral Charles R., USN (USNA, 1921)
    Famous message he sent as Commander Sixth Fleet during the Suez crisis of 1956, 320; relationship with CNO Arleigh Burke, 322

Brumby, Captain Frank H., Jr., USN (USNA, 1932)
    Served as commanding officer of the guided missile cruiser <u>Canberra</u> (CAG-2) in the late 1950s, 358, 363, 379-380

Bryan, Lieutenant Louis A., USN (USNA, 1932)
    Served as regimental commander during his first-class year at the Naval Academy, 1931-32, 13-14; was executive officer of the destroyer <u>Duncan</u> (DD-485) when she rescued survivors from the torpedoed aircraft carrier <u>Wasp</u> (CV-7) in September 1942, 99

Bureau of Ships
    Devised damage control procedures for missile magazine fires on board the cruiser <u>Canberra</u> (CAG-2) in the late 1950s, 373

Burke, Admiral Arleigh, USN (USNA, 1923)
    While serving as ComDesLant in 1955, was selected as Chief of Naval Operations and chose Weschler as his aide, 248-250, 258-259; displays of impatience, 251-252, 271-272, 277-278, 296-299, 332-333; notified Admiral Jerauld Wright in 1955 that he, Burke, had been selected as CNO, 254-255; transition period in 1955 while preparing to take over as CNO, 255-272; knew a lot of men in the Marine Corps, 260-261; sense of humor displayed in playing tricks on people, 265, 272-275; emphasis on the importance of Navy families, 268-269, 333; his wife Roberta had a calming influence on his temper, 270-271; office routine as CNO, 276-281, 293-300, 328-335, 338, 342-345, 347-349; overseas trips while serving as CNO, 281-284; involvement with protocol, 284-286, 288-289; hesitant to become CNO when he was chosen, 286-287; relationship with Secretary of the Navy Charles Thomas, 286-288, 290; decorations in CNO office, 289-290; relationship with Secretary of the Navy Thomas Gates, 290-292; role in the operational chain of command,

292-293; relationship with JCS Chairman Arthur Radford, 302; in 1959 accepted a third two-year term as CNO, 303; later expressed regret for having served so long in office, 303, 316; involvement with the Polaris program in the late 1950s, 304-305, 353-354, 423; developed a humidor as a symbol of his CNO tenure, 307-308; economies forced loss of some missiles and aircraft, 308-309; relationship with Britain's Lord Mountbatten, 310-312, 320; relationship with Rear Admiral Hyman Rickover, 313-314; loss of the Typhon program, 315-316; evacuation of President Fulgencio Batista when Cuba fell in 1959, 319-320; and Suez crisis of 1956, 320-321; regard for Vice Admiral Charles R. Brown, 322; hobby of gardening, 322-323, 325, 336; scrupulous honesty in financial matters, 324-325; operation of CNO living quarters, 325-326; choice of Admiral James Russell as possible successor, 326-327; relationship with VCNO Don Felt, 327-328, 331; friendly association with Japanese, 336-337; showed little concern for his health, 338-340; enjoyed visiting fleet ships, 340-341; congressional testimony, 341-342; taping of office conversations, 344-345; dealings with news media, 345-347; did not demonstrate political leanings, 349-350; reaction to the Soviet satellite Sputnik in 1957, 352; eagerly sought as a speaker by Naval Reserve groups, 386

Burke, Roberta
As wife of the Chief of Naval Operations-designate, moved from Newport to Washington in mid-1955, 253; genuine, unselfish personality, 268; when leaving Newport in 1955, she left two nice steaks in her apartment's refrigerator, 269-270; calming influence on her husband's temper, 270-271, 332; concern when her husband's pants were temporarily lost during a trip to Africa, 281-282; planning of social events when her husband was CNO, 284; spent many evenings at home while her husband was at his office, 294; hobby of gardening, 322-323

Canberra, USS (CAG-2)
Commanding officers in the late 1950s, 358, 362-364, 371, 379-380, 387; participation of in a May 1958 ceremony to select the unknown soldier of the Korean War, 359-362, 379; competence of the ship's officers, 362-364; had a role in the development of doctrine and tactics for the use of guided missiles for antiair warfare in the late 1950s, 364-368; shortage of missiles, 368; slowness of radar operations in the first guided-missile cruisers, 368-369; the ship got a positive response when her Terrier missiles were painted blue and yellow during a visit to Sweden in 1958, 369-370; midshipman training cruise in the summer of 1958, 369-374; damage control procedures for fires in missile magazines, 373; missile-

handling procedures, 374-375; beam-riding fire control system, 376-377; fitted for gunnery but not as a flagship, 377-378; Marine detachment, 379, 381; formality on board, 379-381; habitability, 382; handling characteristics, 382-383; discipline of the crew, 383-384; visit by ship's officers to the estate of Bernard Baruch, Jr., in New York, 386-388

Carney, Admiral Robert B., USN (USNA, 1916)
His term as Chief of Naval Operations lasted only two years, from 1953 to 1955, until he was replaced by Arleigh Burke, 255, 286-287

Castro, Fidel
The U.S. Navy evacuated President Fulgencio Batista and his family when Cuba fell to Castro in 1959, 319-320

Caufield, Captain Cecil T., USN (USNA, 1927)
As chief of staff for ComDesLant in 1955, notified Weschler that he was to be the CNO's aide, 249-250

Cavite Navy Yard, Philippines
The U.S. Navy's Dewey dry dock was operated at Olongapo and Cavite prior to World War II, 120

Central Intelligence Agency
Vice Admiral William Raborn did not do well as director of the CIA in the mid-1960s, 431

Charette, Hospital Corpsman First Class William R., USN
Participated in a May 1958 ceremony on board the guided missile cruiser Canberra (CAG-2) to select the unknown soldier of the Korean War, 359-362

Charts-Navigation
U.S. capture of Japanese charts during the invasion of Kwajalein in early 1944, 109

Clarence K. Bronson, USS (DD-668)
Had a slight collision with the escort carrier Point Cruz (CVE-119) during refueling in 1953, 215-216; patrolled off Korea during the distribution of released prisoners of war following the armistice in July 1953, 217-218; outlook of the local people when the ship operated out of Sasebo, Japan, in late 1953, 219-220; the performance of the crew at the end of the Korean War was disappointing, 220-222, crew reunion in 1984, 222-223, 246-247; trip from Korea to Newport via the Indian Ocean, Suez, Med, and Atlantic in 1953-54, 223-237, 242; training exercises in the Atlantic in 1954-55, 238-248; few married crew members, 246; Weschler was relieved of command in 1955 after having served as Admiral Arleigh Burke's aide for a few weeks, 252-253

Clark, Captain Thurston B., USN (USNA, 1927)
Served as senior aide to the Chief of Naval Operations in the mid-1950s, 275, 293

Coast Guard, U.S.
Administered exams in the late 1930s so merchant marine personnel could qualify for licenses, 33

Collisions
The aircraft carrier Wasp (CV-7) collided in fog with the destroyer Stack (DD-406) in the Atlantic in March 1942, 64-72; the destroyer Clarence K. Bronson (DD-668) had a slight collision with the escort carrier Point Cruz (CVE-119) during refueling in 1953, 215-216

Combat Information Centers
Use of on board the cruiser Canberra (CAG-2) in the late 1950s while developing doctrine for guided missiles, 365-368; slowness of radar operations in the first guided-missile cruisers, 368-369

Computers
Early models used in 1946 by Dr. Dillingham at MIT to solve practical problems, 131

Conolly, Vice Admiral Richard L., USN (USNA, 1914)
Provided excellent leadership while serving as president of the Naval War College in the early 1950s, 202-203

Cornnell, Colonel Walter F., USMC
Service as aide to CNO Arleigh Burke during a trip to Japan in the late 1950s, 282-284

Corsiglia, Chief Yeoman Madeline F., USN
Did an excellent job while working in the office of CNO Arleigh Burke in the 1950s, 280, 293-294, 344

Creed, Chief Turret Captain Euly C., Jr., USN
Did a fine job in the gunnery department of the heavy cruiser Macon (CA-132) in the late 1940s, later moved to the ComCruLant staff, 164-165, 183

Cruiser Force, U.S. Atlantic Fleet
The advent of the rapid-fire Salem (CA-139)-class cruisers in the late 1940s gave a boost to the U.S. Navy's surface force, 158-159, 194; Rear Admiral Allan Smith as type commander in 1949-50, 158, 188, 192; staff's role in the salvage of the battleship Missouri (BB-63) after she ran aground at Thimble Shoal near Norfolk, Virginia, in January 1950, 167-173; Rear Admiral James L. Holloway, Jr., was an energetic, traditional

officer who served as type commander in the early 1950s, 174, 188-191; working styles of the chiefs of staff in running the staff, 177-178; Weschler's interaction with the gunnery departments of the various ships in the type command, 178-188; the <u>Worcester</u> (CL-144)-class light cruisers were disappointing when they joined the fleet in the late 1940s, 186-188; a major role for the cruisers in the early 1950s was as flagships, 193-194; role of the force in supporting the Korean War effort in the early 1950s, 198-200

Cuba
Training for Atlantic Fleet ships around Guantanamo Bay in 1954-55, 238-248; the U.S. Navy evacuated President Fulgencio Batista and his family when Cuba fell to Fidel Castro in 1959, 319-320

Culebra
Shore-bombardment exercises by the Destroyer Division 302 in the mid-1950s, 243-244

Damage Control
Procedures for missile magazine fires on board the cruiser <u>Canberra</u> (CAG-2) in the late 1950s, 373

<u>Dealey</u>, USS (DE-1006)
Shakedown training around Guantanamo Bay, Cuba, in the summer of 1954, 238-240; capabilities, 239-240

Demobilization
The Navy lost a great many experienced men when Naval Reservists were released from active duty at the end of World War II, 125

Destroyer Division 302
Commander B. J. Semmes served as division commander in the mid-1950s, 214-215, 228-232; made an around-the-world cruise in 1953-54, 215, 223-237; skippers of individual ships, 226, 228-229; operations in the Atlantic in 1954-55, 238-248

Destroyer Force, Atlantic Fleet
Welcomed home the ships of Destroyer Division 302 in January 1954 after a long trip from Korea, 237; the type commander, Rear Admiral Charles Hartman, had a real interest in Navy families, 237-238

Dickey, Commander Fred Clinton
Mustang who was the executive officer of the aircraft carrier <u>Wasp</u> (CV-7) at the beginning of World War II, 47-48, 62-63

Discipline
Demerits for conduct by Naval Academy midshipmen in the late 1930s, 26-27; captain's mast cases in the aircraft carrier Wasp (CV-7) in the early 1940s, 52-53; on board the cruiser Canberra (CAG-2) in the late 1950s, 383-384

Dockum, Commander Donald G., USN (USNA, 1936)
Worked on developing his subordinates while serving as the commanding officer of the destroyer Young (DD-685) in 1945, 117-120

Doehler, Brigadier General William Francis, USMC (Ret.) (USNA, 1945)
Marine Corps officer who began his career as a talented enlisted man on board the aircraft carrier Wasp (CV-7) shortly before World War II, 56-57

Draper, Dr. C. Stark
Outstanding professor who was on the faculty of the Massachusetts Institute of Technology in the mid-1940s, 130, 135-137; role in the development of the Polaris missile guidance system in the 1950s, 392, 394, 396-398, 420

Duke, Captain Irving T., USN (USNA, 1924)
Took command of the battleship Missouri (BB-63) shortly before she went to Korea in 1950, 199-200

Duncan, Admiral Donald B., USN (USNA, 1917)
As Vice Chief of Naval Operations in the mid-1950s, reprimanded Captain John McCain for exceeding his authority, 273-275; relationship with CNO Arleigh Burke, 276-277

Duncan, USS (DD-485)
Destroyer that rescued survivors from the torpedoed aircraft carrier Wasp (CV-7) in September 1942, 99-100

Education
Academic routine at the Naval Academy in the late 1930s, 18-21; Weschler's postgraduate study in ordnance engineering in Annapolis and at MIT in 1945-46, 127-140

Eisenhower, Dwight D.
As President in 1957, appointed CNO Arleigh Burke to a third two-year term, 303-304; felt relief when the Suez crisis of 1956 was resolved peaceably, 320-321

Elcano
See Juan Sebastian de Elcano

Elliott, Commander Rogers, USN (USNA, 1922)
Served as chief engineer of the aircraft carrier <u>Wasp</u> (CV-7) at the beginning of World War II, 50-51

Enlisted Personnel
Early in World War II the crew of the aircraft carrier <u>Wasp</u> (CV-7) included some talented enlisted men who later became officers, 56-58

Ensey, Captain Lot, USN (USNA, 1930)
Did an excellent job running the command and staff course at the Naval War College in the early 1950s, 201-202

Erie, Pennsylvania
Early in the 20th century, it was the home of a number of future military leaders, 1-5; schools in the 1920s and 1930s, 5-9; movies, 11; a Navy gunboat was named in honor of the city, 23; Weschler and his family made a vacation visit to the city in 1955, 300-301

<u>Erie</u>, USS (PG-50)
Gunboat that took Naval Academy midshipmen on a summer cruise of the East coast in 1937, 23

Eversole, Midshipman John S., USN (USNA, 1939)
Was not commissioned upon graduation from the Naval Academy in 1939 because of vision problems, 24-25

Fairbanks, Lieutenant (junior grade) Douglas E., Jr., USNR
Actor who served for a time in 1942 as a reserve officer on board the aircraft carrier <u>Wasp</u> (CV-7), 72-75

Families of Servicemen
Housing situation for Navy families in Norfolk, Virginia, in the late 1940s, 166-167; in the mid-1950s the commander of the Atlantic Fleet Destroyer Force had a real interest in the welfare of Navy families, 237-238, 268-269; few married men were in the crew of the destroyer <u>Clarence K. Bronson</u> (DD-668) in the mid-1950s, 246; concern by CNO Arleigh Burke about service widows, 333

Felt, Admiral Harry D., USN (USNA, 1923)
Demanding officer who served as Vice Chief of Naval Operations in the late 1950s, 327-328, 331

Fire
Burning oil on the water impeded abandoning ship after a Japanese submarine had torpedoed the aircraft carrier <u>Wasp</u> (CV-7) in September 1942, 95; damage control procedures for missile magazine fires on board the cruiser <u>Canberra</u> (CAG-2) in the late 1950s, 373

Fire Control
Replacement of the Mark 4 fire control radar with the Mark 12 when the destroyer Sigsbee (DD-502) underwent a brief repair period at Pearl Harbor in the middle of World War II, 106-107; contributions of Dr. C. Stark Draper to the Mark 14 lead-computing gun sight in World War II, 130; role of servo mechanisms in transmitting orders to remote locations, 131-133; GUNAR was an experimental program in the late 1940s to mount fire control radar on a shipboard gun platform, 134; development of the guidance system for the Polaris missile in the late 1950s, 138, 391-399, 403-404, 406-417, 432-433; the Mark 63 director was tested on board the heavy cruiser Macon (CA-132) in the late 1940s, 149-150; limited antiaircraft capability of the destroyer Clarence K. Bronson (DD-668) in 1953, 236; used by the Clarence K. Bronson in shore-bombardment exercises at Culebra in the mid-1950s, 243-244; beam-riding system for the Terrier missiles on board the cruiser Canberra (CAG-2) in the late 1950s, 376-377; installation of Polaris fire control equipment in the submarine George Washington (SSBN-598) in 1959, 406; updates in the early 1960s to produce improved versions of the Polaris guidance systems, 420

Fitness Reports
In the late 1940s Captain Roland Smoot gave a briefing to the staff of ComCruLant on how to write fitness reports that would get officers promoted, 174-176; evaluation of an officer in the Polaris missile program in the late 1950s, 176-177

Fletcher, Vice Admiral Frank Jack, USN (USNA, 1906)
Withdrew aircraft carrier support early during the invasion of Guadalcanal in August 1942, 86-89

Fog
The aircraft carrier Wasp (CV-7) collided in fog with the destroyer Stack (DD-406) in the Atlantic in March 1942, 64-72

Food
The men of the destroyer Sigsbee (DD-502) were eating ice cream while their Marine Corps counterparts were ashore during the invasion of Tarawa in November 1943, 107-108; the Arabs served lamb (Including the eye) to officers from Destroyer Division 302 during a visit to Bahrain in 1953, 228-229; when leaving Newport in 1955, Mrs. Arleigh Burke left two nice steaks in her apartment's refrigerator, 269-270

French Navy
  The U.S. aircraft carrier Wasp (CV-7) kept the French carrier Bearn bottled up in Martinique when the United States entered war in 1941, 47

Galantin, Admiral Ignatius J., USN (USNA, 1933)
  As Chief of Naval Material in the late 1960s, was supportive of the approach used on the Spruance (DD-963)-class destroyer program, 419

Gates, Thomas S., Jr.
  As Secretary of the Navy in the late 1950s, worked closely with CNO Arleigh Burke, 290-291; death of son, 291; substantive knowledge of naval matters, 291-292; reaction to the Soviet satellite Sputnik in 1957, 352

General Electric Corporation
  Received a visit from CNO Arleigh Burke in the mid-1950s to demonstrate development work on a fleet ballistic missile, 304-306; role on Polaris guidance system in the late 1950s, 394, 405-418; some of GE's equipment for Polaris was backed by a second manufacturing source, 412-413; provided training on equipment for early Polaris crew members, 413

George Washington, USS (SSBN-598)
  Installation of Polaris fire control equipment in the ship in 1959, 406; missile guidance systems had a high reliability rate during the submarine's initial patrol, 414-415

Gibraltar
  Long-time British influence was evident at Gibraltar when the ships of Destroyer Division 302 visited in late 1953, 234-235

Gilbert Islands
  The men of the destroyer Sigsbee (DD-502) had it much easier than their Marine Corps counterparts ashore during the invasion of Tarawa in November 1943, 107-108

Giuseppe Garibaldi
  Italian cruiser that was modernized in the late 1950s and early 1960s to take missiles, 423

Gold, Dave
  Highly capable civil servant who was involved in the development of Polaris missile guidance systems while at the Naval Industrial Reserve Ordnance Plant, Pittsfield, Massachusetts, in the late 1950s, 416

Goteborg, Sweden
 The cruiser <u>Canberra</u> (CAG-2) got a positive response when her Terrier missiles were painted blue and yellow during a visit in 1958, 369-370

Great Britain
 Long-time British influence was evident at Gibraltar when the ships of Destroyer Division 302 visited in late 1953, 234-235

 <u>See also</u> Royal Navy

Greece
 Liberty for the crews of ships in Destroyer Division 302 when they were in Athens in December 1953, 232-234

Gross, Ensign Leonard, USNR
 As an officer in the aircraft carrier <u>Wasp</u> (CV-7) in August 1942, he was quite disappointed about the U.S. inability to cope with the Japanese attack at Savo Island, 90-91

Guadalcanal
 Vice Admiral Frank Jack Fletcher withdrew aircraft carrier support early during the invasion of Guadalcanal in August 1942, 86-89; disastrous Battle of Savo Island in early August 1942, 88-89; postwar analysis of the Savo Island action by Rear Admiral Richard Bates, 207-208

Guantanamo Bay, Cuba
 Training for Atlantic Fleet ships around Guantanamo in 1954-55, 238-248

GUNAR
 Experimental program in the late 1940s to mount fire control radar on a shipboard gun platform, 134

Gunnery-Naval
 The destroyer <u>Sigsbee</u> (DD-502) ship served as bait to draw the fire of Japanese shore batteries during the U.S. invasion of Kwajalein in February 1944, 108-111; Weschler's pleasure in being a gunnery specialist during his career, 111-112; GUNAR was an experimental program in the late 1940s to mount fire control radar on a shipboard gun platform, 134; gunnery officers' ordnance school in Washington, D.C., in late 1946, 143; the heavy cruiser <u>Macon</u> (CA-132) switched crews between 8-inch and 5-inch guns to have enough to hold competitive drills in the late 1940s, 150-152; advent of the rapid-fire <u>Salem</u> (CA-139)-class cruisers in the late 1940s gave a boost to the U.S. Navy's surface force, 158-159, 194; Weschler's interaction with the gunnery departments of the various

CruLant ships in the late 1940s-early 1950s, 178-188; the _Worcester_ (CL-144)-class light cruisers disappointed in terms of gunnery when they joined the fleet in the late 1940s, 186-188; role of naval shore bombardment in support of amphibious operations in the early 1950s, 195-198; limited antiaircraft capability of the destroyer _Clarence K. Bronson_ (DD-668) in 1953, 236; shore bombardment practice at Culebra in the mid-1950s, 243-244

See also Fire Control

Hall, Captain John L., Jr., USN (USNA, 1913)
Spent time on board the aircraft carrier _Wasp_ (CV-7) in early 1942 as a liaison officer on behalf of Admiral Harold R. Stark, 72-76

Halpine, Lieutenant Commander Charles G., USN (Ret.) (USNA, 1916)
While serving in Washington in 1940-41, helped Weschler get a reserve commission, 40-41

Hartman, Rear Admiral Charles C., USN (USNA, 1920)
As Commander Destroyers Atlantic Fleet in the mid-1950s, had a real concern for Navy families, 237-238

Hayward, Captain John T., USN (USNA, 1930)
Was commanding officer of the escort carrier _Point Cruz_ (CVE-119) during a slight collision while refueling the destroyer _Clarence K. Bronson_ (DD-668) in 1953, 215-216; personality, 216; role in Navy nuclear weapons delivery programs in the 1940s and 1950s, 427-428

Helicopters
Installation of a helicopter landing platform on the stern of the heavy cruiser _Macon_ (CA-132) in 1947, 144-145, 197; role in spotting for naval gunfire in the early 1950s, 197-198

Hodes, Lieutenant General Henry L., USA (USMA, 1920)
As an Army commander in Germany in 1955 gave Admiral Arleigh Burke a hospitable greeting during a visit, 262

Holloway, Admiral James L., Jr., USN (USNA, 1919)
Energetic, traditional officer who served as Commander Battleship Cruiser Force Atlantic Fleet in the early 1950s, 174, 188-191; as commanding officer of the battleship _Iowa_ (BB-61) in 1944, 191

Hooper, Rear Admiral Edwin B., USN (USNA, 1931)
Specialized in the study of servo mechanisms while at MIT, 133

Hyatt, Lieutenant Commander George W., MC, USN
    Served as a physician for CNO Arleigh Burke in the mid-1950s, 339-340

I-19
    Japanese submarine that torpedoed the aircraft carrier Wasp (CV-7) on 15 September 1942, disabling her so badly she had to be sunk, 94-100

Iceland
    The aircraft carrier Wasp (CV-7) supported the Marine landing in Iceland in 1941, 45-47

Inspections
    A Saturday personnel inspection on board the aircraft carrier Wasp (CV-7) in 1942 led to the disappearance of a pair of Douglas Fairbanks's trousers, 73-74; the Atlantic Fleet Cruiser Force staff conducted inspections of various ships in the type command in the late 1940s-early 1950s, 181-183; the USS Albany (CA-123), slated to become flagship for the Atlantic Fleet Cruiser Force, received a tour de force inspection by Rear Admiral James L. Holloway in 1950, 189-190; conducted by Commander B. J. Semmes as Commander Destroyer Division 302 in the mid-1950s, 231-232

Intelligence
    Use of U.S. merchant ships in an intelligence-reporting network in the 1950s, 386-387

Iowa, USS (BB-61)
    Personality of Captain James L. Holloway when commanding the ship in World War II, 191

Italy
    Crew members from the heavy cruiser Macon (CA-132) visited the Italian Naval Academy at Livorno in 1948, 145-146

Italian Navy
    Crew members from the heavy cruiser Macon (CA-132) visited the Italian Naval Academy at Livorno in 1948, 145-146; in the late 1950s and early 1960s the cruiser Giuseppe Garibaldi was modernized to take missiles, 423

Japan
    Outlook of the local people when the destroyer Clarence K. Bronson (DD-668) operated out of Sasebo in late 1953, 219-220; visit to Tokyo by CNO Arleigh Burke in the late 1950s, 282-284

Japanese Army
  The destroyer Sigsbee (DD-502) ship served as bait to draw the fire of Japanese shore batteries during the U.S. invasion of Kwajalein in February 1944, 108-111

Japanese Navy
  Inflicted a serious defeat in the Battle of Savo Island in August 1942, sinking four Allied cruisers, 87-89; the submarine I-19 torpedoed the aircraft carrier Wasp (CV-7) on 15 September 1942, disabling her so badly she had to be sunk, 94-100; the destroyer Sigsbee (DD-502) was damaged by a Japanese kamikaze at Okinawa in April 1945, 115-116; Japanese naval officers had a high regard for U.S. CNO Arleigh Burke, 337

Joslin, Captain Royal K., USN (USNA, 1940)
  Had a fine career after taking postgraduate education in ordnance engineering right after World War II, 139

Juan Carlos, Prince
  Spanish prince who visited the cruiser Canberra (CAG-2) when she was in Vigo, Spain, during a midshipman training cruise in the summer of 1958, 371-372

Juan Sebastian de Elcano
  Spanish yacht that was moored near the cruiser Canberra (CAG-2) at Vigo, Spain, in the summer of 1958, 371-372

Kamikazes
  The destroyer Sigsbee (DD-502) was damaged by a Japanese kamikaze at Okinawa in April 1945, 115-116

Kelly, Richmond K. (USNA, 1921)
  Former naval officer who ran the marine department of the Tidewater Associated Oil Company in the 1930s, 36-37, 39-40

Kernodle, Commander Michael H., USN (USNA, 1921)
  Served as air officer of the aircraft carrier Wasp (CV-7) at the beginning of World War II, 50, 54

Kinney, Commander Sheldon H., USN (USNA, 1941)
  Visited the Long Island estate of businessman Bernard Baruch in the late 1950s, 387-388

Korean War
  Role of the Atlantic Fleet Cruiser Force in supporting the war effort in the early 1950s, 198-200; the destroyer Clarence K. Bronson (DD-668) patrolled off Korea during the distribution of released prisoners of war following the armistice in July 1953, 217-218; some ship crew members seemed poorly motivated as the war wound down,

220-222; some of the destroyers that served off Korea came from the Atlantic Fleet, 224-225; the guided missile cruiser Canberra (CAG-2) participated in a May 1958 ceremony to select the unknown soldier of the war, 359-362, 379

Kwajalein, Marshall Islands
The destroyer Sigsbee (DD-502) served as bait to draw the fire of Japanese shore batteries during the U.S. invasion of Kwajalein in February 1944, 108-111

Landing Signal Officers
Lieutenant David McCampbell was a top-notch officer who served as LSO in the aircraft carrier Wasp (CV-7) early in World War II, 53-54

Leave and Liberty
Conditions for the crews of the ships in Destroyer Division 302 in Greece in December 1953, 232; opportunities limited in the Persian Gulf region in late 1953, 233; vacation trip in 1955 that Weschler and his family took to Erie, Pennsylvania, on leave, 300-301

Lee, Rear Admiral Fitzhugh, USN (USNA, 1926)
Sent a friendly greeting when Arleigh Burke was chosen as CNO in 1955, 267; helped develop a tobacco humidor for Burke to give away as a memento, 307-308

Lehman, John F., Jr.
As Secretary of the Navy in the 1980s, sought to have too much control over personnel assignments, 351

Leonard, Captain Robert C., USN (USNA, 1932)
Did a poor job of communicating with subordinates while serving as executive officer of the heavy cruiser Macon (CA-132) in the late 1940s, 154-155

Lewis, Lieutenant William E., USN (USNA, 1936)
Had a fire-control radar watch on board the aircraft carrier Wasp (CV-7) when she collided with the destroyer Stack (DD-406) in March 1942, 65, 69-70

Libby, Vice Admiral Ruthven E., USN (USNA, 1922)
Sharp individual who served as OP-06 in the late 1950s, 301

Logistics
Studied at the Naval War College in the early 1950s, 206-207

Long Beach, USS (CG-9)
Cruiser that was fitted to accommodate Polaris missiles in the early 1960s but received none on board, 423

Macon, USS (CA-132)
　　Visit to New Orleans in early 1947, 142; role as a test platform for the Operational Development Force in the late 1940s, 144-150; installation of a helicopter landing platform on the stern in 1947, 144-145, 197; midshipman cruise to the Mediterranean in 1948, 144-147; Captain Olin Scoggins as commanding officer, 1948-49, 147-148, 165; switched crews between 8-inch and 5-inch guns to have enough men to hold competitive drills in the late 1940s, 150-152; crew morale, 153; administrative side of the gunnery department was run smoothly, 164-165

Maintenance
　　Thorough testing of Polaris guidance systems in the late 1950s by General Electric to minimize the need for shipboard maintenance and repair, 413-415

Malta
　　Mediterranean island to which the aircraft carrier Wasp (CV-7) delivered British planes in 1942, 80-81

Marine Corps, U.S.
　　The aircraft carrier Wasp (CV-7) supported the Marine landing in Iceland in 1941, 45-47; the men of the destroyer Sigsbee (DD-502) had it much easier than their Marine Corps counterparts ashore during the invasion of Tarawa in November 1943, 107-108; invasion of Kwajalein in February 1944, 109; role of naval shore bombardment in support of amphibious operations in the early 1950s, 195-198; Admiral Arleigh Burke, CNO in the late 1950s, knew a lot of Marines, 260-261; made a point of sending a representative to greet high-ranking Marines on tour, 263; Marine detachment on board the cruiser Canberra (CAG-2) in the late 1950s, 379, 381

Mark 4 Fire Control Radar
　　Replacement of the Mark 4 fire control radar with the Mark 12 when the destroyer Sigsbee (DD-502) underwent a brief repair period at Pearl Harbor in the middle of World War II, 106-107

Mark 12 Fire Control Radar
　　Replacement of the Mark 4 fire control radar with the Mark 12 when the destroyer Sigsbee (DD-502) underwent a brief repair period at Pearl Harbor in the middle of World War II, 106-107

Mark 37 Director
　　Replacement of the director's Mark 4 fire control radar with the Mark 12 when the destroyer Sigsbee (DD-502) underwent a brief repair period at Pearl Harbor in the middle of World War II, 106-107

Mark 63 Director
   Tested on board the heavy cruiser Macon (CA-132) in the late 1940s, 149-150

Marshall Islands
   The destroyer Sigsbee (DD-502) ship served as bait to draw the fire of Japanese shore batteries during the U.S. invasion of Kwajalein in February 1944, 108-111

Martinique
   The aircraft carrier Wasp (CV-7) kept the French carrier Bearn bottled up in Martinique when the United States entered war in 1941, 47

Massachusetts Institute of Technology
   Provided postgraduate course in ordnance engineering to a small group of naval officers in 1945-46, 128-140; Dr. C. Stark Draper was an outstanding professor on the faculty in the mid-1940s, 130, 135-137; early use of computers, 131; contribution to the development of the Polaris guidance system in the late 1950s, 392, 394, 399-400

McCain, Captain John S., Jr., USN (USNA, 1931)
   While working in OpNav in the mid-1950s received a facetious award for exceeding his authority, 273-275; vision of U.S. role in the Indian Ocean, 311

McCampbell, Lieutenant David, USN (USNA, 1933)
   Top-notch naval aviator who served as landing signal officer in the aircraft carrier Wasp (CV-7) early in World War II, 53-54

McDaniel, Captain Eugene F., USN (USNA, 1927)
   Did an excellent job running the command and staff course at the Naval War College in the early 1950s, 201-202

McMullen, Ensign John J., USN (USNA, 1940)
   Served as officer of the deck of the destroyer Stack (DD-406) when she collided with the aircraft carrier Wasp (CV-7) in March 1942, 70; post-Navy career, 72

Media
   See News Media

Medical Problems
   A number of men in the Naval Academy class of 1939 graduated but were not commissioned because they did not meet vision standards, 24-25, 30-32; Weschler's vision had improved considerably when he was retested in 1941, 41; as CNO in the mid-1950s, Admiral Arleigh Burke showed little concern for his health, 338-340

Mediterranean Sea
   The heavy cruiser Macon (CA-132) made a midshipman training cruise to the Mediterranean in 1948, 144-147; some Royal Navy ships were operating in the area in 1948, 146; fewer British ships by the mid-1950s, 235

   See also Sixth Fleet, U.S.

Mendenhall, Captain William K., Jr., USN (USNA, 1923)
   Served as chief of staff to Commander Cruisers Atlantic Fleet in the late 1940s, 165-166, 177-178

Merchant Marine
   Several members of the Naval Academy class of 1939 went into the commercial maritime industry because they were unable to pass the physical exam at the time of graduation, 24-25, 32-33; hostility toward the Navy in the 1930s and 1940s, 32-33; operations of the Tidewater Associated Oil Company in the late 1930s and early 1940s, 33-38; comparison of watch standing with that in Navy ships, 37-38; recruiting of new employees in 1939, 39-40; use of U.S. merchant ships in an intelligence-reporting network, 386-387

Middle East Force, U.S.
   Received a visit from the transiting ships of Destroyer Division 302 in late 1953, 227-229

Midway (CVB-41)-Class Aircraft Carriers
   Made most of their deployments in the 1940s and 1950s to the Mediterranean, 161-162

Miller, Captain George H., USN (USNA, 1933)
   Gave Weschler advice upon reporting to the staff of Rear Admiral Arleigh Burke in 1955, 251-252

Mine Warfare
   See Paravanes

Mississippi, USS (AG-128)
   Test ship that was involved in the late 1940s with gunnery and missile experiments, 183-184

Missouri, USS (BB-63)
   Salvage of the battleship after she ran aground at Thimble Shoal near Norfolk, Virginia, in January 1950, 167-173; operated in support of the Korean War after being refloated, 199-200

Mountbatten, Admiral of the Fleet Lord Louis, RN
   Relationship with U.S. CNO Arleigh Burke in the 1950s, 310-312, 320

Movies
   Weschler worked as an usher in a theater in Erie, Pennsylvania, in the 1930s, 11

Mumma, Rear Admiral Alfred G., USN (USNA, 1926)
   As Chief of the Bureau of Ships in the late 1950s, made frequent visits to see CNO Arleigh Burke, 334

Naval Academy, Annapolis, Maryland
   Competition for appointments in the 1920s and 1930s, 4, 14-16; in the early years of the century, books for youngsters served as an inspiration for potential midshipmen, 12; experiences of the plebes in the 1935-36 school year, 13, 16-18; academic routine in the late 1930s, 18-21; summer training cruises, 21-23; some members of the class of 1939 weren't commissioned on graduation because of vision deficiencies, 24-25, 30-32; top students in the class of 1939, 25-26; competition for honors by midshipmen and companies, 26-27; athletics, 27; extracurricular activities, which included sailing, 28-29; Weschler taught engineering at the academy in 1941, 41-42; midshipman training cruise on board the cruiser Canberra (CAG-2) in the summer of 1958, 369-376

Naval Industrial Reserve Ordnance Plant, Pittsfield, Massachusetts
   Role in the development of guidance systems for the Polaris missile in the late 1950s, 391-393, 404-418; highly capable civil servant named Dave Gold, 416

Naval Material Command
   Added an unnecessary layer of bureaucracy when it went into existence in the mid-1960s, 335-336

Naval Postgraduate School, Annapolis, Maryland
   Course in ordnance engineering in 1945-46, 127-130

Naval Reserve
   Weschler went through a cumbersome procedure in getting into the Naval Reserve in 1940-41, 40-41; relatively few reservists were in the crew of the aircraft carrier Wasp (CV-7) when the United States entered war in 1941, 55-56; talented group of reservists in the first batch on board the Wasp, 59, 61; potential value of reservists in civilian life, 59-60; in 1945 nearly all the officers in the destroyer Young (DD-685) were reservists, 124-125; reservists eagerly sought CNO Arleigh Burke as a speaker in the late 1950s, 386

Naval War College, Newport, Rhode Island
   Inauguration of a new command and staff course in 1950, 201-202; excellent leadership from Vice Admiral Richard

Conolly as president, 202-203; curriculum, 203-207; detailed analysis of World War II battles by Rear Admiral Richard Bates, 207-208; top instructors, 209; sent a speaking team to the Air War College in the early 1950s, 209-210; conflict of war college work and graduate studies, 210-211; value of war college study, 211-212

Navigation
Taught at the Naval Academy in the late 1930s, 21; one of the officers of the merchant ship Stanley Matthews in 1939 was conversant with a variety of navigation methods, 35

Neutrality Patrol
Operations in the Atlantic on the part of the aircraft carrier Wasp (CV-7) in 1941, 43

New Caledonia
Survivors of the torpedoed Wasp were kept at Noumea for several weeks in late 1942, 101-102

News Media
Coverage of CNO Arleigh Burke in the 1950s, 345-347

Norfolk, Virginia
Housing situation for Navy families in the late 1940s, 166-167; salvage of the battleship after she ran aground at Thimble Shoal near Norfolk in January 1950, 167-173

North Carolina, USS (BB-55)
Fast battleship that was torpedoed by the Japanese submarine I-19 on 15 September 1942, 97-99

Noyes, Rear Admiral Leigh, USN (USNA, 1906)
Flag officer who was ineffectual while embarked in the aircraft carrier Wasp (CV-7) in the summer of 1942, 81-82, 86-89, 91-92

Nuclear Weapons
In the late 1950s the cruiser Canberra (CAG-2) was capable of carrying nuclear weapons but didn't have any on board, 272

Observation Island, USS (EAG-154)
Test ship involved in Polaris missile development work in the late 1950s, 389, 398

Oil
Operation of a fleet of tankers by the Tidewater Associated Oil Company in the late 1930s and early 1940s, 35-37

Okinawa
   The destroyer Sigsbee (DD-502) was damaged by a Japanese kamikaze at Okinawa in April 1945, 115-116

Olongapo, Philippines
   See Subic Bay, Philippines

Operational Development Force
   In the late 1940s tested GUNAR, an experimental program to mount fire control radar on a shipboard gun platform, 134; role of the heavy cruiser Macon (CA-132) as a test platform in the late 1940s, 144-150

P6M Seamaster
   This jet-powered seaplane was developed in the 1950s but did not join the fleet, 310-311; possible strategic value, 311

Paravanes
   Boatswain's Mate First Class Chester N. Spiewak saved Weschler's life in September 1942 by alerting him when it was time to rig paravanes on board the aircraft carrier Wasp (CV-7), 92-94

Paria, Gulf of
   Landlocked body of water off Venezuela that was the site of shakedown training for the crew of the destroyer Sigsbee (DD-502) in 1943, 105-106

Pate, Lieutenant General Randolph McC., USMC
   In 1955, while preparing to take over as Commandant of the Marine Corps, made an orientation tour with Admiral Arleigh Burke, 260-263

Pearl Harbor Navy Yard, Hawaii
   Replacement of the Mark 4 fire control radar with the Mark 12 when the destroyer Sigsbee (DD-502) underwent a brief repair period at Pearl Harbor in the middle of World War II, 106-107

PERT
   Program Evaluation Review Technique used to monitor progress in the Polaris program in the late 1950s, 401

Pickett, Captain Ben B., USN (USNA, 1938)
   Went through postgraduate education in ordnance engineering right after World War II, 139; detailed Weschler to a Polaris missile development billet in 1959, 390-391

Philippine Islands
   Operations in and around the country in 1945 by the destroyer Young (DD-685), 117-120; Lieutenant Charles

Weschler's experiences as a prisoner of war in World War II, 120-122; the Navy's Dewey dry dock was operated at Olongapo and Cavite prior to World War II, 120

Pittsfield, Massachusetts
See Naval Industrial Reserve Ordnance Plant, Pittsfield, Massachusetts

Point Cruz, USS (CVE-119)
Had a slight collision with the destroyer Clarence K. Bronson (DD-668) during refueling in 1953, 215-216

Polaris Missiles
Development of the guidance system for Polaris in the late 1950s, 138, 391-399, 403-418, 432-433; interest on the part of CNO Arleigh Burke in the Polaris program, 304-306; advent of Polaris cost the Navy the Regulus missiles, 308-309; confined to submarines rather than also being in surface ships, 317-318, 423; in the mid-1950s Rear Admiral William F. Raborn, Jr., received a "CNO hunting license" from Admiral Arleigh Burke for development of the Polaris project, 353-354; Rear Admiral Hyman Rickover had a role in the Polaris because he was providing the nuclear submarines, 355; role of the test ship Observation Island (EAG-154) during Polaris development, 389, 398; compressed time schedule for the program, 399-400; technical and management contributions by Captain Levering Smith, 400-401, 424-426, 431-432; use of various methods to monitor development progress, 401-403; reliability of people working in the program in the late 1950s, 410-411; dual sourcing of equipment components supplied by private industry, 411-413; General Electric provided training on equipment to crew members of the early Polaris submarines, 413; thorough testing of guidance systems by General Electric to minimize the need for shipboard maintenance and repair, 413-415; broad, overall role of the Special Projects Office in introducing Polaris to the fleet, 418-419; updates in the early 1960s to produce improved versions of the Polaris guidance systems, 420; role of Commander Paul Backus, 423-424; concern about people getting too compartmented on Polaris, 427-428

Price, Captain Frank H., USN (USNA, 1941)
Top-notch gunnery department officer of the battleship Missouri (BB-63) in the late 1940s, 185-186

Prince Juan Carlos
See Juan Carlos, Prince

Prisoners of War
Lieutenant Charles Weschler's experiences as a prisoner of war in World War II, 30, 120-124; General Harold K.

Johnson, Army Chief of Staff in the mid-1960s, was a prisoner of the Japanese in World War II, 123-124; the destroyer Clarence K. Bronson (DD-668) patrolled off Korea during the distribution of released prisoners of war following the armistice in July 1953, 217-218

Promotion of Officers
In the late 1940s Captain Roland Smoot gave a briefing to the staff of ComCruLant on how to write fitness reports that would get officers promoted, 174-176; in 1955 Rear Admiral Arleigh Burke was promoted over many more senior officers to become Chief of Naval Operations, 248-250, 258-260

Protocol
Appreciation of by CNO Arleigh Burke in the late 1950s, 284-286, 288-289

Raborn, Rear Admiral William F., Jr., USN (USNA, 1928)
In the mid-1950s received a "CNO hunting license" from Admiral Arleigh Burke for resources to use in development of the Polaris project, 353-354; decision-making power, 355, 409; monitoring of progress, 401-402, 426; dealings with personnel, 426, 428; was commanding officer of the carrier Bennington (CVS-20) when she had a fire in 1954, 430; leadership qualities, 430-431; did not do well as director of the Central Intelligence Agency in the mid-1960s, 431

Radar
The fire control radar of the aircraft carrier Wasp (CV-7) had only limited usefulness when the ship collided with the destroyer Stack (DD-406) in March 1942, 65-70; as air group commander in the Wasp in 1942, Lieutenant Commander Wallace Beakley jealously guarded the information available from radar, 82-85; replacement of the Mark 4 fire control radar with the Mark 12 when the destroyer Sigsbee (DD-502) underwent a brief repair period at Pearl Harbor in the middle of World War II, 106-107; use of on board the cruiser Canberra (CAG-2) in the late 1950s while developing doctrine for guided missiles, 365-368; slowness of radar operations in the first guided-missile cruisers, 368-369; beam-riding fire control system for the Terrier missiles on board the Canberra, 376-377

Radford, Admiral Arthur W., USN (USNA, 1916)
As Chairman of the Joint Chiefs in the mid-1950s, seemed to be too evenhanded to suit CNO Arleigh Burke, 302

Radio
Operation of early commercial stations in the 1920s, 10-11

Ramage, Rear Admiral Lawson P., USN (USNA, 1931)
As a cruiser division commander in the late 1950s, had an important role in the use of guided missiles in antiair warfare, 364-369

Reeves, Captain John W., Jr., USN (USNA, 1911)
Strict and demanding while serving as commanding officer of the aircraft carrier Wasp (CV-7) at the beginning of World War II, 48-51; the crew of the carrier had great confidence in Reeves in leading them into war, 51-52; qualified only a few officers of the deck, 61-64; reaction when the Wasp collided with the destroyer Stack (DD-406) in March 1942, 67-68, 71; played tennis with actor Douglas Fairbanks, Jr., 75; departure from the Wasp in May 1942, 77; used senior officers as command duty officers in the Wasp, 78; role when the ship was operating in the Atlantic, 79-80

Refueling
The destroyer Young (DD-685) took on fuel at Subic Bay in the Philippines in 1945, 118-120; the destroyer Clarence K. Bronson (DD-668) had a slight collision with the escort carrier Point Cruz (CVE-119) during refueling in 1953, 215-216

Regulus Missile
Surface-to-surface weapon that was dropped from the Navy program in the late 1950s to help pay for Polaris, 308-309

Rescue at Sea
The destroyer Duncan (DD-485) picked up survivors from the torpedoed aircraft carrier Wasp (CV-7) in September 1942, 99-100; process of accounting for the Wasp survivors, 100-102

Research and Development
Development of the guidance system for Polaris in the late 1950s, 138, 391-399, 403-418, 432-433; compressed time schedule for the Polaris program, 399-400; technical and management contributions by Captain Levering Smith, 400-401, 424-426, 431-432; use of various methods to monitor development progress, 401-403

Ricketts, Rear Admiral Claude V., USN (USNA, 1929)
Had an important role in the late 1950s in the development of doctrine for use of guided missiles in antiair warfare, 364-369

Rickover, Rear Admiral Hyman G., USN (USNA, 1922)
Arranged for CNO Arleigh Burke to visit a nuclear power plant in the fall of 1955, 313-314; concern about safety

in nuclear operations, 314-315; disdain for excess gadgets in nuclear submarines, 315-316; had a role in the Polaris missile program in the late 1950s because he was providing the nuclear submarines, 355

Rider, Commander Eugene C., USN (USNA, 1934)
Served as operations officer of the heavy cruiser <u>Macon</u> (CA-132) in the late 1940s, 154-155

Rudden, Captain Thomas J., Jr., USN (USNA, 1939)
Went through postgraduate education in ordnance engineering right after World War II, 139; while in the Polaris missile program in the late 1950s gave advice on how to write fitness reports, 176-177

Russell, Commander Benjamin Van Meter, USN (USNA, 1926)
Was a fussy officer while in command of the destroyer <u>Sigsbee</u> (DD-502) during World War II, 113-115

Robins, Commodore L. J. J., Belgian Navy
As Chief of Naval Staff in the mid-1950s arranged for CNO Arleigh Burke to tour the Belgian Congo, 281-282

Royal Navy
Benefited from information provided by U.S. ships on neutrality patrol in the Atlantic in 1941, 43; some British ships were operating in the Mediterranean in 1948, 146; fewer British ships in the Med in the mid-1950s, 235

Russell, Vice Admiral George L., USN (USNA, 1921)
As DCNO for Administration in the late 1950s checked into the operations of the living quarters of CNO Arleigh Burke, 325-326

Russell, Admiral James S., USN (USNA, 1926)
Designated by CNO Arleigh Burke in the mid-1950s as a possible successor in the event something happened to Burke, 326-327

Safety
Insistence by Rear Admiral Hyman Rickover in the 1950s about the safe operation of nuclear power plants, 314-315

Sailing
Offered a pleasant break from the usual routine for Naval Academy midshipmen in the late 1930s, 28-29

<u>Salem</u> (CA-139)-Class Cruisers
Advent the rapid-firing ships in the late 1940s gave a boost to the U.S. Navy's surface forces, 158-159; role as Sixth Fleet flagships in the 1940s and 1950s, 159-161; development of doctrine for the guns, 194

Salvage
The battleship Missouri (BB-63) had to be refloated after she ran aground at Thimble Shoal near Norfolk, Virginia, in January 1950, 167-173

Sasebo, Japan
Outlook of the local people when the destroyer Clarence K. Bronson (DD-668) operated out of Sasebo in late 1953, 219-220

Savo Island-Battle of
The aircraft carrier Wasp (CV-7) was kept on the sidelines and not allowed to take part in this battle in August 1942, 86-91; postwar analysis of the action by Rear Admiral Richard Bates of the Naval War College, 207-208

Scoggins, Captain Olin, USN (USNA, 1923)
As commanding officer of the heavy cruiser Macon (CA-132) in the late 1940s, recruited the ship's junior officers into submarine service, 147, 165

Security
As air group commander in the aircraft carrier Wasp (CV-7) in 1942, Lieutenant Commander Wallace Beakley jealously guarded the information available from radar, 82-85; survivors of the torpedoed Wasp were kept at Noumea, New Caledonia, for several weeks in late 1942 because the Navy did not want to divulge the loss of the ship, 101-102; protection of Terrier missiles on board the cruiser Canberra (CAG-2) in the late 1950s, 375-376; reliability of employees working in the Polaris missile program in the late 1960s, 410-411

Semmes, Vice Admiral Benedict J., Jr., USN (USNA, 1934)
As a crew member of the aircraft carrier Wasp (CV-7), helped evacuate shipmates after she was torpedoed on 15 September 1942, 94-95; recruited junior officers to serve in the destroyer Sigsbee (DD-502) when she was commissioned in 1943, 104; during World War II demonstrated his qualities as an energetic, knowledgeable officer, 112-115; as Commander Destroyer Division 302 in the mid-1950s, 214-215, 228-232; style of leadership, 229-232; on DesLant staff in the mid-1950s, 250

Shea, Lieutenant Commander John J., USN
Killed in September 1942 during the sinking of the aircraft carrier Wasp (CV-7), 54

Sherman, Captain Forrest P., USN (USNA, 1918)
Took command of the aircraft carrier Wasp (CV-7) in May 1942 as she was preparing to support the invasion of

Guadalcanal, 77-78; personality, 78-79; emphasis in preparing the ship for combat, 78-79, 81-82, 92, 96; intelligence, 81-82; during the disastrous battle of Savo Island in August 1942, urged Rear Admiral Leigh Noyes that the Wasp should provide support, 88

Ship Design
In the mid-1950s Commander Destroyer Division 302 submitted ideas on improving destroyers, 230; the program for the design and procurement of the Spruance (DD-963)-class destroyers in the late 1960s was modeled on the successful Polaris submarine program, 419

Sides, Rear Admiral John H., USN (USNA, 1925)
Played a major part in the Navy's guided missile program in the 1950s, 307-309; commanded the first cruiser division in the U.S. Navy to have guided-missile ships, 357-358

Sigsbee, USS (DD-502)
Destroyer that went into commission in early 1943 with several officers from the recently sunk aircraft carrier Wasp (CV-7), 104; shakedown in the Atlantic in 1943, 104-106; men of the destroyer had it much easier than their Marine Corps counterparts ashore during the invasion of Tarawa in November 1943, 107-108; the ship served as bait to draw the fire of Japanese shore batteries during the U.S. invasion of Kwajalein in February 1944, 108-111; operations later in 1944, 111; B. J. Semmes as executive officer, 113-115; damaged by a Japanese kamikaze at Okinawa in 1945, 115-116

Singleton, Captain Charles T., Jr., USN (USNA, 1926)
As head of the ordnance program at the Naval Postgraduate School in 1946, helped Weschler augment into the regular Navy, 128

Singleton, Midshipman Henry E., USN
Entered the Naval Academy with the class of 1939 but left prior to graduation to enter the civilian business world, 16-17

Sixth Fleet, U.S.
Salem (CA-139)-class cruisers served as fleet flagships in the 1940s and 1950s, 159-161; Midway (CVB-41)-class carriers made most of their deployments in the 1940s and 1950s to the Mediterranean, 161-162; liberty for American sailors in the Med in late 1953, 232-234

Slack, Captain Leslie M., USN (USNA, 1934)
Served as commanding officer of the test ship Observation Island (EAG-154) during Polaris development work in the late 1950s, 389

Smedberg, Lieutenant Commander William R. III, USN (USNA, 1926)
   As commanding officer of the destroyer Lansdowne (DD-486), had the job of sinking the aircraft carrier Wasp (CV-7) in September 1942, 95-96

Smith, Rear Admiral Allan E., USN (USNA, 1915)
   As Commander Cruiser Force Atlantic Fleet in 1949-50, tried to imbue the force with a feeling of distinction, 158, 167, 188; supervised the salvage of the battleship Missouri (BB-63) after she ran aground at Norfolk in 1950, 169-173; lacking in the ability to inspire, 192; got Weschler into the Naval War College in 1950, 192

Smith, Captain Charles H., USN (USNA, 1932)
   As commanding officer of the cruiser Canberra (CAG-2) in the late 1950s, 363, 371, 380, 387

Smith, Commander Donald F., USN (USNA, 1921)
   Dubious performance as navigator of the aircraft carrier Wasp (CV-7) when she collided with the destroyer Stack (DD-406) in March 1942, 66-67, 71-72

Smith, Captain Harold Page, USN (USNA, 1924)
   Took command of the battleship Missouri (BB-63) after she was refloated in 1950, 199-200

Smith, Lieutenant (junior grade) John C. H., USN (USNA, 1938)
   Recruited Weschler for the personnel office of the aircraft carrier Wasp (CV-7) in 1941, 45

Smith, Captain Levering, USN (USNA, 1932)
   Technical and management contributions in the late 1950s to the Polaris missile development program, 400-401, 424-426, 431-432

Smoot, Captain Roland N., USN (USNA, 1923)
   Served as chief of staff to Commander Cruisers Atlantic Fleet in the late 1940s, 166, 177, 198; advice to staff on writing fitness reports, 174-176, 178; had a role in getting Weschler into the Naval War College in 1950, 192

Snyder, Rear Admiral J. Edward, Jr., USN (Ret.) (USNA, 1945)
   Demonstrated capability as a junior officer in the heavy cruiser Macon (CA-132) in the late 1940s, 147-148, 162-163

Sonar
   Training for prospective ship captains in the mid-1950s, 214

Spain
Prince Juan Carlos visited the cruiser <u>Canberra</u> (CAG-2) when she was in Vigo during a midshipman training cruise in the summer of 1958, 371-372

Special Projects Office
Technical contributions in the late 1950s to the Polaris missile development program by Captain Levering Smith, 400-401, 424-425, 431-432; broad, overall role of SP in introducing the Polaris system to the fleet in the late 1950s and early 1960s, 418-419; SP has proved to have enduring value, even after the completion of the initial Polaris development, 421-422; concern about people getting too compartmented on Polaris, 427-428

Spiewak, Boatswain's Mate First Class Chester N., USN
Saved Weschler's life in September 1942 by alerting him when it was time to rig paravanes on board the aircraft carrier <u>Wasp</u> (CV-7), 92-94, 96

Spitfire
British fighter plane delivered to Malta by the aircraft carrier <u>Wasp</u> (CV-7) in 1942, 80-81

<u>Spruance</u> (DD-963)-Class Destroyers
The program for the design and procurement of the class in the late 1960s was modeled on the successful Polaris submarine program, 419

Sputnik I
Artificial earth satellite that caused much consternation in the United States after it was launched by the Soviets in October 1957, 352-353

<u>Stack</u>, USS (DD-406)
Collided with the aircraft carrier <u>Wasp</u> (CV-7) in fog in the Atlantic in March 1942, 64-72

<u>Stanley Matthews</u>, SS
World War I-era oil tanker operated by the Tidewater Associated Oil Company in the late 1930s, 33-35

Strategy
Studied in the senior course at the Naval War College in the early 1950s, 206

Stump, Admiral Felix B., USN (USNA, 1917)
While serving as Commander in Chief Pacific in 1955, went out of his way to make CNO-designate Arleigh Burke feel welcome during a visit to Hawaii, 257-258, 266

Subic Bay, Philippines
   Operations in the port in 1945 by the destroyer Young (DD-685), 118-120; the Navy's Dewey dry dock was operated at Olongapo and Cavite prior to World War II, 120; Lieutenant Charles Weschler was a prisoner of war in the Olongapo area in World War II, 121-122

Submarines--Nuclear
   Rear Admiral Hyman Rickover had a role in the Polaris missile program in the late 1950s because he was providing the ships, 355

Suez Canal
   Americans felt relief when the Suez crisis of late 1956 was resolved peaceably, 320-321

Sweden
   The cruiser Canberra (CAG-2) got a positive response when her Terrier missiles were painted blue and yellow during a visit to Goteborg in 1958, 369-370

Tactics
   Role of the cruiser Canberra (CAG-2) in the development of doctrine and tactics for the use of guided missiles for antiair warfare in the late 1950s, 364-365

Tarawa
   The men of the destroyer Sigsbee (DD-502) had it much easier than their Marine Corps counterparts ashore during the invasion of Tarawa in November 1943, 107-108

Terrier Missiles
   Development of doctrine and tactics for use of the missiles in antiair warfare in the late 1950s, 364-368; shortage of missiles on board the cruiser Canberra (CAG-2), 368; slowness of radar operations in the first guided-missile cruisers, 368-369; the Canberra got a positive response when the missiles were painted blue and yellow during a visit to Sweden in 1958, 369-370; damage control procedures for missile magazine fires on board the Canberra, 373; missile-handling procedures in the Canberra, 374-376; beam-riding fire control system on board the Canberra, 376-377

Thomas, Charles S.
   As Secretary of the Navy in 1955, selected junior Rear Admiral Arleigh Burke as Secretary of the Navy, 254, 258-259, 286-287; desire to be a strong man posed a problem for uniformed officers, 261-262; working relationship with CNO Burke, 287-288, 290

Tidewater Associated Oil
  Company that ran a fleet of commercial oil tankers in the late 1930s and early 1940s, 24-25, 33-40

Torpedoes
  The Japanese submarine I-19 torpedoed the aircraft carrier Wasp (CV-7) on 15 September 1942, disabling her so badly she had to be sunk, 94-100

Training
  Summer cruises for Naval Academy midshipmen in the late 1930s, 21-23; routine for new deck officers serving in tankers of the Tidewater Associated Oil Company in the late 1930s, 36-38; shakedown cruise for the destroyer Sigsbee (DD-502) in the Atlantic in 1943, 104-106; inadequate training for the crew when the Sigsbee received a new fire control radar in the middle of the war, 107; gunnery officers' ordnance school in Washington, D.C., in late 1946, 143; the heavy cruiser Macon (CA-132) made a midshipman training cruise to the Mediterranean in 1948, 144-147; the undermanned heavy cruiser Macon (CA-132) switched men between various gun mounts during training exercises in the late 1940s, 150-152; Weschler received some preparatory training en route to command of the destroyer Clarence K. Bronson (DD-668) in 1953, 213-214; various exercises conducted by the ships of Destroyer Division 302 as they returned to their home port following the end of the Korean War in 1953, 226; refresher training around Guantanamo for Atlantic Fleet destroyer types in 1954-55, 238-248; midshipman training cruise by the cruiser Canberra (CAG-2) in the summer of 1958, 369-376; General Electric provided training on equipment to crew members of the early Polaris submarines, 413

Trinidad
  The destroyer Sigsbee (DD-502) conducted shakedown training in the nearby Gulf of Paria in 1943, 105-106

Triton Missile
  The Navy developed this weapon in the 1950s, but it essentially priced itself out of existence, 308-309

Typhon
  Air defense system that was canceled in the 1960s because it got too big for the ships intended for it, 315-316

Uniforms-Naval
  Survivors from the torpedoed aircraft carrier Wasp (CV-7) were reimbursed afterward for the uniforms they lost when the ship sank in September 1942, 103; problems with uniform items when CNO Arleigh Burke was on overseas tours in the late 1950s, 281-284

Unknown Soldiers
   The guided missile cruiser Canberra (CAG-2) participated in a May 1958 ceremony to select the unknown soldier of the Korean War, 359-362, 379

Vietnam War
   U.S. use of amphibious raids in the mid-1960s, 204-205

Vigo, Spain
   Prince Juan Carlos visited the cruiser Canberra (CAG-2) when she was in port during a midshipman training cruise in the summer of 1958, 371-372

Wake Island
   The destroyer Sigsbee (DD-502) accompanied carrier forces for raids on the island in late 1943, 105-106

Wallin, Rear Admiral Homer N., USN (USNA, 1917)
   As commander of the Norfolk Naval Shipyard in 1950, was the technical director of the salvage of the battleship Missouri (BB-63), 169, 172-173

Walker, Commander Thomas J. III, USN (USNA, 1939)
   Had an early liaison role in the Polaris missile development program in the mid-1950s, 354

Wasp, USS (CV-7)
   Size of the crew in 1941, 14; sinking in September 1942, 31; neutrality patrol operations in 1941, 43, 45; personnel office, 45; support of U.S. Marine landing in Iceland in 1941, 45-47; brief foray to Martinique, 47; Captain John W. Reeves, Jr., as commanding officer at the beginning of World War II, 48-51; disciplinary cases in the early 1940-s, 52-53; Lieutenant David McCampbell as LSO, 53-54; relatively few reservists were in the ship's crew when the United States entered war in 1941, 55-56, 59-61; talented enlisted men in the crew later became officers, 56-58; officers of the deck, 61-64; collision in fog with the destroyer Stack (DD-406) in the Atlantic in March 1942, 64-72; actor Douglas Fairbanks, Jr., was on board as a reserve officer in 1942, 72-75; transition from the Atlantic to Pacific in mid-1942, 76-77; Captain Forrest P. Sherman as commanding officer in 1942, 77-82, 92, 96; senior officers as command duty officers, 78; operations with the British Home Fleet in 1942, 79-81; Rear Admiral Leigh Noyes was ineffectual as embarked flag officer in the ship during the Guadalcanal operation, 81-82, 86-89, 91-92; as air group commander in 1942, Lieutenant Commander Wallace Beakley jealously guarded the information available from radar, 82-85; the ship was on the sidelines during the disastrous Battle of Savo

Island in August 1942, 86-91; sinking of after being torpedoed by a Japanese submarine in September 1942, 92-101; process of accounting for the Wasp survivors after the sinking, 100-102; reimbursement of the crew for lost uniforms, 103

Weather
The aircraft carrier Wasp (CV-7) collided in fog with the destroyer Stack (DD-406) in the Atlantic in March 1942, 64-72; blizzard that the Weschler family went through in 1955 during a vacation trip to Erie, Pennsylvania, 300-301

Weisner, Ensign Maurice F., USN (USNA, 1941)
Got married in 1941 while serving in the aircraft carrier Wasp (CV-7), 43-44, 156

Wertheim, Rear Admiral Robert H., USN (USNA, 1946)
Engineering duty officer who spent many years with the Special Projects Office in strategic missile systems, 429-430

Wesche, Commander Otis A., USN (USNA, 1938)
Top-notch gunnery officer of the battleship Missouri (BB-63) in the late 1940s, 185-186

Weschler, Lieutenant Charles J., USN (USNA, 1932)
Older brother of Thomas Weschler, graduated from Naval Academy in 1932, 1-5, 10, 12-14, 128, 154; did postgraduate work and became an engineering duty officer, 13; as prisoner of war in World War II, 30, 120-124

Weschler, Vice Admiral Thomas R., USN (Ret.) (USNA, 1939)
Relatives in military service, 1-5, 12-13; parents of, 1-2, 4, 10-11, 15-16, 300; other ancestors, 1; siblings not in military service, 2-3, 11, 42; boyhood in Erie, Pennsylvania, 4, 7-11; education of in Pennsylvania, 4-10; appointment to the Naval Academy in 1935, 4, 14-16; brief period in Boy Scouts, 7; as a Naval Academy midshipman, 1935-39, 13-28; vision problems as a midshipman, 24-25, 30-32; merchant marine service from 1939 to 1941, 32-40; wife of, 39, 136-137, 140-143, 249, 253-254, 268, 300, 388-389, 393; process of getting a Naval Reserve commission in 1940-41, 40-41; duty as a Naval Academy instructor in 1941, 41-42; service in the aircraft carrier Wasp (CV-7) in 1941-42, 43-104, 113; served in the destroyer Sigsbee (DD-502), 1943-45, 104-115; duty as executive officer of the destroyer Young (DD-685) in 1945, 117-126; postgraduate study in ordnance engineering in Annapolis and at MIT in 1945-46, 127-140; augmentation into the regular Navy in 1946, 128; served in the heavy cruiser Macon (CA-132), 1947-49, 141-156,

163-164; duty on the staff of Commander Cruisers Atlantic, 1949-50, 164-201; as a student and faculty member at the Naval War College, 1950-53, 201-212; command of the destroyer Clarence K. Bronson (DD-668) from 1953 to 1955, 213-248; as personal aide to Admiral Arleigh Burke from 1955 to 1958, 248-356; children of, 249, 254, 300, 381; service as executive officer of the guided missile cruiser Canberra (CAG-2), 1958-59, 356-388; duty in 1959-62 in the Polaris program at Pittsfield, Massachusetts, and Washington, D.C., 388-434

West, Midshipman Joseph M., USN (USNA, 1939)
Entered the Naval Academy in 1935 after initial medical difficulties, 15, 17-18, 24

Wilson, Charles E.
As Secretary of Defense in 1955, directed the promotion of Rear Admiral Arleigh Burke to four stars, 260

Wilson, Vice Admiral Ralph E., USN (USNA, 1924)
While making a tour to Japan with CNO Arleigh Burke in the late 1950s, provided an extra cap when Burke was missing his, 282-284

Worcester (CL-144)-Class Cruisers
These light cruisers were disappointing when they joined the fleet in the late 1940s, 186-188

Wright, Admiral Jerauld, USN (USNA, 1918)
As Commander in Chief Atlantic Fleet in 1955, was a candidate for CNO, but Arleigh Burke was selected instead, 251, 254-255, 287; relationship with CNO Burke, 347-348

Young, USS (DD-685)
Operations around the Philippines in the middle of 1945, 117-120; Commander Donald Dockum as commanding officer, 117-119; relationship among officers, 117-118; nearly all the officers in 1945 were reservists, 124-125